Early Praise f

"The insights in this book are ⫿
in their clarity and in their valu⫿
just your perspective—it can change your life!"

YASMIN DAVIDDS
Television Talk Show Host, Author of *Take Back Your Power*
Empowerment Specialist

"*Find Your Courage!* is an up-front, to-the-point, and honest masterpiece. You can't go wrong with this one."

RICHARD CARLSON
Author of *Don't Sweat the Small Stuff…and it's all small stuff*
and *Don't Get Scrooged*

"At a time when our world is facing seemingly unsolvable problems, we must all learn to adapt our long held assumptions and beliefs about how life works. This takes courage. Margie's practical book is here to help us all garner the personal courage to take responsibility, show personal leadership and do things differently. Timing is everything—and the timing for this book could not be better."

JOSIE McLEAN
Director, The Tactical Partnership
Director, Be The Change Australia
Past President, ICF Australasia

"We all start out in life with goals and dreams but too often we let our doubts and fears take over and pull us onto the sidelines of life. *Find Your Courage!* will empower you to overcome those obstacles and reconnect with your dreams by getting off the bench and back into the Game of Life!"

RUDY RUETTIGER
Inspiration behind the TriStar movie *RUDY*

"Courage is about having the ability to be who you *really* are and do what you *really* want, especially when it is challenging, scary, or inconvenient. In this smart, eloquent book, Margie Warrell gives you all the tools you need to live life with greater courage. Read it, apply it and live into your greatness!"

KIM GEORGE
Bestselling Author of *Coaching Into Greatness:*
4 Steps to Success in Business and Life
CEO, The AQ Institute

"This book is a must read if you want to live your life to the fullest. Margie has masterfully laid out in simple terms how to take control of your life and make it yours. Her authenticity, real-life examples and reflective exercises will cause you to take a look at who you are and find the courage that lies within you. This book is a road map to help you get where you want to go and become who you were meant to be."

LAWANA S. GLADNEY, PhD
Author of *If I Have to Tell You One More Time…*
6 Keys to Motivating Your Kids
President, Gladney & Associates

"Courage is one of the key tenets to living an extraordinary life. *Find Your Courage!* is an insightful yet entertaining book that explores the many ways that we can add courage to all aspects of our lives. Margie's stories and examples make it easy to capture the valuable lessons contained in this profound read."

CAROL FRANK
Author of *Do as I Say, Not as I Did!*
Professional Speaker
President, Avian Adventures

This book is, in my assessment, an excellent, no-nonsense, easy-to-read book that is a must read for all people of all ages and in all walks of life. Margie addresses the key issues that limit most people from achieving their dreams and individual greatness whilst carefully taking the reader through great strategies on how to overcome them. *Find Your Courage!* includes many examples you will find relevant to your own life experiences. I will be recommending this book to many of my clients as their personal handbook."

GRAEME J. SCHACHE
Psychologist & Corporate Ontological Coach

"*Find Your Courage!* is a profound resource for summoning inner bravery. Discover how to step outside your comfort zones, take important risks, and improve your levels of effectiveness in all areas of your life. Margie's guiding principles will help you tap into and leverage the many kinds of courage essential to fulfilling your dreams."

MARTA C. WILSON, PhD
Author of *Work Miracles and Live A Difference*
CEO of Transformation Systems

"In *Find Your Courage!*, Margie Warrell provides such depth of information on the subject, from so many angles, that readers are bound to find the courage they need to confront any situation."

JENIFER MADSON
Financial Success Coach
Author of *A Financial Minute*

"So many of us live in the 'comfort zone' yet are seeking more. *Find Your Courage!* compels you to release your limitations and move beyond what's easy or comfortable—and tells you why you should. Margie's sharp but sweet lessons prove to us that the ensuing personal growth is in fact necessary in our universal quest for fulfillment. She gives us the tools and motivation to blast through the comfort zone, and ultimately, to reach fulfillment. Margie's wisdom provides not only a pathway but the inspiration to go there."

RITA ROY, MD, MSC
President, Astute Technology
Assistant Professor, The George Washington University Medical Center

"Margie Warrell delivers on her promise to show readers how to create the life they really want. Her frank talk about taking responsibility for your life, whatever shape it's in, is right on the mark, and her methods to create the life you desire work in the real world."

MAUREEN RADLICK
Editor-in-Chief
Women's LifeStyle Magazine

"Margie Warrell's writing style and stories wonderfully touch and inspire, as well as give the needed kick from behind. I would recommend this book to increase fulfillment in your personal life and for professional growth and anything in between. This book is not for wimps—be prepared to take on your life (again and again)!"

REBECCA HEINO, PhD
Professor of Management and Communication
McDonough School of Business, Georgetown University

"A powerful framework for inner growth to create a life of meaning and happiness. Buy it. Read it. Live it."

RANDY GAGE
Author of *Why You're Dumb, Sick, and Broke... and How to Get Smart, Healthy and Rich!* "

"Wherever your life is right now is not nearly as important as where you want it to go. *Find Your Courage!* will propel your life forward in the direction you want it to go. This is a must-read book you won't want to miss."

JIM DONOVAN
Author of *This is Your Life, Not a Dress Rehearsal*

"Written with spirit and heart, *Find Your Courage!* will touch your heart, inspire your spirit and help you to live a more purposeful and rewarding life. The insights and strategies in this book are relevant, accessible and doable no matter who you are or where your life is at."

CAMILLE L. PRESTON, PhD
President, AIM Leadership

"Margie's words are magical as she helps you tap into your brilliance, live into your dreams and live a truly authentic, meaningful and extra-ordinary life."

SHERI McCONNELL
President and Founder, National Association of Women Writers

"Find your courage and you find so much more. You find strength, insight, and the power to do all you ever wanted to - and it is all found in this marvelous book!"

KIRK WILKINSON
Professional Speaker
Author of *The Happiness Factor: How to Be Happy No Matter What*

FIND YOUR
COURAGE!

Unleash Your Full Potential
& Live the Life You Really Want

MARGIE WARRELL

Synergy Books

Find Your Courage!: Unleash Your Full Potential & Live the
Life You *Really* Want
Published by Synergy Books
2100 Kramer Lane, Suite 300
Austin, Texas 78758

For more information about our books, please write to us, call
512.478.2028, or visit our website at www.bookpros.com.

Warrell, Margie.
        Find your courage! : unleash your full potential &
    live the life you really want / Margie Warrell.
        p. cm.
        LCCN 2006932155
        ISBN-13: 978-1-933538-70-9
        ISBN-10: 1-933538-70-8

        1. Self-actualization (Psychology) 2. Courage.
    I. Title.

    BF637.S4W37 2007   158.1
                                  QBI06-600703

ISBN 13: 978-1-933538-70-9
ISBN 10: 1-933538-70-8

Edited by Vida Jurisic

10 9 8 7 6 5 4 3 2

Dedication

This book is dedicated to my four beautiful children—
Lachlan, Madelyn, Ben and Matthew.
Thank you for the many "cuddle breaks" during the
writing of this book. You fill my days with more joy, love,
laughter and noise than I ever dreamt possible.
May you live boldly and shine brightly.

Contents

SECTION TWO—COURAGE IN ACTION

SECTION THREE—COURAGE AS A WAY OF BEING

EXERCISES

Acknowledgments

How does one acknowledge all the wonderful people in their life without having it turn into a long rambling Oscar acceptance speech? They don't. But, with brevity in my mind, I'd like to thank a few truly fabulous people for supporting me along my journey to becoming a coach, a speaker, a writer and now, an author.

Firstly, a heartfelt thank you to each of my clients for their trust, honesty and willingness to grow. In an effort to protect their privacy and honor confidentiality I have changed their names and altered identifying characteristics and details whilst still, I hope, conveying the essence of the challenges they faced and how they courageously rose to overcome them.

Secondly, I would like to thank some of the key people who have trained, mentored and guided me in becoming a coach. Graeme Schache, my own coach, mentor and teacher for generously sharing with me his many years of experience, knowledge and wisdom. Chris Chittenden, for the body of work that he has put together to grow my understanding of the ontological distinctions and how they apply to individuals and organizations. I also want to acknowledge Julio Olalla and Newfield for their leadership in the field of Ontological Coaching and the valuable work they do in training people to make a profound and lasting difference in the lives of individuals and the organizations they are a part of. Merely being in the presence of Julio is a gift. His love and wisdom have deepened my appreciation for life, for learning and for the importance of gratitude immensely.

I would also like to thank the many people in my life whose "fabulousness" makes my life so much more meaningful, rich and fun. Anna, Janet, Mona, Susie, Andy, Michelle, Joan, Mez, Fletch,

Sarah and the list goes on and on. And to my beautiful Mum, Dad, brothers and sisters—Frank, Pauline, Steve, Annie, Pete and Cath— you are gold in my life and I feel blessed to be part of such an extra ordinary family.

Lastly I want to acknowledge my wonderful husband Andrew. Thank you for believing in me more than I often do myself, for calming me down when I get my knickers in a knot, for loving me even when I'm being a crankpot (which is, of course, only rarely!) and for helping me find my courage to write this book. You are truly an extraordinary man, a beautiful husband, a loving dad and the greatest cheerleader this woman could ever have wished to have at her side through life. I love you dearly.

> *"Courage is the first of human qualities because it is the one quality which guarantees all others."*
>
> —Aristotle

Introduction

Helen Keller once said, "Life is a daring adventure, or nothing." No matter how unadventurous, timid, scared, cynical or resigned you think you are, you possess the ability to live with far greater courage than you have up until now. But not only do you have a lot more courage than you think you do, you also have the ability to live a bigger, more daring and more adventurous life that is rich in all you seek.

You see, courage has many faces and is not confined to the traditional definition involving some extraordinary feat of bravery or physical risk. The reality is that most of us do not find ourselves with opportunities to lay down our life to save another, march bravely into battle, slay the dragon or heroically respond to some unexpected and overwhelming challenge. Because of this we mistakenly assume that we don't possess the sort of courage we witness in others. But that just isn't the case. The truth is that you possess no less nor more courage than the people you hail as heroes—you just haven't found yourself in circumstances where you've felt compelled to draw on it.

Ultimately, courage has little to do with heroic acts and everything to do with the choices you make moment-by-moment, day-by-day, right throughout the course of your life. Every time an opportunity challenges you to be more than who you presently are—to take responsibility for the state of your life, express yourself authentically, act with integrity, pursue your dreams, open your heart wide to the experience of life, say no to what doesn't inspire you and yes to what does— you are acting with courage. Such opportunities to act with courage arise every day of your life.

During the writing of this book I was often asked, "Why a book on courage?" Throughout the course of my life—from my experiences growing up as one of seven children on a farm in rural Australia, traveling and living around the world, working for Fortune 500 companies and in my more recent career as a coach, speaker, writer and also as a mother of four children—the one consistent factor I have found that keeps people from fulfilling their potential and creating the life they really want is fear. Fear of failing, being rejected, looking foolish or just being inadequate. The way this manifests for people has differed greatly, but it has been consistently present in some form. Given that courage is not the absence of fear, but rather action in the presence of it, I became inspired to write a book that would help people find the courage to live bigger and more rewarding lives.

That said, I have not written this book for you to get something you don't already have. Rather I have written it to help you connect with the courage that already lies within you. The word "courage" comes from the Latin word *cor* meaning heart and so the essence of courage is about living "wholeheartedly". Therefore, so long as you have breath in your body, you have all that it takes to live a whole-hearted courageous life. In fact, your life is waiting on you to do just that. Not because you might die if you don't act with courage, but because without it you may never truly live. Choosing to live without courage, giving in to your fears and doubts, will have you continue to play it safe on the sidelines of life. There you will gradually lose touch with that sacred part of your being that yearns for growth, for expression and for wholeness. At the end of the day, without courage you will fail in the only true mission you ever really have—to do the best you can do with what you have been given.

What courage means for you is unique; what it can unlock for you is unimaginable. By connecting with what inspires you deeply, you will be able to find the courage to powerfully address those areas of your life that aren't working for you, and to play a bigger game in those areas that are. With courage you will be able to reclaim the power fear and self-doubt has wielded in your life, to boldly step into action and to stay the course toward that which tugs at your heart and brings your life a deeper sense of meaning and fulfillment.

As you step beyond your comfort zone onto unfamiliar ground, new possibilities will open up for you that currently lie beyond the horizon of what you can now see. Will it be uncomfortable at times? Sure. In fact, at times it may be terrifying. However, sometimes you are called to do what you fear most since doing so is the only way you can ever come to experience just how powerful, resourceful, brave and amazing you really are. With courage, possibility takes bloom.

Whilst it is the intention of this book to challenge and guide you to living with more courage, I do not pretend to cover every way courage can be expressed. The 12 acts of courage in this book have been carefully chosen, because I believe they are those most fundamental to your ability to live fully. They are divided into three main sections. The first section addresses the *Foundational Acts of Courage*: the courage to take responsibility, to live with integrity, to challenge your stories and to dream bigger. Although you may feel like skimming over these chapters, I strongly encourage you not to as they set the foundation for the subsequent acts of courage to follow. Without a solid commitment to each of the specific acts of courage explored in this first section, you will find it very difficult, nigh impossible, to find your courage to persist in achieving your goals and resolving the issues that led you to pick up this book in the first place. In the second section of the book, *Courage in Action*, the focus moves from inward to outward. Chapters 5 thru 9 guide you through five acts of courage that will have you stepping courageously out of your comfort zone to make real and meaningful changes in your life through your words and your actions. The final section in chapters 10 thru 12, *Courage as a Way of Being*, are about living with courage in the deepest sense and exploring how it influences not only what you are *doing* but also who you are *being*. It will guide you in becoming a person who has the courage to open their heart fully to life and those you share it with, to let go having to control the outcome of your efforts, to trust more deeply in yourself, to blossom into your full brilliance and, in so doing, become a leader by inspiring others so do the same.

In writing this book I have risked the possibility that I will be insufficient for the task of helping you find your courage. I have written it anyway. Why? Because I believe that, as David Grayson once said, "We fail far more from timidity than we do from over daring." It is my hope that the words which have come from my heart onto the pages of this book will resonate with yours. I do not promise you that after reading this book you will no longer have to contend with fear or doubt in your life. Rather, I promise you that after reading this book you will be empowered with the tools you need so that fear and doubt no longer have the power to stop you from doing what inspires you—in your career, in your relationships…in your life.

Each chapter serves as a practical guide to help you draw from you own life experiences and connect to your personal "courage bank" to transform your life as it is now into the one you want it to be. Don't try to digest this book in one hit. Rather aim for just a few pages or a chapter at a time. I strongly recommend that you get yourself a notebook or journal in which to do the exercises, and write down any observations or insights that come to you as read along. I also invite you to underline whatever rings true with you. Of course, some chapters will resonate with you more than others. When they do, take notice! It is your heart calling you to pay attention to something you have left unattended for too long. And when you hear objections and excuses shouting loudest in your head, take even more notice! They are the surest sign that the time has arrived for change and for confronting those issues which have been limiting your success and happiness up until now.

Initially the path of courage may appear fraught with risk, but as you read on, you will come to see that the far riskier path is to take no risk at all. Your life is but a blink in eternity. Really. While you have no choice in the matter of your death, you do have a choice in the matter of how you will live. What a shame it would be for you to one day arrive at your death only to look back and realize you had never fully lived. Honor the sacred spark inside you; don't let it lay dormant a moment longer.

No matter how great or "ungreat" your life is right now, I challenge you to ask for more out of life and give more to it. For regardless of how much you have accomplished or failed to accomplish until now, you are capable of more, much more, than you think you are. Don't let your doubts keep you playing small, don't let your fears stop you from aiming high and don't let your feelings of inadequacy about your ability to turn your dreams into a reality deter you from getting started.

Never again do you need to say "If I just had the guts," because you do! All the courage you need is available to you at this very moment; it's just waiting on you to tap into it to create a life that makes you feel truly alive, that reveals your unique greatness to the world and allows you to enjoy the deeply fulfilling, purposeful and happy life you have it within you to live. Dream bigger dreams for yourself, and trust that whatever direction your dreams may take you, you have the courage to travel.

> *"Life shrinks or expands in proportion to one's courage."*
> —Anais Nin

Section One
Foundational Acts of Courage

The Courage to Take Responsibility
The Courage to Live with Integrity
The Courage to Challenge Your Stories
The Courage to Dream Bigger

"There are better things ahead than any we leave behind."
—C.S. Lewis

Chapter 1
The Courage to Take Responsibility

"In a word, each man is questioned by life; and he can only answer to life by answering for his own life; to life he can only respond by being responsible."

—Viktor E. Frankl

The first and greatest courage is the courage to take responsibility for your own life. Like it or not, you alone are responsible for the person you are today, the state of your heart and the shape of your life. You can point your finger 'til the cows come home but, at day's end, the buck stops with you. This is *your* life and, since I'm assuming you'd like to enjoy it, then you need to own your experience of it—fully! By fully, I mean every single aspect of it from your relationship with your mother or boss or children, to the satisfaction you get from your daily roles—at work and home—to your experience of getting up this morning! Only by doing so will you be able to muster up the courage you need to take the chances and make the changes that will allow you to create a life you *wholly* and *fully* and *truly* enjoy living!

But, let me be up front with you—the path of responsibility has its share of potholes. You see, if you are fully responsible for your life, it means you can't blame other people or circumstances for the things that aren't going so well. You can't blame your boss or the HR department for not moving ahead in your career; you can't blame the banks or department stores for your credit card debt; you can't blame your spouse or kids for the quality of dinnertime conversation; you can't blame McDonalds or the festive season because your clothes no longer fit and you can't blame your parents for your succession of failed relationships, imperfect physique or any of the million and one wrongs we like to hold our parents responsible for. As I said, the choice to take responsibility has its downsides and can be tough going at times.

If it were easy to take ownership of all the not-so-great aspects of your life, everyone would be doing it. Facing your problems head on isn't easy and takes guts, sometimes lots of it. We humans are wired to seek pleasure and avoid pain—physical, emotional, mental—and responsibility can be pretty darned unpleasant at times. Though not physically painful, the psychological discomfort that taking responsibility sometimes requires us to endure explains why so many people, perhaps even you, choose to take the softer option of abdicating responsibility for your problems onto people or sources beyond yourself. In the short term (which is where our sights are often focused), it really is much more attractive to take the comfortable option, the easy option, and pass the buck for those things that aren't working in life.

Taking responsibility for your life creates a clearing for creating your life.

But here's the hitch and the key reason finding the courage to take responsibility is so crucial. By failing to take responsibility for the problems in your life you are, by default, handing the reigns of your life to sources over which you have little, if any, control. Sure, you may not have 100% control of your circumstances *in* life but you have no power unless you take 100% responsibility for your experience *of* life.

Think about it: Can a doctor effectively treat an ailment that has been diagnosed incorrectly? No. Likewise, neither can you effectively address the "ailments" in your life that you have misdiagnosed. Instead, what starts out as a small issue in one area of your life slowly grows bigger and insidiously spreads out to affect other parts of your life. Therefore, unless you accept full and complete accountability for your experience of life, you will continue to misdiagnose the problems in your life. In turn, you will fail to respond to the circumstances you find yourself in every day that would have you creating the life you want. Only by owning what you've caused in your life (however unintentionally) can you move into a position of power from which you can effectively address whatever concerns are weighing you down and undermining your success and happiness.

The Pay Offs for Not Being Responsible

The reason so many people fail to take responsibility is because they receive a "pay off" from abdicating responsibility. Pay offs support the continuation of destructive behaviors and limiting choices. Some pay offs, such as social acceptance or financial gain, are easy to spot. Others need a little more digging to uncover, as they can support behaviors that you might not consciously want. For example, a pay off can be:

- the validation of feelings of unworthiness or being unlovable
- the satisfaction of having something be *all* somebody else's fault
- being able to continue playing the "*Oh, poor me*" victim and getting the sympathy that comes with it
- an excuse for playing safe and avoiding risk

Let me assure you of one thing; no matter how destructive the behavior appears to be or how unhappy one might be about a situation, there is *always* a pay off on some level. *Always!* We humans can be mightily misguided creatures at times, but we're not totally stupid and we never do anything unless we judge (however poorly) that *on some level* we will get some positive value or reward from it. Until you identify the pay off you get from whatever problem or circumstance you've got on your hands, it will be damned hard to do something about it. Likewise, until you identify the pay off you get from failing to take responsibility you will be unable to get more of what you *really* want in life. Period!

Stacy came to me for coaching because she was unhappy. Unhappy about her weight, unhappy about her career and unhappy about her relationships (or lack thereof). In her early 30's, Stacy had been on the diet merry-go-round for years and despite losing hundreds of pounds along the way, she'd put on even more weight. She was convinced that her "fat genetic programming" and slow metabolism were the reasons she had failed to slim down. On top of that, she had always had asthma and argued that this made it more difficult for her to exercise. When it came to her relationships, she said she'd been waiting to get down to what she felt was an "attractive weight" before she would go out and try to find "Mr Right." As for her career, Stacy was also waiting to get "the weight thing" sorted out before she did anything about her unfulfilling job working in hospital administration. She was afraid that if she got promoted into a more senior position with greater responsibilities (which all the jobs she wanted would involve), she would end up eating more to cope with the additional stress, which would thwart her dieting efforts.

I knew we'd need to do some digging to get to the core of Stacy's pay offs (there are often more than just one) and when we did, we struck gold. It emerged during our conversation that while Stacy was growing up, her father often made sarcastic remarks about her "plumpness" which contrasted with the comments he made about her older sister being "as skinny as a bean pole." Her mother also weighed into the picture by making disparaging remarks about Stacy being "good for nuthin'" around the house. Stacy admitted that she hated doing household chores and would get out of them whenever she could.

Despite being "good for nuthin'" at home, Stacy did well enough at school to go on to college to study hospital administration. However, she never was able to shake off her parents comments, which she processed not just as being "unattractive and good for nuthin'" but, "fat and good for no one," as well. This was her truth, her "story" (which we'll explore more in chapter 3), and her behavior served to validate the fact that she was indeed unattractive and unworthy of love from the kind of man she'd like to love her. There lay the pay off for overeating. At one level she loved the idea of losing weight, meeting someone special and having a successful and rewarding career. At a deeper level she felt unworthy of doing so and proved it to herself by keeping herself large, unattractive (by current social standards) and sitting at home, away from any opportunity to meet Mr. Right. Her asthma was a convenient excuse for not exercising, and her weight was a great excuse for playing it safe and avoiding the risks involved in career advancement or social situations.

Once Stacy became aware of the pay offs that were driving her life and the excuses she'd been using to avoid taking responsibility for it, everything changed. She started an exercise program that actually improved her asthma and she began eating and living as though she was good for something and good for someone. Her body slimmed down (in spite of her supposed "fat genetic programming"), her world opened up and she stepped out into the dating scene, her bosses office and her life with a new-found confidence she'd always envied in others, but never thought she could possess.

The Upside of Responsibility

Many upsides come when you find the courage to take full ownership of your life. For starters, when you hold yourself accountable for your circumstances, you don't depend on others to behave in certain ways in order for you to get what you want. The ball is in *your* court and *you* get to decide what your next shot will be. You aren't waiting for the stars and moon and planets to all line up perfectly in order for your life to be great. You decide to make your life great regardless of the planetary movements, your mother's nagging, the state of the economy or whether or not your boss, your spouse or Wall Street is having a good day.

> *"The price of greatness is responsibility."*
> —Winston Churchill

Life also becomes a whole lot more rewarding when you realize and accept that you alone are responsible for creating your reality. Want to run your own small business or move up in your organization? You alone will get yourself there. Want to go on an adventure holiday, expand your business, improve an important relationship or remove yourself from a destructive one, sort out your finances, make new interesting friends, get back into shape or run a marathon? It's there for the taking (or should I say the "making") *if you so choose!* Whatever it is you feel dissatisfied with in your life, I promise you, by mustering up your courage to take full and complete responsibility for the life you *are* living, there is no limit to how rich and rewarding your life can become.

Della, a client of mine shared with me recently how taking responsibility for her relationship with her mum has completely changed their relationship. Previously, Della had always felt like her mother nagged her all the time and she related to her mother as someone who was forever trying to "fix her." Of course, she knew her mom loved her, and she valued her relationship with her mom enormously, but every time her mother would say anything, Della would bristle. She heard only nagging. This meant that Della often was unable to enjoy conversations with her mum, and more often than not, their time together would include at least one or two tense interchanges as Della rebuked her mum. Sometimes she would just avoid being around her when she wasn't in the mood for her "constant pestering." But by taking responsibility for how she listened to her mum and making the decision to relate to her mother as someone who really cared for her, rather than someone who was always trying to fix her, it allowed her to drop her defenses and enjoy their time together much more.

Linda, another client, had a similar experience regarding her daily commute to work from her home in New Jersey to her office on Wall Street where she works as a broker. During our conversations, I noticed that Linda often complained about her commuting experience. In great details she would describe how she had to leave home by 5:30 a.m., drive 15 minutes to the station, ride a train for 30 minutes, jump on a ferry across the Hudson River to Manhattan and then catch a second train to her office. Now I'm not saying that if faced with this commute, I would wake up excited every morning, but the facts were that *she chose* to move from her apartment in Manhattan to a larger home in New Jersey when she had her first child. And *she chose* to stay in her high-paying Wall

Street job, rather than look for another job closer to home with less commute. Linda's continual complaining about her commute served no positive purpose and only added unnecessary negativity to her day. Why perpetuate the pain by adding five, ten or 30 minutes of unpleasantness to her day moaning about it? Linda began to see that she was accountable for the quality of her day regardless of her commute. With that perspective, she began to use the commuting time each day to enrich, rather than erode, the quality of her day. I won't go so far as to say that she woke up every day excited about commuting to work, but I know it no longer makes her feel so miserable, stressed and annoyed. The good news is that by taking responsibility for her experience of her daily commute, Linda now arrives at work less physically sapped and in much better spirits than she did previously.

As a parent, I have experienced a similar situation myself with raising my children. It's very easy to get caught in a trap complaining about the behavior of our children. The fact is that children are children and sometimes—shock horror—they act childish! Babies wake up at night, two-year-olds throw tantrums, three-year-olds wet their beds and all children get tired and grumpy and go through phases where their behavior is less than…well…adult like! What's to be gained by complaining about it? Sure there are days that can be more challenging than others, but that's true for all of life. So, if you have children, instead of having your children be a key source of complaint in your life, take responsibility for enjoying the experience of parenting them—and quit whining about how they disrupt your life (and your sleep) and behave so…childishly! After all, it is a privilege that you have them to raise in the first place. I know from experience that raising children is a lot more enjoyable when you come at it from that approach. It's a whole lot more fun for your kids too!

We Are All "Response-Able"

The word "responsible" comes from two words: *response* and *able*. Therefore, being responsible means that whilst you can't always choose your circumstances in life, you are always able to choose how you respond to those circumstances. Put another way, while you are not always responsible for your experiences *in* life, you are always responsible for your experiences *of* life. This is an important distinction to make!

Perhaps you have known someone who has overcome adversity such as cancer or personal tragedy, and is thankful for the difference this experience has made in their life. They are grateful because they choose to respond to their circumstances in a positive way. In doing so, the tremendous inner growth that took place because of this event transformed their day-to-day experience of being alive and deepened their appreciation for all that is good in their life. Sadly, for some the wake-up call that life is precious, short and to be lived fully comes too late. So, regardless of the state of your life right now, don't wait to be confronted by a life-threatening situation to decide to live your life the way you *really* want to.

It is no accident that the people who are the unhappiest and least successful in life are also the most fiercely resistant to the idea that they are response- *able* for their life. Ask them how they got where they are and you will likely hear a long tale of misfortune and lack of opportunity. They will share how some person or event (or series of them) "ruined" their life: they became redundant in a corporate downsize, their spouse walked out on them, their children turned to drugs, their business partner swindled them…the list is endless. Such people refuse to acknowledge not only their role in the situation, but also their ability to respond to it differently. In doing so, they choose the path of blame and victim hood, rather than the path of courage.

Choose How You Will Let Your Childhood Impact Your Adulthood

Perhaps you are a "tough case" and, as you read this you are still resisting what I'm saying. You may think, "I've heard all this responsibility stuff before and I still think it's a load of crap." If that's the case, then maybe there is something that happened to you that you are still resentful about and for which you adamantly refuse to take responsibility. Don't get me wrong though, I agree that there are events that can happen to people for which they cannot be held responsible: events that have truly left them a victim of forces and circumstances beyond their control, events which they actually have a responsibility for remembering so they can ensure they never happen again.

For instance, you had no say in how your parents parented you, nor can you be blamed for having placed your trust in them (or other caregivers). Sadly, many children are not raised in loving and secure homes. Millions don't even have clean drinking water or sufficient food much less an opportunity to gain education. These are facts, which as adults we must take joint responsibility for trying to improve for future generations. However, despite the lack of control children have on their circumstances as they grow into adults, it does not change the truth that as adults they need to take responsibility for their life lest the circumstances of their childhood continue to have the power to determine their experience of adulthood. Therefore, if something from your past still plagues you, I invite you to take a look a little deeper into what this idea of being fully responsible is all about.

Obviously, you can never change the past, but you can change how you choose to think about it. Your past doesn't need to define who you are or the future you will have. As an adult, you have the power to choose how you react to the events of your childhood and to choose to stop letting the past determine your future.

Yes, placing the blame on someone else's shoulders reduces the load you carry on yours, but it also undermines your personal power. As much as you may have developed a comfortable habit of blaming *other* people or circumstances for *your* problems today, they are still *your* problems. All the blaming in the world isn't going to change that one iota.

> *You can never change the past, but you can change how you choose to think about it.*

The only thing that blaming does is to keep you stuck in a rut that prevents you from taking actions needed to create the life you want.

Letting the past go and leaving it squarely in the past is *not* about denying the very real experiences you had to endure. It *is* about cutting the chains that keep you bonded to the past so you can move forward to create whatever your heart desires for your future, free of resentment, anger and bitterness. It is *your* choice how you respond, and *you* alone are accountable for the impact your childhood has on your life today and the life you want to create for yourself tomorrow.

How Have You Contributed to Your Problems?

Whilst I believe there are times when people can truly be victims, we are still responsible for our experience of life. This was the profound lesson learned by Victor Frankl a Jewish psychologist interned in the concentration camps of Nazi Germany where thousands around him were being taken off to their deaths in the gas chambers. The Nazis robbed him of his clothes and everything he owned. They sent his father, mother, brother, wife and friends to the gas chambers. They starved him, beat him and forced him to undergo the most humiliating and degrading things possible to any human being. However, what they could not do was take from him his ability to choose how he would respond to his circumstances. Most importantly, they could never take away his dignity. He could give it away or relinquish it in despair, but that would be his choice, and unless he chose that path, he would preserve his dignity. As Frankl later wrote in his book *Man's Search for Meaning*, "Everything can be taken from a man but one thing; the last of the human freedoms—to choose one's attitude in any given set of circumstances, to choose one's own way."

Fortunately, most of us have never had to endure the torments and atrocities Frankl suffered. Until you acknowledge that you have actively contributed to your circumstances, you will be incapable of changing those you are dissatisfied with. This doesn't imply that you made your decisions recklessly or with poor intent. Neither does it imply that your decisions were unjustified. It simply means *you* made the decisions.

There are three ways you contribute to creating problem areas in your life:

1. *As a causative agent*—The choices you made led to creating your current situation. For example: You lived beyond your

means and ended up having to get a 2nd mortgage on your home; You didn't study hard enough and failed an exam. (Exercise 1.1 will help you identify these choices.)

2. *By your response*—The event or circumstances may have been completely out of your control, but the way you responded did not improve the situation and possibly worsened it. For example: Your child crashed the family car and you completely over reacted saying hurtful things that damaged your relationship: You found out your partner was cheating on you so you cheated too and now your marriage is in tatters.

3. *By your lack of response*—Once again, you may not have contributed to your circumstances, but instead of responding to your situation, you chose to do nothing (perhaps pretending that everything was okay when it really wasn't or convincing yourself that any response on your part was futile). The fact is you cannot choose not to choose. If you choose not to respond, then this is your choice. For example: Your doctor told you to watch your weight but you didn't change your lifestyle and now your health is suffering; you noticed that your business partner was spending money foolishly, but you said nothing and now you've had to declare bankruptcy.

Be Honest with Yourself!

Sometimes it's all too convenient to lie to yourself by either misrepresenting the truth or by only telling half the story. "No mum, I promise I didn't eat all the candy in the jar," I recall my then four-year-old daughter, Madelyn, pleading with me. When I told her the consequences she would face if I found out she was not being truthful with me, she guiltily conceded "Well, not *all* the candy. I gave one piece to each of my brothers." *Oh, the tangled webs we weave when we practice to deceive.* These lines from a poem by Sir Walter Scott extend to deceiving oneself. Small fibs, if let go, gradually, insidiously, grow into bigger ones as the truth becomes harder and harder to look in the face. (Of course I am hoping Madelyn will learn this lesson whilst she is still young.)

When it comes to holding yourself accountable for what is amiss in your life, failure to be fully honest will cost you. In fact, denial of reality can be deadly. Literally. I mean how many people have you heard of who turn a blind eye to their health problems until it deteriorates dramatically, then go to the doctor only to find they have advanced cancer with just a few months to live? Too bloody many! Behavioral scientists have dubbed this tendency to avoid facing realities that don't make us feel all warm and fuzzy inside the Perceptual Defense Mechanism. Of course, this phenomenon may have a positive role in coping with extremely traumatic circumstances. For instance, if you've ever been in an accident you simply may not have been able to recall moments leading up to or directly following the actual accident. However, it also can have a negative outcome if it prevents us from accessing information we need for our well-being. Here are a few more examples of Perceptual Defense in "negative mode."

- Someone cheats on his or her spouse and the spouse says they had no idea what was going on until they literally caught their partner red-handed, despite the telltale evidence staring them in the face.
- A teenager gets involved with drugs and his or her parents refuse to believe it could be happening to *their* child.
- A company downsizes in response to market changes, yet employees say they didn't see it coming, even though the writing was on the wall.

Exercise 1.1: Identifying Your Role in Your Problems

This exercise is designed to help you identify how you have contributed to those areas in your life, which cause you to feel dissatisfied. You may think of them as problems, or you may just think of them as aspects of your life that you are "tolerating," but are less than happy about. Given the tendency we all have to avoid facing unpleasant realities in our lives, you may find yourself resisting taking the time to do this exercise. However, unless you are prepared to feel the discomfort that goes with taking responsibility, you aren't going to enjoy the benefits of doing so. I therefore encourage you to do this exercise in spite of any resistance you have.

(A) In each of the following areas of your life write down a problem or issue that is causing you to feel dissatisfied, angry, resentful or unhappy in some way. If nothing comes to mind, just move on to the next one.
- Relationship with Spouse/Family
- Career/Professional Development/Business
- Finances
- Personal Health/Sense of Wellbeing
- Recreation/Social Life
- Physical Environment (where you live, work, etc.)

(B) Answer as honestly as you can the following questions to identify how you may have contributed to this problem or issue. Repeat the exercise for each issue you identified above:
1. What choices did you make that led to the result you didn't want?
2. What did you do or fail to do?
3. Did you trust someone foolishly?
4. What did you fail to be proactive about or do as well as you could have?
5. How did you underestimate your ability to accomplish something?
6. Did you fail to trust someone when you could have (by delegating to them or developing a more meaningful relationship with them)?
7. Did you settle too soon or for less than what you really wanted (in your career, relationship or life)?
8. Did you commit yourself to something for the wrong reasons (e.g., to please someone, to earn a quick buck, because it seemed like fun, to avoid conflict, to prove a point)?
9. Did you compromise your values and integrity for the sake of immediate peace or pleasure?

10. Was there something you could have said "yes" to, but instead held back and missed out?

Career Specific —

11. Did you fail to put in the effort required to fulfill your responsibilities well?

12. Did you fail to address an issue with an employee or co-worker effectively?

13. Did you let the excuses, "I don't have time," or, "I 'm too busy," stop you from attending to other important (but not urgent) matters?

14. Did you choose not to respond to feedback from a superior about your performance?

15. Did you fail to prioritize your time and manage your commitments effectively?

16. Did you choose to stay in a job you should have left, or left one you should have kept?

17. Did you make a high-risk decision, but failed to mitigate the risks?

18. Did you fail to ask for what you really wanted?

Relationship Specific —

19. Did you allow someone to treat you continually with a lack of respect or dignity?

20. Did you choose not to confront someone about something that was bothering you?

21. Did you fail to let someone know what your needs were?

22. Did you choose to focus on your career instead of your relationships?

23. Did you walk away, withdraw or give up instead of staying to express how you felt?

24. Did you fail to truly listen to someone to gain a better understanding of their perspective?

25. Did you withhold love, affection, time, attention or information from someone that undermined or damaged your relationship with them?

26. Did you lose your temper or say something intentionally to hurt someone?
27. Did you fail to apologize when your behavior caused hurt?
28. Did you choose to go with the crowd when you knew it wasn't the right thing to do?
29. Did you make a decision in the heat of the moment that caused a lot of damage?

Money Specific —
30. Did you jump into something without enough thought or properly assessing the risks?
31. Did you choose to invest in something that failed?
32. Did you choose to not make an investment or sell funds that were profitable for others?
33. Did you fail to budget appropriately?
34. Did you spend money you didn't have (or someone else's money) for short-term gain?
35. Did you fail to take corrective action when things started to go off the track, hoping it would just get better?

The Buck Stops with You!

If there is any aspect of your life you are unhappy, angry, hurt or upset about, you own those feelings and you're 100% accountable for them. As I said earlier, our innate instinct for self-preservation wants us to avoid the pain of owning our part in creating certain situations. It's just no fun taking the blame for our unhappiness, so we blame other people or circumstances for our failure to *have* what we want, to *be* who we want and to *feel* as happy as we want.

> *"You cannot solve a problem by condemning it."*
> –Wayne Dyer

Given that the life you are living today is the lump some of all the choices you have made up to this point, what would you like your life to be like 1, 5, or even 25 years from now? Whatever it is that you want, whether in your relationships, your career or your life in general, you alone are responsible for making the choices that will bring it into being. So no matter what challenges you face, no matter what impossible people you have to deal with, no matter what the tea leaves say (or don't say) lies ahead for you, the buck stops firmly and squarely with you!

Learning Responsibility the Hard Way

I learnt this lesson the hard way. During my early teens, I began to develop bulimia, an eating disorder. I was, as my parents put it, "a big framed girl" who developed early reaching my full adult height by the time I was 14. "It's in the family," I was told, which seemed pretty evident from my 220 pound nana and her rather rotund siblings in the black and white, sepia photographs that sat on the mantle. At the time, I would have much preferred to have developed a good case of anorexia, which would have been far trendier and not have involved any of the messy throwing up that is the hallmark of bulimia. However, I didn't have the self-control (something I further chastised myself for) to permanently starve myself. Instead, I found myself trying to starve myself all day at school, but when I arrived home at 4.30, I would completely pig out on whatever I could find in the kitchen. Growing up on a dairy farm, that meant I consumed an abundance of butter, bacon, cream and extra, full-cream milk and a marked lack of low cal, waist-friendly foods.

Needless to say, my daily binges left me putting on more padding and moving further and further away from the skinny, bony, waif look that I thought would guarantee the end to all my adolescent problems (i.e., all the boys would think I was cute). As the years passed, my bulimia became more and more entrenched. It became second nature for me to go outside to the toilet after my afternoon binge and purge whatever I could. Then after dinner, and a second or third helping of bread and butter pudding, or golden syrup dumplings (my very favorite) I would do it again.

By my final year in high school, I had decided that it was all my mum's fault for never having nice fruit around the house. Having gone through years of drought with a near zero income, and having to feed, clothe and raise seven kids, she considered foods such as nice crisp apples to be a luxury we could ill afford. We always got the big cheap bags of bruised, flowery, soft apples, which usually sat there since none of us had much desire to eat them. Yes, I decided, it was completely my mum's fault for not having enough healthy food around the place and for always making dessert, which, of course, I just *had* to eat.

My dad didn't get off the hook either. He was to blame for having imbued in all of us, from the first spoon of cereal that went in our mouths as babies, that leaving food on your plate (or in your cereal bowl) was a sin. Though I was not a child of the depression, my nana, who lived with us until I was about eight, was. Hence, the "waste not, want not" ethic was firmly emblazoned in our young minds. What's more, both sides of my family had produced many women who had big builds—another cross against my parents for passing down to me what I perceived was an oversized body and which I felt powerless to change. So with the blame for my eating disorder laid squarely at my parents feet, I concluded that, once I was out of their home, I would be able to control my eating problem, or more appropriate, my spewing problem, and be "normal" again, just like all my girlfriends. (Unbeknownst to me at the time, many of them were struggling with their own eating hang-ups and body image demons.)

At eighteen, after finishing high school with top grades, I moved to Melbourne to go to the University. Now a three and a half hour drive from my rural home and mum's puddings, I was sure that in new surroundings I would be able to conquer my bulimia. Of course, the reality of being suddenly and completely on my own wasn't quite as glamorous as I'd envisaged. In fact, food became something I turned to more and more for a quick hit of comfort. Instead of getting better, my bulimia deteriorated! Now I could no longer blame my parents. But aha! I could now blame the awful little ground floor apartment I was living in with a couple other country girls. A malfunctioning fridge prevented me from buying fruit and vegetables and preparing decent meals and required me to live off toasted cheese sandwiches! This, compounded with drinking more alcohol than I'd ever drunk before, caused my skin to break out into terrible and very unattractive cystic acne. This depressed me more. To numb the ache, I binged more, purged more and on the cycle went, snowballing to where I felt completely and miserably out of control. Somehow I managed to keep up my "got it together" front at school, where I was getting good grades, but I kept this dark secret from my many new friends. This only increased my self-loathing and shame, as I felt like a complete fraud. Once again, I blamed my parents, throwing in the extra charge of not being able to assist me financially as other kids parents did. (For the record, my parents did offer to help me financially many times—I always refused their money, as things were very tight for them on the farm due to drought and the other five kids still at home.) I also blamed my environment and the awful flat I was living in. If I lived in a nice flat, I just knew things would be better, or so I kept wishfully telling myself.

The following year I moved in with some other friends into a much nicer little place. The only hitch was that I had to share a bedroom to afford it. The bulimia abated...a little. This time I added the people I was living with to the list of reasons I couldn't get my eating sorted out. If only I lived with people I didn't know, I could start anew. After six months, I decided to move to a ramshackle old house that I shared with two complete strangers. Though the house was a dump (what else could you call something where the toilet was an outhouse with no door?), it was in a great location, and the people I lived with were fun. Life in general improved, but I *still* wasn't able to get my bulimia under control, despite determinedly declaring to myself countless times that I was never ever *ever* going to overeat or throw up again. It was around this time that I had a major breakdown—and reached a turning point—after eating a whole package of my favorite mint slice cookies during a long study session. Once I had eaten one, I figured I'd blown it and may as well eat the entire package. I recall trying to bring up (i.e. purge, vomit) the cookies unsuccessfully and kneeling on the floor in front of my wardrobe mirror, tears of complete and utter self-contempt and loathing streaming down my face. I felt utter despair and hopelessness about ever overcoming my bulimia. It was then that I realized a simple but profound truth: *wherever I go, I take myself with me.*

Sure, some of the environmental circumstances were at times aggravating my "disease" (which I have since learnt is what bulimia is rather than just a distasteful deficiency in character), but no matter what I changed about my environment, I still had the same internal struggle. I vividly recall thinking that if the rest of my life is going to be like this, preoccupied with food 24 hours a day, unable to control what I eat, consumed with feelings of utter disdain, loathing and shame, then I don't want to live it.

Now I am not saying that I felt suicidal. I just knew that if I was going to spend another 50 plus years on this earth, I had to do something more than just wishful thinking about my eating disorder. Like the saying goes, "keep doing what you've always done, keep getting what you've always got." The truth of this suddenly hit home like a ton of bricks. I realized that I had to take full responsibility for my eating disorder. I had to stop looking outside of myself for *why* I was stuck in this horrendous cycle, and I had to humble myself enough to accept that my efforts to date had been completely unsuccessful.

It was soon after this that I shared with one of my closest friends, Anna, that I had bulimia. I was expecting her to show total disgust (as so many people do —picturing the bulimic person with their head stuck down a toilet bowl). Instead, she responded without judgment and with consideration. "Margie, you need to get some professional help," was all she said. A part of me was resisting this advice because getting "professional help" was tantamount to acknowledging I had a serious problem. In my mind, only people who had "mental problems"—not a label I was rapt about putting on myself—saw psychologists. (In Australia then, as now, therapy has a rather negative stigma attached to it.) Up to this point, I'd been able to convince myself that I just had a little issue with food and that I could overcome it myself if I just tried hard enough. Getting help was akin to admitting defeat and making a public declaration that I did in fact have a problem, a big, whopping, serious problem. At the same time, taking complete responsibility for doing whatever it took to get out of this debilitating cycle, including seeing a psychologist, gave me hope.

The following week I went to see a psychologist who worked at the university I attended and so began my weekly visits, which continued through my final year at university. Susan was compassionate and completely non-judgmental, and to this day, I feel deeply grateful to her. She helped me see that although my environment, growing up in a large family on a farm, was a factor that contributed to the development of my eating disorder, I could not blame my bulimia on that. It was how I responded to that environmental that caused my problem. During that year, I began slowly but surely, to get my eating and my life under control. I learnt new strategies for dealing with stress and began to transform my attitude toward food. As I did, I started losing weight. I cut my hair and my skin began to clear up. By the end of that final year in university, I felt like I was emerging from a long dark tunnel. What I had learned in the intervening period was that although my environment were factors that contributed to my eating disorder, it was the choices I made along the way that got me to the crisis point. Yep, my mum did make a delicious bread pudding, but I put it in my mouth. By taking complete responsibility for my

> *Only by taking responsibility for your predicament, however humbling that may be, can you take the actions to address it effectively.*

situation, as humbling as it was at the time, I was able to take the actions needed to work through my bulimia and overcome it. I no longer have an ongoing pre-occupation and struggle with food and weight. In making peace with food and myself, my body weight dropped to the perfect weight for me (as distinct from the unhealthy weight of the super models I had aspired to look like), and in between my pregnancies, has stayed very near the same ever since.

Of course, the circumstances surrounding my own experiences of learning to take responsibility will most likely be very different from the circumstances you find yourself in now. However, a common thread ties both you and I together in that we each have to learn to take a critical and sometimes painful look at where we are not fully owning the circumstances of our lives. Only by finding the guts to take full responsibility for those aspects of your life that you feel less than great about—whether it be a low-grade irritation or a high-grade upset—can you take the actions you need to create the wonderful life that you wish to have.

Ultimately, the point at which we choose to take responsibility is different for each of us. How much pain one must feel before they are prepared to let go of the pay off they get from blaming varies from person to person. It's up to you whether or not you want to wait for the elevator to descend to the basement before you get off. My recommendation is the sooner the better, because the longer you wait the harder and more painful it is going to be and the higher the cost to your career, your sense of wellbeing, your relationships and your overall quality of life.

If nothing changes, nothing changes. If you are okay about the idea that your future is going to be pretty similar to what you've been experiencing up until now, then by all means, keep doing what you're doing now. However, if the thought that your future will largely resemble your past gives you a sinking feeling in the pit of your stomach, regard it as a signal that it's high time to pull your finger out (as we Aussies like to say) and get on with turning your life into one that really delights you.

Finding the guts to take absolute responsibility is the crucial first step in recreating your life the way you *really* want it to be. Your willingness to do this is a vital and huge step forward in the direction of your success and happiness. Does more work lie ahead? You bet it does. But don't let that worry you as within you lies all the courage you need to unleash your unique greatness on the world and create a future that gives you a far more meaningful, fulfilling and enjoyable experience of being alive in the world.

Chapter 2
The Courage to Live with Integrity

*"Integrity is one of many paths you can follow in life.
It distinguishes itself from others because it is the only
path upon which you will never get lost."*
—Author Unknown

If you can cast your memory back to your days in the classroom you may recall (*if* you were paying attention) learning that "integers," from which the word integrity derives, are whole numbers. Likewise, integrity is also about wholeness. This wholeness comes through having alignment between what you believe is the right thing to do and what you are doing, and on a deeper level, between who you were born into this world to be and who you are being. At its core, integrity is about being true to yourself.

Although the path of integrity is not always an easy one to follow, it is the only path that will allow you to experience real peace of mind, contentment and harmony in your life. Indeed, only by building your life on a solid foundation of integrity can you live the fulfilling and fabulous life you wish for. Why? Because without integrity, nothing works!

Just think about the foundation on which your home is built. If it was built on unstable soil, when the wind blew hard or the rain bucketed down, it would not be able to withstand the onslaught and its walls would eventually begin to crumble. The same would also occur if you wanted to expand it by building a second or third story. Unable to cope with the additional pressure placed upon it, it would begin to sink in places due to the extra weight and render your home uninhabitable. It's the same for your life. If you want to live a bigger, more rewarding life, then you'd better have a rock solid foundation upon which to build it. Indeed, the higher you climb, the harder the wind blows so if there are any cracks in your foundation—any areas where your integrity is compromised—then those cracks will begin to give way under the pressure of mounting expectations, responsibility, power and status. And if the foundation crumbles, the consequences can be devastating for you and those around you.

Whilst writing this chapter, I attended a ball in Dallas where several local businessmen were made laureates of the Dallas Business Hall of Fame, among them Ross Perot, the computer billionaire and twice presidential candidate. Of all the things he could have spoken about during his speech—leadership, business success, finance, risk, or entrepreneurship—he chose to speak about integrity. He stated that to succeed in business one must be a person of their word with a steadfast commitment to integrity. I'm going to take this a step further and state that to be successful in *life*, and I mean *truly* successful, you must be a person of your word with a steadfast commitment to living with integrity in every aspect of your life. Given that integrity is the foundation upon which Perot achieved his extraordinary success (it's no small feat to get from breaking horses to running for President), I'm confident he'd agree that integrity is essential to enjoy success, not just in business, but in *every area* of life.

So what does the concept of integrity mean to you? I've found that integrity means different things to different people, from honoring their commitments and being ethical in their business dealings to not cheating on their tax return, or for that matter, on their spouse. Of course, integrity is not to be confused with morality. Morals are societal standards, which can change over time and be different across cultures (think mini-skirts in 18th Century England) and so what is morally right for one person may not be so for another. Integrity transcends morality for integrity is timeless and universal.

As Isaac Asimov once said, "Never let your sense of morals prevent you from doing what's right." Accordingly, integrity does not require you to look outward to society for direction, but to look inward to your heart. Doing so provides a compass to guide your choices moving you away from disharmony and into wholeness.

Integrity of the Spirit

Often people have a narrow concept of what integrity means and accordingly, are not fully present to where they may be living with a lack of integrity in their life or how this may be undermining their ability to feel truly content and powerful. I therefore invite you to reflect on what integrity means to you and the level of integrity you have in your life.

It is very easy to live under the illusion that because in the *outer areas* of our lives we are good, honest, hardworking people who never cheat a soul that we have full integrity. However, we may be completely unaware of the lack of integrity in the *inner areas* of our lives. That is, not just in what we are *doing* in the world, but in whom we are *being* in the world. You see, at its core, integrity is far more than just being honest in your external dealings—obeying the law, paying your taxes and being a "good" person. It is also about being honest in your inner dealings and honoring the sacred nature of who you are.

> *"We have the responsibility to listen and honor the siren call of our souls—too often silenced by our egos."*
> —Lance Secretan, author of *Inspire: What Great Leaders Do*

Psychologist Harry Frankfurt spent many years studying the concept of integrity and concluded that living with integrity was akin to living "wholeheartedly". Given that psychologists generally like to stay in the realm of the head and cognitive processes (where things can be quantified), it is interesting that Frankfurt felt compelled to refer to the heart (which goes beyond measurement) in describing integrity. Since we must live from the heart in order to have courage, then it makes sense that we must have a *whole* heart in order to do so (as distinct from a heart that is filled with compromise and disharmony).

In relation to our lives, the virtue of integrity allows us to experience a sense of wholeness and unity between not just our mind (what we *know* intellectually to be right) and our actions, but between our heart (what we *feel* to be right) and our actions. So at its deepest level, the level at which the most profound transformation occurs and which the greatest courage is found, integrity is about unity between *what* your heart calls you to *do* and what you are *doing*; between *who* your heart calls you to *be* and who you are *being*. When you are living fully in integrity, you can experience wholeness and harmony at every level of your being: body, mind and spirit.

Yes, that's right—body, mind *and spirit*. You see it is my belief that who we are is not just a physical being born into this world to hang out and make the best of it for however long we get to live, without any particular purpose. Rather, each of us is a spiritual being born into this world with a unique set of gifts and talents and with the ability to contribute to the world in a way no other human being ever has before or ever will again.

At its core, integrity is about wholeness on every level of your being: body, mind and spirit

Sometimes people react with cynicism and resistance at the mere mention of the phrase "spiritual being" because they confuse spirituality with religion. Allow me to clarify. When I speak of spirituality, I am not talking about any particular set of religious beliefs or dogma, but something that transcends all religions and goes beyond what we can experience physically. In the words of William Bloom, "I simply mean that whole reality and dimension which is bigger, more creative, more loving, more powerful, more visionary, more wise, more mysterious than the daily human existence." It is my deep conviction that we are all spiritual beings and that there is a sacredness within each of us (and yes, that includes you) that longs to express itself in the world. This sacredness holds the wisdom to guide you in fulfilling your greatest potential and expressing your uniqueness fully in the world.

Having faith in a divine power and wisdom greater than ourselves, in something that touches and runs through all of life connecting all that ever was with all that ever will be, is not something you gain by being told about it. Rather it is something you come to know through experiencing it. For instance, recently I caught up with a Scottish friend of mine, Bill, who has been living in Singapore for the last three years. He recounted how he and his wife Fran recently took their children and their Amah (the name for housemaids in Asia) to Europe for a ski holiday. They had told their Amah, a 37-year-old woman from the Philippines who had never lived outside the tropics, that it would be very cold where they were going. However, their describing the cold to her was simply insufficient for her to grasp just what it meant to be cold. Only when they arrived at their mountain top destination did she really come to know through direct experience what it was to feel cold. The same would be true if you tried to explain to someone who had never left the confines of their small village in the middle of the Amazon rainforest what it is like to walk through the busy, noisy, vibrant streets of New York. No matter how brilliant and articulate your description, they would not be able to appreciate the experience and know the feeling of being in New York surrounded by skyscrapers and thousands of people briskly walking from one place to another.

The same is true when it comes to faith in something bigger than yourself. People can tell you about God, or their Higher Power, or whatever they like to call it, until they are blue in the face, but really *knowing* about something bigger than yourself is not something you get by being told about it. Rather it requires that you open yourself to the possibility of its existence. For then, and only then, however doubtful you still are, can you become available to experiencing it in a very intimate way. Only then can you move from a theoretical, intellectual understanding to a deep and personal knowing.

Sometimes it speaks to you through your intuition or a gut feeling, sometimes through your dreams, sometimes through a strange and amazing coincidence (or a series of them), and sometimes you just get a sudden insight about something from out of nowhere. The more closely you are connected to your innate wisdom, the better it can serve you. Too often, though, we ignore our inklings or fail to pay attention to the messages that are being presented to us. Spending time in silence provides an opportunity for you to get in touch with what is sometimes referred to as your "inner voice." For some people, meditation provides a powerful way to access wisdom and intuition, for others it is journaling, spending time out in nature or in prayer.

Perhaps my words are resonating with you on some level. Given that truth lives in the heart, it makes sense that what comes from my heart resonates with yours. However, perhaps you are finding it difficult to swallow the idea that there is more to your life than what you can experience with your physical senses. If that's the case, then that is okay too. You are where you are and wherever you are in your beliefs is perfect in itself. But have the courage, at least, to open your mind and your heart to such a possibility. Take a moment to reflect and behold the wonders of nature that surround you—from the perfection of the seasons, the majesty of the stars, the miracle of a newborn baby, the rhythm of the tides and earth and the beauty and mystery of the life that exists within it. As you do, you may sense on some level that there is something far bigger and far greater than yourself at play in the world even if you cannot understand, much less articulate, what it is.

Maybe your struggle with the idea of a power or life force greater than you—and the very notion that there is an entity such as God—stems from seeing so much suffering in the world. "After all" you argue, "If there was such thing as God or some Higher Power that is all loving and all knowing and all powerful then why would they allow such suffering to happen?" But in the words of Marianne Williamson, "The question is not, 'What kind of God would let children starve?' but rather, 'What kind of people let children starve?'" Ultimately, having faith in the sacredness that lies within you and in something greater than yourself does not imply the absence of doubt on your part. Rather, when confronted by a choice to believe or not believe in something beyond what you can see, touch or physically experience you choose to believe even though you don't comprehend it and you have many more questions than you do answers about the nature of its existence.

It is not my intention in this book to convince you to forego your beliefs or to adopt mine. However, I do see it as my responsibility to challenge your thinking and encourage you to being open minded about the nature of the universe and your place in it. Regardless of what you do or don't believe, the fact is that most of us are so busy with the business of living that we aren't tuned in to the wisdom that comes through our hearts to be able to live with integrity at its deepest level. And when the messages persist for long enough that we have no choice but to pay them attention, we too readily try to discredit them as they often nudge us in a direction we just don't want to go, or more accurately, in a direction we feel too scared to go.

The Integrity/Courage Connection

But that's exactly where courage kicks in. Integrity takes courage because the path of integrity is often not the easiest path nor most convenient one to travel. We all experience occasions when it is much easier to just go with the status quo, take the politically expedient and socially acceptable route and step away from our principles or the voice of our conscious. So, unless you're committed to a personal foundation built on integrity, you will not be able to muster up the courage you need to make the right choice when it really counts. Without this commitment, you will find it very difficult, nigh impossible, to remain true to your deepest values and core principals, and as a result, unable to do honor to the unique potential you have within you.

When you are committed to living fully with integrity, you are compelled to take the actions you know are right for you, however great the doubt, large the risk and daunting the challenge. You simply cannot help but choose to follow the path that stirs your heart, however great the price and scary the prospect, for you know that the price you will pay for not doing so will be far greater.

During the writing of this book, I contacted Dr. Patch Adams. You may recall him from the MCA/Universal Studios movie named after him in which his character, played by Robin Williams, defied conservative corporate medical care. He became famous for his clown-like antics that cheered up children who were hospitalized. Like so many truly great men and women, Patch Adams' life is one which epitomizes real integrity and because of this, demonstrates great courage. I asked Patch how, throughout his life, he found the courage to do all that he had despite the many setbacks and obstacles he has faced. He replied that he simply did what was true for him so that he didn't have to "live a lie." This very humble man also said, "I would claim that everything that I do is because I am only brave enough to do what's true for me. It's never felt like a big deal. *Not* doing it would feel like a big deal."

Like Patch Adams, we all have enough courage to do what is true for us (for that is all the courage we need anyway). However, unlike Patch Adams, most of us are not connected closely enough with our hearts to know what is true for us. Hence, why it is so important to take the time to reflect on how, in going about the business of our daily lives, we may in fact be "living a lie" and how our doing so may be undermining our happiness and limiting the potential we have in the world.

You are no doubt familiar with the famous words of Shakespeare, "*This above all: to thine own self be true.*" These words echo the essence of spiritual integrity as Shakespeare's reference to the self is not merely to the physical self, but to the spiritual self. Maybe you are familiar with the expression, "I couldn't live with my*self* if I did that." This expression refers to "I" and "self" as two separate entities with "I" being the person you think of yourself as in everyday terms and "self" being the spiritual dimension of who you are. In other words, if you do not act in accordance with the voice of your spirit "self" (that speaks through your conscious and the gentle or not so gentle tugs on your heart), there will be conflict between "I" and the "self". The path of integrity—which has you being true to your self—allows you to harmoniously live with your *self*, and even better, to feel truly great about your*self*!

> *When you are fully committed to a life of integrity, you are compelled to take the actions you know are right for you, however great the doubt, large the risk or daunting the challenge.*

A Life of Integrity—Why Bother?

Given that most people would like to feel whole and good about themselves, why then do so many people act in ways that lack integrity? I'm so glad you asked! Because they are too attached to the pay offs and not sufficiently aware of the costs of their behavior to admit it, much less change it. As with all choices, there are pros and cons whichever way you go. And when people make a judgment that doing the right thing is going to be more troublesome and less convenient than doing the easy thing, it's no surprise they choose the road *more* traveled. So, why even bother?

By reflecting on how a lack of integrity may be affecting your life, you will be far better equipped to find the courage to live with integrity and to do the work required to restore your personal foundation to one of uncompromised integrity. Of course, owning up to where you are failing to live with integrity takes not only self reflection but also brutal honesty and a good dose of humility. So if you have not been running your life with a conscious and strong commitment to integrity, I urge you to think about how profoundly your choices may be impacting the true quality of your life.

Settling for "Less Than" What You Really Want

One of my favorite sayings in life is, "You get what you tolerate!" So if you have been settling for "less than" what makes you feel really good in any aspect of your life—from your relationships and physical well-being to your career and pay check—then you are not living a life of integrity in its deepest sense. Integrity means not tolerating anything that involves selling out on what brings you a deep sense of joy, fulfillment and satisfaction. Integrity therefore compels you to speak your truth about issues of concern, ask for what you want, stand your ground and run your life in a way that doesn't involve settling for "less than" in any way. So what things are you "putting up" with in your life—in your work, your relationships, your home environment, your health and well-being? For instance, if you have a job you really don't enjoy very much, but you are staying in it, then you are settling for "less than" what you would like for yourself in the way you earn money and in the way you spend a huge proportion of your time each week.

Inner Conflict

When I met Bob, he had been married for nearly 20 years. Whilst discussing the issue of integrity and the impact a lack of it can have on one's relationships, Bob shared with me how about 15 years earlier he had a brief affair with another woman. It ended not very long after it began and given that it had meant little to Bob at the time, he decided there was no point in telling his wife about his infidelity since it would only be hurtful to her and may have jeopardized their marriage. So for the last 15 years Bob had been living with the knowledge that he had cheated on his wife and whilst they had remained married, their marriage had long since lost its passion.

> *"Courage is the price that life exacts for granting peace."*
> –Amelia Earhart

I asked Bob to think about how it would feel for him not to be living with this lie and to share with his wife not only what he had done, but how, ever since then, he had failed to have integrity and then to ask her for her forgiveness. Initially, Bob was pretty resistant to the idea of coming clean with his wife. But as he got present to the huge toll it had taken on his own sense of self and on his marriage, he began to realize that as difficult as it would be to confess his transgressions to his wife, the price he would continue to pay for continuing to withhold was even greater. Only by mustering up the courage to act with integrity with his wife, whom he loved very much, would he be able to enjoy the peace of mind he'd long since lost, and open up the possibility of creating with his wife the kind of loving and passionate relationship he truly wanted to have with her.

You see, peace of mind cannot exist unless your conscious is at rest, and the call of your heart has been heeded. Acting in ways that violate what you know is right and true for you results in a marked absence of inner harmony and a marked presence of inner unrest. Any significant withheld truth in a relationship will sabotage harmony and poison passion. For Bob, his failure to restore integrity in his relationship with his spouse only served to undermine his happiness and the joy available to both of them in their marriage. This lie lay between them in their bed each night and would continue to do so until he took responsibility for addressing it. You see, as much as you might like to, you can't compartmentalize your life and be selective about where you will practice integrity. It just doesn't work that way. As Mahatma Gandhi once said, "A man cannot do right in one department of life whiles he is occupied with doing wrong in another. Life is one indivisible whole." Acting in ways that lack integrity in *one* area of your life undermines your integrity in *every* area of your life.

Psychologists have coined the term "Cognitive Dissonance" to describe the inner conflict that results when there is discord between our behavior and beliefs. In order to quiet the dogfight going on in their heads, most people put in one huge effort to justify their actions. Here are some of the excuses I have heard justifying acting in ways that lack integrity:

- "They don't pay me enough, so it's only fair I get a little extra compensation this way."
- "My husband has checked out of our marriage so why shouldn't I?"
- "Everyone else does it— I can't see why I shouldn't."
- "What's the point of saying anything? It won't change anything."
- "If I didn't do it, someone else would have."

Just think of all the energy you lose trying to make yourself feel good or right and bridging the gap between who you truly want to be as a person and who you are being. It's not only wasted energy, it's also used in vain as, no matter how hard you try, you will never escape the unpleasant gnawing that eats away at your sense of worthiness. At day's end, self worth can only come from doing worthy things. If your mind is full of conflict, it's bloody difficult to enjoy peace of mind or a healthy sense of self worth. I know this to be true because I used to act in ways which constantly diminished my sense of integrity and made me feel less than great about myself.

> *"Self worth can only come from doing worthy things."*

Back in my teens (at the same time I was struggling with bulimia), I...ugh...this is even more humbling than my last confession... shoplifted. Yes, lipstick was my downfall. Of course, at the time I justified my behavior to myself with arguments that I was a poor student (who could not live without red lips), from a poor family who couldn't afford to give me the money other parents gave their kids. I also rationalized that the large companies I stole things from had so much money that my small bit of pilfering wouldn't even be noticed. To vindicate my moral stance on this, I only took things from large store chains and never from small businesses. "That," I self-righteously argued to myself, "just wouldn't be right!" Anyway, like so many people who shoplift, eventually I got caught. I cannot begin to convey the depth of the shame I felt when this happened. Shame not so much for what I had done, but rather for the possibility that what I had done might bring dishonor to my family, particularly my loving and "honest as the day is long" dad whom I felt so proud of and whom I wanted to make proud of me. As dishonorable an experience as this was, you might think that that would have been my wake-up call. It wasn't. Instead, my "Aha!" moment came several months later while reading a prayer book my mother had given me. I read something that made the distinction between the consequences of an act and whether an action was right or wrong. Though I'd probably heard similar stuff many times before from my parents, this time it hit me right between the eyes that it had *nothing* to do with whether or not that large retail chain would be hurt by my actions, and it had *everything* to do with the fact that it was just plain wrong to steal. As obvious as that distinction may be to you, I had just never truly gotten it before. (Some of us are slower learners than others.) At last, I got it. My dishonest behavior was hurting myself *much* more than it was harming anybody else. Duh.

Every time I took something that did not belong to me without paying, my brain went into overdrive justifying my actions. However, because I knew in my heart what I was doing was wrong (even though I wasn't consciously admitting it) it always left me with a big knot in my stomach. Did I feel good about myself afterward? Of course not! Sure I enjoyed the feeling of thinking

I'd gotten something for nothing, but what impacted my sense of self far more profoundly was that I had done something I would be ashamed of if anyone were to find out. Something I knew wasn't aligned with who I wanted to be and how I wanted to operate in the world. That knot in my stomach represented everything. It stood for the lie that I was living and the size of the gap between what I knew was the right thing to do and what I was actually doing. Only by bringing the two into alignment, by restoring integrity into my life, was I able to untie it.

We can justify our actions until we are blue in the face but that will never make them right. Ultimately, integrity requires that we give up justifying what we are doing (or what we've done) and just get on with doing what we know is right (which may mean going back and cleaning up any mess we've made.) Heck, think of the atrocious things human beings have done to one another and justified for reasons they felt were valid. Were they able to enjoy peace of mind? I think not. Spending every moment of every day being someone you don't feel *really* good about is no fun at all!

That's why people who choose to act in ways that lack integrity also avoid their own company like the plague, filling their days with as much activity as possible to drown out the voices of their conscience. And at night when the activity slows? They quiet the voices with alcohol, drugs, food, sex (if they can get it!) and sleeping pills. But whilst the behavior persists, so too does the conflict. At the end of the day, you cannot improve your life until you address those aspects of it that are out of integrity.

Remember Bob who I introduced to you earlier? When he found the courage to restore integrity in his marriage his whole experience of being alive transformed. Understandably, his wife was initially very hurt to learn about his infidelity. What made it worse for her was that he had kept this a secret for so long and made her feel as though the last 15 years of their marriage had been one big lie. But because she did love Bob very much and because she knew that he truly did love her and wanted to create a more loving and passionate relationship with her in the future, she forgave him. Needless to say, Bob felt as though a huge weight had been lifted from his heart.

When I saw Bob after this event, his whole demeanor was radiant and somehow, he looked younger to me than he had before. It was a true pleasure to witness.

Building Your Foundation of Integrity

So, what is stopping you from feeling 100% fabulous about your life and how you are operating in the world? Perhaps you've already have had a flash in your mind about an area of your life you don't feel quite right about. If this is the case, then just know that you had that flash for a reason. It jumped into your mind because at your core level of being, you yearn to feel the wholeness that comes from having alignment between who you truly want to be and who you are actually being. Heed that voice!

Restoring your personal foundation of integrity requires that you restore alignment between what you do and what you know is right to do—as distinct from what "everyone else" is doing, what is the least hassle or what you reckon you can get away with! Now I am not saying that the process of doing so will be painless. In fact, I once heard integrity described as being a bit like giving birth—really painful but the rewards are more than worth it. The pain comes from having to give up some of the payoffs that you have gotten rather attached to (e.g., financial, an absence of confrontation, getting more than your fair share, living a double life, being a victim). This takes courage. However, as you begin to build a solid foundation of integrity, you will start to feel more powerful about what you can do with your life. It will soon become apparent that what you get in your life far outweighs what you have to give up.

If you can't readily identify any areas of your life with a shortfall of integrity, take a moment to do the *Personal Integrity Audit Exercise* that follows.

Exercise 2.1: Personal Integrity Audit

Ask yourself each of the questions below in relation to the different areas of your life to see where your behavior is not fully reflecting your values. As you answer, think about whether those whom you live and work with would agree with your answer. If not, perhaps you're not being completely honest with yourself.

Workplace: Do you undermine/sabotage other people's efforts to your advantage? Do you engage in behavior you'd hate others to know about? Do you take credit for work that isn't all yours? Do you always treat those whom you work with and whom work for you with respect? Do you do your fair share in your team/ business? Do you fulfill your responsibilities ethically? If you are in a position of authority, do you give people honest feedback about their performance in a respectful way that they can use to further develop themselves? Are you settling for less than what you really want from your position or job? Are you standing your ground about workplace issues you feel are important or just going with what is politically expedient?

What must I do to clean it up? When am I going to do this?

Relationships: What issues are you not addressing in your relationships? Whom are you failing to be honest with? What are you not speaking up about that is undermining your relationships? Are you treating people with a lack of dignity and respect? Are you saying things you think people want to hear even though you know you are being untruthful? What are you doing (by your action or your inaction) in your relationships that are hurting another person? Do you say things knowing they will be hurtful?

What must I do to clean it up? When am I going to do this?

Health & Wellbeing—Do you treat your body the way it should be to stay in good health? Do you regularly consume an excess of alcohol, drugs or other substances that are damaging? Do you take the time to exercise? Do you eat foods you know will nourish your body? Do you take time to quiet your mind and get centered? Do you seek medical attention about health issues that concern you?

What must I do to clean it up? When am I going to do this?

Money/Finances—Are you managing your finances responsibly? Do you owe money that you aren't paying back? Are you spending beyond your means? Are you engaging in dishonest or unethical behavior with your money or with someone else's money? Are you using money to manipulate someone? Do you feel good about the amount of money you are giving to those less fortunate than you? Are you honest in how you keep your financial records?

What must I do to clean it up? When am I going to do this?

Commitments—Are you a person of your word? Does what you are committing to on a daily basis reflect what you are most committed to in your life? Do you fulfill your commitments and responsibilities properly and on time? If you can't keep a commitment or fulfill a responsibility, do you let people know immediately? Do you say yes to requests you know you aren't going to follow through on? Are you generally punctual? Do you get back to people when you say you will? Are you someone others know they can depend on? Do you sometimes fail to say no when asked to take on an additional commitment that will mean compromising an existing one (even one to yourself)? Do you make offers to people that you fail to fulfill?

What must I do to clean it up? When am I going to do this?

What You're Doing with Your Life—Are you being the kind of person you really want to be? Is there any behavior you engage in you would hate others to find out about? Is there something that you would love to be doing with your time, energy and talents that you are not? Are there aspects of your life in which you feel dissatisfied or resigned and are doing nothing about?

What must I do to feel good about how I am spending my energy, my talents, my time…my life? When am I going to do this?

Hopefully, you have identified some areas of your life which could do with a little "spring cleaning" in the integrity department (or maybe a complete overhaul!). Integrity sometimes compels you to do what is right rather than what is convenient. For Ross Perot, it meant running as an independent for President against all the odds in 1992, failing and then running again four years later. Of course, we don't all feel called to run for President of the United States, but often we are still called to play a bigger game in life than we have been playing up until now. Only when your actions are in sync with that "inner voice" (or whatever you want to call it!) will you be able to have what you want most in life.

Integrity is the foundation for your future happiness and success—in all aspects of your life. Make it solid! Doing so will open up the door for you to live the life you *really* want. Of course, it may also take you on paths you would otherwise never have journeyed, and it may require letting go of circumstances to which you may have become rather attached, but keep in mind that the greatest thing in life is having the courage to let go of who you are for who you can become. By failing to live with integrity, you dishonor yourself. By honoring integrity, you honor yourself. Doing so will unleash in you the power, the courage and the sense of confidence that you need to become the person you aspire to be and to live the life to which you aspire.

> *"The time is always right to do what is right."*
> –Martin Luther King, Jr.

> *"I want you to listen to what your conscience commands you to do and go on to carry it out to the best of your knowledge."*
>
> –Viktor Frankl

Chapter 3
The Courage to Challenge Your Stories

"We don't see the world as it is; we see it as we are."
—Humberto Maturana

In my early twenties, I spent a couple months backpacking around Thailand, which included a week-long hike through the hills in the northern part of the country bordering Burma and Laos, near the infamous Golden Triangle. Whilst there, I stayed in small villages, spending time with the local people gaining a wonderful insight into their lives. One day I noticed that the elephants they used for carrying lumber and transporting people through the jungle always stayed close by. When I inquired as to why they didn't just wander off and disappear into the jungle, I was given an explanation that I found most intriguing.

When an elephant is born, a chain is put around its leg tethering it to a small tree planted nearby to keep him from wandering off. Because it is young and not yet very strong, it is unable to break the chain. However, as the years pass and the elephant grows (a full grown elephant is 10-11 feet tall and weighs around six tons) it continues to live with the assumption that it is unable to move more than a few feet from the tree to which it is chained. In fact, the chain is no longer even attached to the tree and all that is on the elephant is a tiny metal bracelet. So there you have this massive elephant, unaware that it is capable of traveling so much further than in a circle a few feet from the tree it was tethered to as a baby and living a much more confined existence than it necessarily has to live.

Of course, we laugh at how simple minded the elephant is for not realizing the folly of its belief, nor challenging the assumption that the anklet around its leg restricts where it can travel. Yet in our own lives, we too can find ourselves living under outdated assumptions, beliefs and "stories" that limit what we see as possible for ourselves. They define for us a reality that keeps us shackled in one way or another.

You see, your world is different than mine. It's different because the way you observe the world is different from how I observe the world. Likewise, the stories you have created to explain your observations (whether they have been handed down to you from others, or which you have made up all by yourself) are different from mine. The reason is that as human beings, we each have our own unique way of processing our experiences and the information we receive. We do this through language. Through your conversations—both the 'private ones' you have with yourself (sometimes called "self talk") and the 'public ones' you have with others—you have developed "stories" about yourself and the world which have created the reality in which you live. Through the power of words, you have crafted your own unique universe. Through the power of stories, you have created your own reality, and what you see as possible for yourself in every area of your life

Your stories are a melting pot of your opinions, assumptions, interpretations, prejudices, biases and beliefs, which you have created to make sense of the world in which you live and your place in it. Cognitive Psychologists have studied the phenomena of how we create our "stories," or to be technically accurate, how humans process and interpret sensory input (information and experiences) and assimilate it into "schemas" that provide a cognitive framework for abstract knowledge. This is psychological lingo for how we all live in a world shaped by interpretation. Given that our actions are based on the realities our stories paint for us about who we are and what we are capable of, our lives are either limited or expanded by the stories we have. Indeed, how we observe either opens up the choices we see as available to us or closes them down.

The Power of Stories

There is a wonderful saying in Alcoholics Anonymous that goes *"Your best thinking got you here,"* which is another way of saying that your best stories got you the experience of life you have today. Given the tremendous power your stories wield in your life, it is well worth taking a step back from your stories, acknowledging them as such, evaluating their validity, assessing whether they are now serving or limiting you, and if the latter, crafting more empowering ones.

Of course, letting go of anything you have invested a lot of time and energy in can be painful and so it takes real courage to give up the personal narrative you have been living in. However, the pain will be worth it, because only by finding the courage to challenge your stories will you be able to rise above the limits they have placed on you and be free to step into your life more assertively and successfully than you ever have before.

So where do your stories come from and why do they wield so much power in your life? Human beings have always needed to create stories to make sense of the world, but about 2,500 years ago our quest for owning "the truth" took on new ferocity. Around this time the great "thinkers"—the ancient Greeks, Plato, Socrates and Aristotle—created the adversarial style of thinking which still forms the basis for much of western thinking today. This thinking style taught man to rationalize an argument to establish

> *"Assumptions are the death of possibilities."*
> –James Mapes

"the truth." This quest to possess "the truth" has become embedded in western thinking, so that once we've decided (consciously or not) that we own "the truth," we don't bother to question it and will become pretty bloody defensive, pretty bloody quickly when someone questions what we deem to be "the truth."

It is interesting to see what an impact a shared truth can have. In the first half of the 20th century there was an overwhelming consensus of opinion that man could not run under a four minute mile. Everyone agreed it just could not be done; human beings were simply not made to move at this speed. But then in 1954, an Englishman, Roger Bannister, did just that, clocking in at three minutes and 59.4 seconds. An extraordinary feat at the time, it is still regarded as one of the greatest athletic achievements of all time. But what I think was even more extraordinary was that within six weeks, Australian, John Landy, toppled Bannister's record, running three minutes and 58 seconds. In the years that followed, the world record was broken again and again to where it is now down below three minutes and 43 seconds. What Bannister did was prove that man's ability to run under 4 minutes was not a hard fact but merely an opinion. Whilst I do not know how much faster man will run I do know that in the years ahead, many more "truths", about what is possible for each of us and for humankind, will be found to be equally untrue.

It takes great courage to challenge your stories—to put your beliefs and assumptions through the ringer—and to revise or discard altogether those which are unable to stand the pressure. So let me make clear that I am not suggesting that you abandon all your stories. This would obviously be not only ridiculous but impossible.

Often we are trapped inside stories we are not even aware we have.

Your stories generally serve a positive function allowing you to make sense of your experiences and observations, to process the ongoing "sensory input" and make predictions about the future. Without them you would be completely dysfunctional. However, what I am suggesting is that not *all* of your stories serve you and that having the courage to acknowledge those which don't is vital to achieving what you want most in your life.

Here are some of the stories my clients, chance acquaintances and friends have shared with me over the years. Though some of these may sound ludicrous to you, I can assure you that the people who shared them with me felt they were the absolute truth:

- *"I just can't save money. Never have. It's in my family to be hopeless with money."*
- *"Once you have kids, you not only lose your figure, you lose your life."*

- *"It's impossible for me to change careers now. I'm 39 and it's just too late. I could never work with all these young 20-year-olds."*
- *"You should never trust someone completely because just when you do, that's when they will take advantage of you."*
- *"All men, given the opportunity, would be unfaithful."*
- *"Over 80% of the people I work with are narcissistic."*
- *"Obesity is in my family so there's no point even trying to lose weight."*
- *"No one in management has any idea of what's really going on in the organization. They are a bunch of complete idiots."*
- *"You can't raise kids and have a career at the same time and hope to do a good job of both."*
- *"I'm too young to become a university professor. You have to be old and I've only just turned forty."*
- *"Everyone at my work would shun me if they knew I was a lesbian. They are all homophobic—it would spell the end of my career for sure."*
- *"It's impossible not to put on weight during the holiday season."*

Often we are trapped inside stories we are not even aware we have. Instead of consciously choosing to have our stories, our stories have us! Julio Olalla, a leader in the field of ontological thought whom I have been fortunate to learn from said it beautifully, "We are so full of answers to questions we have never even asked." And so it is time to ask some new questions. Doing so will help you identify those stories which are limiting your ability to take effective action in your relationships, career, health and well-being, finances...in your life!

Challenging your stories means challenging the way you have been observing the world. Given that your stories have in some part defined who you see yourself to be, this also means being prepared to challenge the way you have viewed yourself and the identity your stories have created for you.

"The real voyage of discovery consists not in seeking new landscapes but in having new eyes."
–Marcel Proust

Letting go of old stories requires changing the perspective from which you view not only yourself, but also how you observe other people and the way the world operates in general. It has been said, "When your horse dies, get off." I would say, when your stories are no long working for you, ditch them and get new ones. This takes courage. It also takes a lot of humility to let go of old stories you've invested so much in, to accept that you don't own the truth and acknowledge that your view of reality may have been slightly (or completely) off the mark and that you've been living with a blind spot you didn't know you had. Put bluntly, it's admitting you got it wrong.

Why Bother Challenging Your Stories?

Given the amount of effort that's required to challenge your stories, you may be asking the question, "Why should I?" By keeping the stories you've always had, you will keep living the life they've confined you to. Does the thought of more of the same life you've been living up until now excite and inspire you or fill you with dread and dismay? Unless you are prepared to see your stories for what they are and let go of those which are limiting your ability to enjoy your life fully, you will continue to struggle with the same issues you are struggling with now (and which I am guessing probably are the same issues that have been shadowing you all your life). Though your past is no longer your current reality, you are constrained by the past through the stories you created in it. Like the elephants in Asia, you are shackled by chains that no longer exist except in your mind.

As I said before, the problem is *not* that we have stories, for we need to interpret what we see around us to make sense of things. The problem arises when we delude ourselves into thinking that our interpretations (our stories) are the absolute truth, rather than just our perspective on something.

I've certainly had my fair share of stories that required a major rewriting. One of them was my belief I adopted growing up on my parents dairy farm—that people who didn't have a lot of money were generally more decent than the "rich" people who did. Those who fell into this "rich" classification were people who bought a new car (or worse, one of the fancy European ones!), owned more than one television, had a house with stairs in it, or took vacations that required air travel. I also believed that only baptized Catholics would get through the pearly gates of heaven, that once women had children they never did anything else except bake cakes and grow frumpy and that all Americans wore glary Hawaiian shirts, were overweight, loud and pushy. (This last example was based on a sample size of about 6, comprised of the few tourists that traveled to the rural area of Australia in which I grew up.)

Whether you find these truths ridiculous and laughable (as I now do) or not, the point is that we often adopt the truths of our parents, or unconsciously create ones for ourselves. We then carry them through life without ever challenging them. Can you see the parallels between our stories and the chains used on elephants?

Many adults suffer because they are trapped inside "truth-filled" narratives they created en route to adulthood that prevent them from enjoying their lives fully and knowing just how much they are capable of. They think they know the truth—about how the world is, how life is, how they are—but the only truth that exists is that we will never have a monopoly on "the truth."

If you really take a step back to think about this mysterious inexplicable phenomena we call the universe, it really is kind of audacious to think that with our miniscule knowledge and experience we can ever truly claim to own "the truth." All that we can ever really know is what feels true for us. At the same time, we must also take responsibility for continually challenging the stories we are crafting and the truths we are adopting in our daily lives.

> *Though your past is no longer your current reality you are constrained by the past through the stories you created in it.*

In writing this book I do not claim to own "the truth." Rather it is my intention to challenge your mind to question your "truths", to touch your heart and to stir your spirit. What I write is based on what I have experienced in life and what resonates as being "true" for me. It is my belief that the perspectives I am sharing will be as helpful to you as they have been for others. Just think of them as though they were new reading glasses you were trying on—if they allow you to see your life more clearly and can help you get from where you are now in your life to where you want to go then wonderful, keep them. And if they don't, then at least you've had an opportunity to view your circumstances through a different angle lens than you would have otherwise, which is a valuable experience in itself.

Identifying Your Stories

Your stories will either move you forward or hold you back; they will either expand your ability to enjoy your life or shrink it. So if you want to identify your limiting stories think about those aspects of your life which are not moving forward as you would like them to be. The better you can identify the limiting stories that run your life—and the assumptions behind them—the more freedom you will have to create new stories that will predispose and empower you to take the actions you need to create the changes you want.

Of course, spotting other people's stories is often way easier than identifying your own, because when you're smack in the midst of your story, it's difficult to view it objectively. Think back to your days in school when the most important thing for you was to be selected for the school athletic team or to be in the "in group." You had a story at the time that getting onto that team would make you a "winner" and that not being invited into the inner sanctum of the really cool group would render you a "loser." Your mother may have tried to tell you at the time that in the big picture of your life being in the "in group" really wasn't

Your stories will either move you forward or hold you back; they will either expand your ability to enjoy your life or shrink it.

the "be all and end all" (as mine did). You probably thought (like I did), "What would mom know anyway!" At the time it was as though your life depended on these things to go your way, and your language probably reflected your desperation, "I'll just die if I'm not invited," or "It will kill me if I don't make the team." Such drama!

Now, a decade or three later, you see things differently. You realize your mother wasn't quite so clueless and that being invited to Miss Muffett's 15th birthday party really wasn't "the be all and end all" after all. Though we continue evolving after our days in the classroom, we haven't always evolved and matured as much as we would like to *think* we have. We think, very naively and often rather arrogantly, that the way we see the world is the way the world is. But, as difficult as this may be for you to swallow you do not see the world as it is, but as you are. You see it only through the filtering lens of your own eyes which has been shaped by all the experiences in your life. Sure, "perception creates reality," but your perception is *not* reality and the same dynamics that were at play in your life at 15 are still at play in your life today. The only difference is that now the stakes are higher: it's your career, marriage, relationships, health, finances, business or family we're talking about.

It is likely that as you have been living out your stories, there has been little if any room for considering fresh perspectives—about yourself, the people around you and your circumstances—that would allow you to intervene in your life in ways that would make it more rewarding to live. You see, your stories impose on your ability to effectively intervene in your environment to get the results you want in your life. So unless you are willing to take a fresh look at how you have been observing the world and are willing to challenge the stories that run your life (and, believe me, they do run your life!), then there is little chance that anything is going to significantly change in your life.

We human beings treasure being right, so it takes a lot more guts to change your stories (even the ones causing you all sorts of trouble) than it does to keep them. However, unless you do you will be unable to effectively address those aspects of your life that aren't really working for you. Why? Because the core of the problem does not lie in your actions, but in the stories generating those actions. As Albert Einstein once said, "We cannot solve problems on the same level of awareness at which they were created." Therefore what will make a difference for you is not focusing on your actions, but challenging the very stories that have you seeing things the way you do. Ultimately you will only be effective in resolving your problems and creating the life you really want if you are prepared to see yourself and the world in which you live from a new enlarged perspective and to rewrite your stories accordingly.

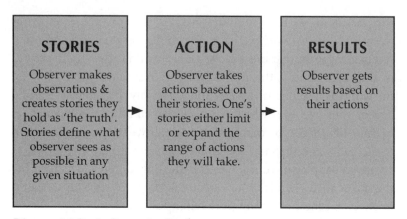

Diagram 3.1 Stories Determine Results

Perhaps as you read this, you have started to become aware of some of the stories you've been living in. If you haven't, don't worry. By finding the courage to really question what you hold to be true, you will eventually become aware of which stories are limiting you and be able to move to that next level of awareness that Einstein referred to. For now, the most important thing is that you are prepared to challenge your perspectives—however attached you are to them!

I'd like to share with you a story about a client who found the guts to challenge her long-held stories about money. At the time I was working with Robyn, she was in her early 30's, single, and doing relatively well in her career, working in sales for a sales training company. She was curious about coaching because she found herself depressed, but couldn't understand why given that she was living the life she had dreamed of back in college. In the Intake Form I ask all new clients to complete before commencing coaching, she wrote down that she had a tendency to go shopping to "treat herself" even when she couldn't really afford to. So during our initial conversation, I asked her to tell me more about this. She divulged that she had maxed out several credit cards, but that she nevertheless felt she had her financial situation under control. She went on to say it didn't stress her out because she didn't believe in getting stressed out about money. "It just isn't worth it. Life's too short," she said. My "story-buster" ears pricked up (so to speak). Robyn's "Money is to be enjoyed" mantra did not seem to extend to financial responsibility, but rather was about spending on whatever brought her maximum in-the-moment pleasure—ski trips, great wine, eating out at least twice a day ("I'm useless in the kitchen and always wanted to earn enough money so I could pay someone else to cook for me."), a stunning designer wardrobe...you get the picture.

She said she liked the idea of having money set aside for the future, although she felt that the odds of her getting married were pretty slim given her comment that, "All the decent guys are already snapped up." But she said that she simply couldn't afford to buy a home in the inner city, which was where she wanted to live, because of the "ridiculous boom in inner city real estate." When, out of sheer curiosity, I asked why she'd never decided to put aside some money on a regular basis, she muttered something about how all the people she knew that saved money were boring and having no fun. She continued explaining how one time when she was young, she had saved up a piggy bank full of money, but it had been stolen and her parents never replaced the money. She went on to defend her behavior, "There's no point trying to save money. I'll never have any anyway so I may as well spend it now and enjoy it. You've got to live in the present, right?"

What I often find interesting when people have a strong story about something is how completely unaware they can be of the absence of logic in the arguments they use to support it. I also find they use a lot of absolutes just like Robyn did—*all* the decent men were gone and *all* the people she knew who saved had *no* fun and she'd *never* have money anyway. Many people, just like Robyn, are so enmeshed in their story that they cannot see (or just don't want to see) where it fails to make sense.

Over a period of several months, Robyn and I slowly went through the process of grounding her stories about money (and men and life, amongst other things). By shifting the way she was viewing her circumstances and her finances, she began to create new stories, which in turn paved the way for her to make different choices and take different actions than she had been in the past. During the process of acknowledging her story for what it was and how it contributed to the situation it had created (and her lack of real contentment), her depression began to lift. Robyn began to get this aspect of her life sorted out, and as she did it helped shift her perspective on others areas of her life also. That was a couple years ago. Robyn is now married to one of those decent guys that *hadn't* been snapped up and will have had her first child by the time this book is published.

Ralph Waldo Emerson once said, "People only see what they are prepared to see." Whilst confronting your stories may be painful, you have within you the courage you need to take a good hard look at how you've been looking at your life. You have absolutely nothing to lose and a whole world of possibility to gain.

The exercise below will help you identify any stories that are limiting you. As you do it I encourage you to think about what things, circumstances or people really trigger you emotionally (e.g., Do people who are really extroverted bug you or do you just hate when people start discussing money?) The reason I suggest this is because often when *something* or *someone* really "gets to you" and upsets you (more than it does to others) it's a strong sign that you have a story related to this issue that is not fully serving you, and which, if uncovered, would allow you to enjoy much greater ease, power and success in that area of your life.

Exercise 3.1: Busting Your Life-Stifling Stories

A. In each of the following areas of your life, I'd like you to write about anything that you are outright unhappy with or which you are perhaps just not fully satisfied with.
   1. Health and Wellbeing
   2. Financial Position and Money Management
   3. Life Balance
   4. Family Life /Children
   5. Relationship with Spouse
   6. Recreation/Social life
   7. Career or Business Success/Work Satisfaction
   8. Direction of Future

B. Then write down the reason why you are in this situation, for each of the issues you've listed above. Here are a few examples of what clients have come up with whilst doing this exercise:

Career:
- I'm not happy in my job because I am not recognized for my hard work and talent.
- *Why?* Everyone in management is too busy looking after their own careers to bother with mine, and since the restructure everyone has too much on their plates to notice what I've got on mine. I can't really blame them for not having enough time to focus on me.

Health and Wellbeing:
- Ever since I had my two children, I've been unable to lose the extra weight. I just hate feeling so flabby and just squeezing into my pre-baby clothes, but I don't want to go out and buy new ones.
- *Why?* It's near impossible to getting out the door much less to the gym with a young baby and a toddler because they take turns napping all day, and I just haven't got enough energy.

Finances:
- I seem to not be getting ahead financially and that is really frustrating me.
- *Why?* I never have the time to sit down and figure out how to better manage my money or structure things for taxation purposes. I'm just so busy with my job, and then, when I'm not working, too busy with my family and other commitments to get around to it. On top of that, I don't know a trustworthy financial planner.

Grounding Your Stories: It Ain't Necessarily So!

Sometimes we can be so sure of the way we think things are that we fail to search for alternate explanations or perspectives. In the book, *The Road Less Traveled*, M. Scott Peck wrote about the importance of being dedicated to reality if we want to solve life's problems. Using the analogy of a map, he wrote that, if our maps are accurate, we will be able to negotiate life's terrain and get to where we want. If our maps are inaccurate—"befuddled by falsehood, misperceptions and illusions"—then we'll be less able to make wise decisions.

The process of grounding your stories will enable you to determine the validity of your stories, stories which define your reality and determine how you will navigate your way through life. By going through this process, you will be better able to identify and rewrite the stories which are restricting your ability to have more of what you want in your life and less of what you don't.

Don't think that grounding your stories is a one-off event. Not at all! Throughout your life you should be continually in the process of grounding your stories so as to avoid falling into the trap of living out your future based on the past's outdated facts, beliefs and assumptions.

> *"The illiterates of the future are not those who cannot read or write. They are those who cannot learn, unlearn and relearn."*
> —Alvin Toffler

The process I take clients through to ground their stories consists of the following three key steps

1. Get Your Facts Straight

While your stories are not the truth, they do represent what is true for you. To help you see your stories for what they are, it is important to separate the facts from your opinions of the facts (or put another way, your "story" about the facts). Now remember, facts are things that are concrete, verifiable and that, regardless of what your opinion about them may be, are beyond dispute. For instance, as I write this today George W. Bush is the President of the United States, I am the mother of four children and the temperature in Dallas is on average higher than it is in Montreal. Get the drift? These are facts. A fact is either true or it is false. There is no gray.

Diagram 3.2 Distinguishing Facts from Opinions

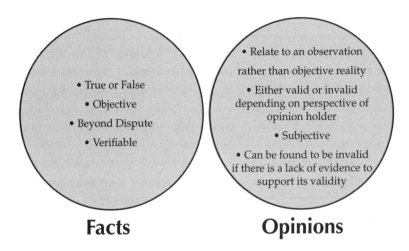

Facts
- True or False
- Objective
- Beyond Dispute
- Verifiable

Opinions
- Relate to an observation rather than objective reality
- Either valid or invalid depending on perspective of opinion holder
- Subjective
- Can be found to be invalid if there is a lack of evidence to support its validity

Then comes the spin that we put on the facts...our "opinions". Opinions, which I use interchangeably with stories, are a different kettle of fish altogether and depend entirely upon the perspective of the person making them. Opinions are not true or false as much as they are valid or invalid, depending upon the perspective of the person making the opinion and the quality of the evidence they have to support them (sometimes people have a lot of factual evidence, other times disturbingly little!) When someone expresses an opinion, it generally tells you far more about the person than it does the person or thing they have an opinion about.

For instance, is George W. Bush a good or bad president? It all depends on which end of the political spectrum you swing to. Is Dallas weather better than Montreal's? Again, depends on who you ask. Are four kids too many or too few? Depending on what day of the week you ask me, you might get either answer!

Escaping the Linguistic Trap

Your opinions about politics, women in the workplace, the weather, the ideal family size or anything else will be just that—*your* opinions. They will most certainly *not* be shared by everyone.

My point here is that too often we collapse our opinions about things with the facts—the two circles become one—and when we do, we fall into the *linguistic trap*. That is, in our language, we treat opinions as though they were facts, and in doing so, we become trapped by them. By treating a story as the one and only truth, it shuts out any possibility for you to see things differently, and because your actions are determined by your stories, it limits how well you can address your problems, achieve your goals and live the life you *really* want.

> *By treating your story as the one and only truth, it shuts out the possibility to see things differently, to take more effective actions and to achieve more satisfying results than you have before.*

For instance:

- If you have no college degree and believe it is impossible for someone without a degree to get on in the corporate world, you won't take the actions required to get ahead.
- If you are a woman who believes it is not possible to have a rewarding career, be a good mother and raise great kids, you won't take the actions required to pursue your professional goals whilst raising your children. You will feel you have no choice but to decide on one or the other.

So often our stories become self-fulfilling prophecies. That is, we behave in accordance with our stories and, sure enough, the results we get reinforce their validity to us. Remember how Robyn said that she knew that she would never have any money (the "truth" that had her trapped) and spent what money she did have on whatever gave her immediate gratification? It's no surprise that people like Robyn (and there are lots of people just like her, male and female; educated and uneducated) who find they are absolutely right when they find themselves in debt up to their eyeballs, broke and feeling smug about how well they could predict their future.

Martin is another example of how a story is reinforced simply by behavior that perpetuates and bolsters our opinions. Martin was a client of mine who had had a pretty rough time growing up. His father had been an alcoholic and had been very abusive, physically and emotionally, to him and his mother. On one occasion he had walked into their home to find his father beating his mother. When he tried to intervene, his father turned on him calling him stupid and worthless. His mother, likely feeling powerless and scared for her own life, had done nothing.

From this experience and many others like it, Martin had grown up with the belief that he was indeed worthless and stupid, for if his father had said it was true, and his mother had never said it wasn't, then it must have been "the truth." Moreover, he was bullied quite a bit during his school years, which served as further evidence to support his story that he was not a person who was worth liking. Fast-forward 25 years and every encounter he had had since then he had interpreted through the lens of, "I'm not worth liking." Martin left school at 16 and began working with a small printer. He learned enough about printing to get a job with a local newspaper and he's been working there ever since. He had never married and had had very few, short-lived relationships.

This story he has about himself has been his reality: he is not likeable and no one worth spending time with would find his company enjoyable. This truth has been the premise of his life, every day, for over two decades. By having the courage to see his story about himself as just that—a story and not "the truth"—he began to climb out of the trap he'd been caught in and develop a new story about himself, one that didn't have him avoiding friendships and feeling like a loser in life. Though it has taken a lot of hard work, on a daily and sometimes hourly basis, Martin now thinks of himself as a worthwhile and likeable guy, someone other people would enjoy spending time with. This is the positive version of a self-fulfilling prophecy since it is actually serving Martin and his ability to enjoy his life. It has opened up the possibility for him to develop rewarding and lasting relationships with people that before, he thought he could never have.

As you can see from diagram 3.2, the facts and opinion circles don't even overlap. They are two separate circles, each standing alone. Likewise, your stories are not factual; rather they are based on your opinion of the facts. This is a very important distinction to take with you in life.

As I said earlier, this book *is not* about throwing out everything you believe in, because many of your beliefs, your personal truths, will be serving you in a positive way. It *is* about taking a second look at the stories you have, which may not be serving you so well (the issues you identified in Exercise 3.1). It *is* also about your willingness to admit that what you think is true about yourself and other people may not be "the truth" after all, but rather a disempowering story you have created. Most of all, it is about helping you become aware of exactly where you have been caught in a linguistic trap and helping you get out of it.

2. Look for Evidence That Doesn't Support Your Story

When we have a story about something we actively seek out information that supports our story, and we either ignore or discredit information that contradicts it. Numerous psychological studies have found that we are prone to a phenomenon called "Information Bias." This resembles an internal spin-doctoring and occurs when people are presented with information that conflicts with their established opinions

It doesn't matter in what area of your life you have a limiting story; what matters is your willingness to do the work to ground your story, which includes searching for evidence that either:

a) doesn't support or contradict your stories' perspective, or

b) actually supports an opposing perspective.

Here are a few examples of former clients I have taken through this process:

- Jane said her spouse was disinterested in their marriage, but the fact was that her spouse had not walked out on her or filed for divorce.
- Will said that his boss was "a complete idiot," yet the facts were that his boss had had a successful career to date, skillfully managing several multi-million dollar projects.
- Gina was very concerned that moving up to partner level in

her firm would entail longer hours in the office, more travel and greater stress. She admitted she knew several partners who traveled less than her, weren't working longer hours and appeared less stressed than she was.

A few examples of the latter:
- Brad said there was no opportunity to advance in his company, yet reported that at least two people had been promoted to the next level during the previous quarter.
- Ellen said that she couldn't return to college to finish her Masters with two children under the age of three at home, yet she learned that at least a dozen women attending the college she wanted to attend had children similar in age.

What evidence contradicts your story? You may need to search a little harder and look a little deeper for evidence that conflicts with the opinion you have about a problem you are facing or a part of your life you just don't feel great about. For instance, I recently met a woman who was of the strong opinion that there really is no such thing as a happy marriage. She had grown up in a home in which there was a lot of tension between her parents, had gone to a school where nearly all her friends parents were divorced or on the brink of one and had never had any close first hand experience of people enjoying a loving marriage. When she shared with me her cynicism, I challenged her to look a little harder amongst her friends and work colleagues to find some examples of happy marriages. I shared my belief that there is indeed such a thing as a happy marriage and that only by shifting her story and opening her mind to the possibility that one was possible for her would she ever be able to be happily married herself.

3. Be Cautious to Whom You Give Authority

It pays to be careful about assuming that something is true simply because other people—even lots of other people—believe it to be so. Just because many people believe the same thing doesn't necessarily make it any more "the truth." Five hundred years ago everyone believed the world was flat. Sixty years ago we believed men couldn't run a mile under 5 minutes and fifty years ago there was still consensus among those running the U.S. that dark-skinned people deserved fewer rights. And what about all the stories that we hold on to today—whether about religion, politics, women in the workplace, in the boardroom, in the oval office or in the priesthood— that with hindsight we will see were completely invalid? If the number of people agreeing with any particular belief or story validates its truthfulness then we'd be able to assess the truthfulness of any world religion or ideology simply by counting the number of people who subscribed to it.

> *"You can tell whether a man is clever by his answers. You can tell whether a man is wise by his questions."*
> –Naguib Mahfouz

My point here is that stories can run deep within our societies, our cultures and our lives and that we should always be careful about what we are buying into and be willing to challenge our stories. Doubt is often the beginning of wisdom.

Too often we buy into the opinions of others without much thought and with very little doubt. Because someone else says it is so, we automatically assume it is so for ourselves. When we do this, we are giving others authority. Sometimes it makes sense to do this. For instance, when the weatherman says there's going to be a tornado tomorrow, it would be foolish to decide not to accept his opinion unless you could verify it. However, before giving someone authority, you need to ask yourself:

- How much knowledge does this person have about a particular subject/issue compared to me (i.e., what facts do they have that I either do not have or cannot readily access?)?
- How might they be biased in their interpretation of the facts?
- How might it serve them (psychologically, monetarily, emotionally, professionally, etc.) for me to accept what they are saying as the truth?

When I had my first child, I gave enormous authority to a friend who had two young boys. As I didn't know anything much about how to care for a baby, initially I took every word she spoke as fact. Thou shalt not let the baby cry lest it grow up feeling unloved. Thou shalt not give the baby a bottle lest it then refuse the breast. Thou shalt not leave the baby's side. Thou shalt keep the baby in the room with you, even better, in the bed with you. Though shalt not use a pacifier and on it went…for about three months, at which point it started to dawn on my sleep-deprived brain that this woman, as well meaning as she was, didn't necessarily know the "best" way for *me* to care for *my* baby, and that her style of mothering wasn't necessarily going to be mine. Of course, it took another few months for me to seek out alternative opinions, and then to start implementing a few different strategies with my by then, six-month-old darling son, who, as gorgeous as he was, would not nap more than 20 minutes and had me up at least three times every night to feed . Eventually, my husband Andrew and I (now three months pregnant with our second child) checked into what we dubbed "Sleep School" where we were taught how to get our insatiable, nocturnal, party boy to sleep through the night and nap properly during the day. Though it was an unpleasant few days, it turned out to be a highly worthwhile investment of our time. It made all the difference over the following five years, as we applied what we learnt to get our three consecutive children into more "mother friendly" routines.

Of course, there will be times you need to rely on someone else's opinion and place trust in their authority. However, you should also always be open to alternative sources of authority whose opinions may differ and who may have a broader base of information and experience than your current source. On this occasion, I gave authority to someone who, in hindsight, was not the authority I took her to be. At the time I was also going through a period where I felt uncertain, unsettled and lacked confidence in my ability to be a mother. The lesson I learned is that when you give someone authority, you need to be conscious you are doing so and continue to ask yourself whether or not it is in your best interests.

Cassy had a similar experience when she returned to her job as a buyer for a large, department store chain after having her second child. She had considered cutting back to part time after her first child, but decided not to based on the advice of a female manager. This manager, an informal mentor, told her if she did, she would never be able to advance in the company and might even have to take a less senior job than the one she held. However, nearly a year after returning to work after her second child, Cassy found she was not enjoying juggling long hours and the demands of two young children. As we discussed her

> *Sometimes you need to take back the authority you are giving others and place more trust in yourself.*

situation, she told me that she really hated the thought that working part time would eliminate her chances for career advancement and possibly result in a demotion. I asked her why she felt so sure of this. Cassy replied that she had it on good authority that this was the reality in the company. So I asked if she could discuss this matter with other senior people in the company. She did and decided she would cut back to three days a week. That was two years ago. Since then, Cassy has been promoted to the position previously held by her boss. How did she achieve this? She decided not to follow the advice of the person to whom she had originally given so much authority and make the part-time option work for her. She took extra initiatives that gave her exposure to senior management and increased her visibility within the organization. As Cassy said, if she had questioned the authority she'd given to the female manager earlier, she would have opted for the three-day week sooner.

Just remember, other people's opinions are simply that—other people's opinions. Period. They are not fact and they are certainly not "the truth." It is your responsibility to question the authority you give others, to question opinions they want you to adopt as your own and to question how it is they are observing the world themselves that has them see things as they do. Sometimes you need to take back the authority you are giving to the opinions of others and place a little bit more trust in yourself. When it comes to motherhood, whenever a new mom asks me for advice, I always like to tell them, "You know more than you think you do—trust your instinct." Indeed in all areas of life, it often pays to trust your own intuition more and others' opinions less.

Throughout your life, it will serve you well to be continually taking a step back to acknowledge your stories and question the assumptions and opinions that perpetuate them. You see, neither you nor I can stop ourselves from creating stories. We are compulsive story makers programmed to come up with our own little theories about why things are the way they are and to extrapolate out meaning about ourselves and the universe at large. However, once we realize that we are constantly interpreting things and forever in the process of story creation, then—and only then—can we step back and see our stories for what they are and, like the elephant realizing it is no longer chained to the tree, be liberated from them.

By having the courage to challenge your stories, you can shift your perspective on life to one that puts you in a position of far greater power with a future filled with vast possibilities. Armed with courage and ready to walk through the door of humility to acknowledge all that you don't know, can open the door of possibility to grow into all you can be.

Chapter 4
The Courage to Dream Bigger

"Cherish your visions and your dreams as they are the children of your soul; the blueprints of your ultimate achievements."

—Napoleon Hill

Dreaming is risky. While only some dreams put you at physical risk, all dreams require that you take an emotional risk. By their very nature, dreams create a gap between your present reality and the reality you want to have, causing you to question whether or not you can bridge the gap. This risk alone can be so daunting for people that they prefer to leave their dreams in their childhood, or buried away beneath layers of fear, doubt and resignation. That's why dreaming bigger dreams than you presently are takes courage—because it means risking the possibility that your dreams may not come true. But to paraphrase Michelangelo, the greater danger is not that your dreams are too big and you fail to reach them, it's that they are too small and you do.

Given the high stakes of dreaming, you may feel overwhelmed at the mere thought of daring to dream about creating a life bigger, more exciting and more fulfilling than the one you have now. Believe me, you are not alone. In fact, I doubt there is a person on this planet who hasn't dreamt about doing something which seemed, at the time, so much bigger than them. However, those who go on to follow their dreams do so not because they have some genetic immunity to fear, but because they find within themselves the courage to risk the possibility that their dreams will not become reality. They pursue their dreams anyway, despite their doubts and despite the many challenges that line the path they have dared to travel.

You too have that courage. Even if you have long since lost the knack of dreaming and, instead, adopted a very grown up "responsible" and "realistic" approach to life, you still have the ability to dream. For you have never lost the longing that dreams can fulfill. Instead, your resignation about your ability to move them forward has just numbed it. Fortunately, there is no "Statute of Limitations" on how much you can dream, how long you have to make a dream come true before you have to ditch it or how many dreams you can have in any one lifetime. Beginning today, start to bring some dreaming back into your life and with it a new experience of living each day that is more inspiring, more meaningful and much, *much*, more fun.

To Dream or Not to Dream: That Is the Question?

Let's face it, no one enjoys the feeling of disappointment when things don't work out as hoped. However, as with every choice, the pros and cons of living a life with dreams or living a life devoid of them go both ways. So it is important to ask yourself, "How much will it cost me *not* to dream?"

First off, when you choose not to dream, you are giving up a unique, precious gift—the gift of dreaming dreams that only you have the ability to dream. Yes, *only* you! Given there is no one else on earth who has the same talents, skills, life experiences and imagination as you, then it makes sense that there are wonderful things that you, and only you, will ever be able to dream of doing. Regardless of how much you feel you lack in resources and ability, you are uniquely positioned to make your dreams come true in some way, shape or form. So, if you do not choose to have a dream, you are aiming lower in life than you are worthy of. In doing so you are selling out on everyone else on planet earth who would also benefit, however indirectly, from you finding the courage to dream bigger in your life. But even worse than selling out on your spouse or your children or your parents or your friends or your community or your country, you are selling out on yourself.

One of my clients articulated this beautifully when I asked her how she would feel if she didn't leave her corporate job to pursue her passion for photography. Though this would mean leaving behind the security of her weekly paycheck and taking on the challenge of running her own small business, she didn't hesitate before replying, "It would be worse than eating glass."

Saying you are selling out on yourself is a pretty harsh statement to make, but let's just try to take a look at this from an objective point of view. There are 24 hours in a day, 7 days in a week, 52 weeks in a year. If you sleep 8 hours each night, that leaves 5,840 hours to spend on other activities throughout the course of any given year. Now, one way or another (unless you are dead or in a coma) you are going to spend those hours doing something. It may be driving to work in your car, running after your children, cleaning your bathroom, shopping, cooking, eating, sitting in meetings, doing your income taxes (or last years taxes), watching TV, playing sports, exercising or whatever…you get my drift. Some of these things you will enjoy more, some you'll enjoy less and some you will positively not enjoy at all. My point is that 12 months from today you will have spent your many waking hours doing something!

Now imagine if, during those waking hours, instead of feeling a general sense of resignation about your life, you were working toward something (however slowly) that actually excited you in some way. And imagine if, whilst you were cleaning your bathroom, driving to work or cooking your dinner, you had a dream in your head that you were playing with—a dream that inspired you at the deepest level. How would that shift your experience of the next 12 months? What difference would that make to how you felt about yourself and your life? You know, however old you are, it is never too late to begin to want more from your life and to dare to give more to it.

The French writer Anais Nin wrote, "Life shrinks or expands in proportion to one's courage." Given how much courage it takes to dream big, exciting dreams for yourself and your life, I believe that life also shrinks or expands in proportion to one's dreams. Dreams have a profound impact on your experience of being alive and enrich the quality of your life exponentially.

Whenever I begin working with a new client who is neither excited nor inspired about their future, it is generally because they do not have a dream that they are working toward. Of course, this is not why they engage me to coach them. More often, it is because there is something going on in their life that's causing them to feel stressed, anxious, frustrated or completely hopeless that they will ever feel really happy. They are generally so absorbed with whatever the particular problem is that they are not the least bit present to the fact that, in between sorting through all their problems, they are journeying towards…well…err…nothing.

Dreams can help keep the small problems in life in perspective. When I am able to help people move to what I call a "space of possibility" and muster up the guts to dream about what they would really love to be doing with their life, suddenly the many problems they have been struggling with seem to either just fade into the ether, or they are able to address them far more effectively with less angst and more ease. As the space of what is possible for them grows, the anxiety and stress about the "small stuff" abates. Having a dream opens the door for inspiration to flow into one's life and, as it does, it lifts the gray mood of resignation that some people have grown so accustomed to they've come to think of it as a normal, completely acceptable state of living.

Take Terese, age 27, who contacted me about coaching after reading an article I'd written for a magazine about harnessing the power of vision. Terese was working at the reception desk at a large upscale hotel. Although she liked her job, she didn't like the hours she worked and thought she could do her boss's job better than her boss could.

Life shrinks or expands in proportion to one's dreams.

She earned enough money to live comfortably, but found it difficult to save much and didn't have any clear financial goals. Her health was fine, but she wasn't as fit as she wanted to be. Terese had a lot of friends but realized she was growing bored with them or, more accurately, with the same small-minded conversations she was having with them. She couldn't put her finger on anything in particular but realized when she read my article that her life would be pretty much the same in five years as it was then. That thought depressed her terribly. She was hoping I could help her figure out how to stop feeling so "ho hum" in her life. I began by asking her a few questions. If she had no fear of failing: What would she *really* love to do with her life? What type of people would she *really* love to hang out with? And most importantly, what kind of person would she *really* love to be herself? Initially, Terese was a little uncomfortable with my line of questioning. It was scary. She felt vulnerable just talking about it. After a couple of coaching sessions, Terese was finding her courage and talking more freely about the kinds of things that she would love to do. Her dream was coming to life. She told me she would really love to return to school to get a degree in hotel management. She would also like to meet new people who were doing interesting things in their life and she would like to get into great shape. Soon she was talking about maybe joining the team for her company in the corporate half-marathon event that was scheduled for later that year.

As I have now witnessed many times with people who find the courage to begin to dream, suddenly Terese's face became radiant. Truly. Her eyes got a twinkle in them and her expression was akin to a kid in a candy store. It was magical. With a vision that really lit her up, we began to work out a plan that helped her take action to realize each of these dreams (something we'll get to in the second section of this book). As she found the courage within herself to dream, Terese not only discovered she was capable of more than she'd ever imagined previously but exciting opportunities opened up for her that she'd never expected. As they did, the problems and annoyances in her life that she'd initially sought coaching for became inconsequential in light of the new goals she was now enthusiastically working toward. In fact, Terese and I are still in touch and she is now engaged to a lovely man she met whilst in training for her first half marathon.

The Power of Dreams

Often we humans resist even dreaming about what we would really love to do, and when our imagination does start to wander, we start chastising ourselves immediately with, "What's the point? It's stupid and foolish to get carried away with such fantasies." Dreaming to some can seem like a futile activity—a big waste of time and energy. But the point of dreaming is that before anything can become tangible it must first be imagined. For instance, I have a world globe sitting on my desk in front of me that was a wedding gift from my sister Pauline. It sits on a carved wooden base and is attached with a brass stand and has two sunflowers carved into it. Before that globe could be made, the designer had to imagine it in their mind's eye. They had to picture those flowers, where they would be positioned and how they would be carved. They could never have created it had they not first imagined it. Likewise, I would never have donned a backpack at 21 and set off for a year traveling around the world if I had not imagined myself doing so first in my mind's eye. The dreaming had to precede the creating. The same applies to everything around you—from the clothes you are wearing to the picture hanging on your wall and the meal you ate for dinner. It didn't just appear. It had to first exist in your mind.

Let me share with you a story about Brenda, an attorney who had been working ten years for a large firm specializing in family law. She dreamt of having her own small practice, because with two young children, she felt it would give her a little more flexibility. However, she hadn't done anything about it for several years. After a few sessions, Brenda became very clear in her head about what her dream family law practice would look like. She imagined where the offices would be, what her clients would be like, her ideal business partner, how large a staff she would have…the works! Gradually, all the pieces began to fall into place. She called me one day and said to me, "You won't believe this, but an opportunity has just come up to start a practice with someone I have admired and respected for many years—an opportunity I never thought I would have." Did she have to get "out there," share her vision and do all the legwork involved in starting a law practice? Of course she did. The point is that once you get the courage to paint your dream with enough detail, you begin to know what you need to make it happen. You will be astounded at how the universe will present you with the opportunities, the circumstances and the people you need to make it a reality.

There are three huge benefits you get once you find within you the courage to dream bigger for yourself. Firstly, your dreams propel your life in a direction that inspires you and so bring a greater sense of meaning and purpose to your present moment-by-moment, day-by-day experience. Secondly, dreams empower you to ask for more from life than you otherwise would. Why?

> *Before anything can become tangible it must first be imagined.*

Because the most you ever get from life is what you ask for but without a dream you can't know what it is you want to ask for. The dreaming must precede the asking. With a dream fixed in your mind's eye, you will be far more powerful, because you will be able to ask for what you want from those who may have the ability to give it to you, or refer you to someone who can. In fact, any area of your life that you fail to hold a vision for yourself you also fail to have any real power. Finally, dreams connect you to the sacred source from which your creativity and intuition comes. Dreams have the power to unleash a positive flow of energy into and around your life. Once you have a dream in your heart and mind that is inspiring you, *extra* ordinary coincidences begin to occur. Life becomes serendipitous in ways you've never experienced before.

The story of Ryan Hrelja is another case in point. In 1998, when Ryan was six years old, he learned from his first grade teacher that millions of people in Africa were ill or would die because they lacked a basic need—access to clean water. His teacher explained that children had to walk many miles to find water and that $70 would be enough to drill a well and save many lives. Discovering this, Ryan went home with the dream of raising money to build wells for people who didn't have the clean water he took for granted in his home in Ontario, Canada. He begged his parents to help him by paying him for doing simple household chores around his family home. Four months later, he had earned $70 and contacted a charity that drills wells in Africa. He found out that building the well would actually cost $2,000. Determined not to give up on his dream of making a difference for those in Africa who so desperately needed fresh water, Ryan said at the time, "I will just have to do more chores." He did just that, and as he did, others, inspired by the size and importance of his dream, rallied around to support him in making his dream a reality. Within seven years the money raised by Ryan's Well Foundation had built over 200 wells in nine countries changing forever the lives of many thousands of people.

What's Keeping You Playing Small?

Not All Dreams Come True

Of course not everyone's experience is the same as Brenda's or Ryan's. Indeed, as you're reading this chapter, there may be a little voice in the back of your head that is saying, "All this dream stuff is pie in the sky, positive thinking fluff. It all sounds very nice, but the reality is that not everyone's dreams come true and it's irresponsible to get people's hopes up." Naturally, you're entitled to your opinion. As much as I advocate a positive approach to life, I'm also a realist. I know, as well as anyone, that not all dreams come true, otherwise we'd all have won the lotto years ago. But if our dreams did all come with a guarantee of success, it wouldn't take any courage to dream in the first place!

However, the good news is that the courage you call on to dream bigger will also give you the strength to deal with any disappointment should your dream fail to turn into your reality. Simply by daring to create a vision for your future that touches your heart and ignites your spirit, you will realize that you are more resourceful and more capable than you have previously given yourself credit for. That in itself is quite a gift regardless of whether or not you end up living bang plonk in the middle of the dream you originally envisaged.

Tall Poppy Syndrome & Your "Small Poppy Committee"

Growing up in Australia I couldn't help but be affected by the "Tall Poppy Syndrome". Whilst it might sound like a rare medical condition it's actually a cultural condition peculiar to the sun burnt country I call home. Born from our convict ancestry, Tall Poppy Syndrome came about from a desire for a more egalitarian society than existed back in class conscious England. A society where, regardless of heritage, all men are equal and no bloke (or 'shiela') is better than the bloke next to him; where anyone who gets too "up themselves" is quickly put in their place, and where being called "down to earth" is a great compliment (and rightly so!).

Something many Americans love about Australians is our self-deprecating humor. No doubt about it, we are the best in the biz when it comes to putting ourselves down. Taking yourself too seriously and being filled with self-importance does not go down well in Australia. But whilst humility (and good humor) is admirable, and arrogance (and being "up yourself") never a virtue, any strength overdone can become a weakness. In this case, the culture that once proudly coined the term Tall Poppy Syndrome also created, however unwittingly, an environment which made people wary of aiming too high or daring to accomplish things that could put them at risk of standing out, being criticized, ostracized or, like the tallest poppies, cut down. In doing so, it has not only held many people back in life and kept them from fulfilling their potential, but it has also stifled creativity, wealth creation, opportunity and excellence. As Australia's Prime Minister John Howard once stated, "If there's one thing we need to get rid of in this country it is our tall poppy syndrome".

Whilst the influence of the Tall Poppy Syndrome has waned in recent years, the fear which drives it is universal and stronger than ever. We all have what I like to call a "Small Poppy Committee" in our own heads which wants us to play safe, stick with the status quo and sabotage our dreams with questions like, "But who are you to do that?" No one wants to fail, make mistakes, look foolish or have others think poorly of them. Sure, for some of us the nagging voices of our Small Poppy Committee are louder, more persistent, more cautious, and more over-bearing than others, but the reality is that we all have them!

The problem is not that we have a Small Poppy Committee; the problem is that we allow it to run our lives and determine the size of our dreams!

Being a "Tall Poppy" is not about you being better than anyone else; it's about you being better than you used to be. It's about having the guts to dream bigger and take on goals that stretch you, that put you at risk and that require you growing into a bigger person than you would otherwise have become. As Marianne Williamson wrote in *A Return to Love*, "We ask ourselves, 'Who am I to be brilliant, gorgeous, talented, fabulous?' Actually who are you not to be? You are a child of God: playing small doesn't serve the world. There is nothing enlightened about shrinking so that other people won't feel insecure around you." Your Small Poppy Committee is all about playing safe and small and avoiding unwanted attention. The question is: how much authority will you give it?

Dreams Create More Challenges

Let's face it. Dreaming bigger doesn't necessarily make life easier. In fact, dreaming bigger dreams for yourself means inviting more challenges into your life. Yes, that's right, *more* challenges. Perhaps your initial reaction to this may be to withdraw from your dreams, or discard them outright, especially if your biggest goal in life has been to keep your challenges to a minimum. If this is the case, I'll bet your life is also not particularly inspiring to you. It may be comfortable, it may be easy, it may be a picture postcard of an "ideal life," but it won't give you buzz. You see, it's the challenges your dreams present you that gives your life its edge, its excitement. It's the challenges that make life interesting and ultimately, by facing them courageously, give you the deepest sense of fulfillment (something we'll get into more in Chapter 8).

> *"The aim, if reached or not, makes great the life."*
> –Robert Browning

When Martin Luther King, Jr. said, "I have a dream…." do you think he was under any illusion about the obstacles he would face in achieving his dream? No way. He knew that he was bringing a heck of a lot more challenges into his life for daring to dream so big. I am sure he was acutely aware that one of the many challenges he faced would be the threats to his own life for having the courage to speak up and demand change as he did. Did that stop him? No. The ironic thing about life's problems is that you can judge the size of a person by the size of their problems. Think about the problems that people such as Gandhi, Mandela, Mother Teresa, Bill Gates and Bono have chosen to take on. If someone's biggest problems in life are how to improve their golf par, keep their nails from chipping or selecting the perfect mural for their child's bedroom—then it's likely they are playing pretty small in life and keeping both dreaming and risk taking to a minimum.

Of course life is a never-ending stream of challenges however big or small you play it, so why not make them meaningful challenges, however lofty! Then, as they come your way, greet them as opportunities to think outside the box, to discover inner resources you didn't know you had, to strengthen your "life muscles" and with them, your ability to live life fully. Ultimately, it is my intention that, after reading this book, you will have much bigger problems and challenges than before you started reading it!

Let me share with you one of my dreams, which I had several years ago on the beach in Mexico. Six months prior to finding myself lying under the Mexican sun, I'd had my third child in 3 ½ years, packed up my house in Australia (the same week as 9/11), lived out of suitcases for three months, moved to the U.S. (a trip which took 36 hours due to post 9/11 flight scheduling changes), found myself covered head to toe with psoriasis and had an all round difficult time. Kathy, a "Fairy God mother" cousin of my mum's living in California, sensing my need for respite, had flown to Dallas and sent Andrew and me to Mexico for a few days of much needed downtime. So there I was laying on the beach counting my psoriasis spots when I was hit with the inspiration to do a little meditation exercise about what I really wanted my life to look like ten years out. In one part of my vision, I was doing what I am doing now—helping people to live happier lives. But what I saw in the other part of my vision knocked my socks off! Strike me down, I can't tell you how totally perplexed I was when into my mind's eye appeared four children. FOUR! "No, God, not four. Three, please God, make it three. You've made a mistake here…can't you see these spots? I've barely kept my head above water since having my third and whilst the idea of four children has always been very inspiring to me, as I sit here right now it absolutely terrifies me." But the picture that emerged in my mind's eye had left its mark…my dream life had me the mother of four, not three, children. Ukurumba…how would I ever manage?

My husband Andrew took no convincing about the merits of a fourth child. Five months later, the week Ben turned one, the marker on the home pregnancy test came up positive. Eight months later, just as my oldest child Lachlan turned five, Matthew was born. Did having him throw in a whole range of extra challenges? Sure it did. Were there many days that I was exhausted and struggling to keep all the balls in the air? Sure there were. However, too often we lump challenges into the category of things that are "bad" and to be avoided. Challenges are neither good nor bad. Rather they are things to be managed and worked around. Sure, life would be easier if I'd stopped at three children, it would be easier still if I'd stopped at two and wow, imagine how easy it would be if I'd never stopped taking that pill! But easy doesn't mean rich. Easy doesn't mean joyous. Easy doesn't mean anything if you aren't doing something with your life that is aligned with your deepest passions and your most inspiring dreams.

What I have since learned is that if you muster up the courage to pursue your dreams, the ones that may terrify you as much as they inspire you, you will find a way to "manage" the challenges as they arise. Sure a life without dreams may have fewer and smaller challenges, but oh, what a flat barren place to live.

Don't get me wrong, I am not advocating large families. Though I do cherish coming from a large family of seven and absolutely love the family Andrew and I have created, I know that having four children—or having *any* children—isn't something that inspires everyone. As I said earlier, we each have our own special dreams to dream, and so what inspires you doesn't necessarily inspire your best friend and it doesn't need to. Each person has his or her own gifts, dreams and contributions to make in the world. The only thing that matters is that you are doing with your life something that makes you feel fully alive, that resonates with your spirit and honors the person have you it within you to become. What everyone else is doing is irrelevant. Period.

You Have Your Dreams for a Reason

So, back to the question, *To Dream or Not To Dream?* I believe that once you grasp how much it costs you to live a life without a dream—whatever package your dream comes in—you will find within yourself the courage to dream of whatever ignites your spirit.

We each have different passions, abilities, gifts and personalities which provide inspiration for different dreams. Not everyone dreams of climbing Kilimanjaro. Not everyone dreams of starting up their own cake shop, running a day-care center, a B&B, or being a professional organizer. Not everyone dreams of managing a large company. Not everyone dreams of opening an animal shelter, teaching migrants how to speak English or writing a book on courage (I couldn't resist popping that one in) and not everyone dreams of sailing single-handedly around the globe on a 30-foot yacht (me least of all!).

Whatever dreams you have, you have for a reason. I mean think about it, you wouldn't be able to dream about something if it weren't already inside you. The thoughts that make up the dream have to be inspired from within you. Not within me…*within you!* Sure someone else might help to nurture your dream, give it the space to breath and the water to grow, but no one can create a dream and give it to you (as much as the model home builders might tell you otherwise). That is why your dreams are different from mine and those around you.

Dispelling the Dream Myths

For some people the word "dream" conjures up a particular image, sometimes not always a very positive one. So before going further, I think it is important to dispel any preconceptions you might have about what your dreams "should" or "should not" look like in order for them to make a difference in your life.

Dreams Come In Many Shapes and Sizes

First of all, dreams don't have to fit a "stereotype" to be valid and inspiring. What are you dreaming about? Are you looking for a new job, to meet someone special or get your teenager through adolescence in one piece? Whatever your dream, don't start comparing it to someone else's. Just because a dream may seem small and insignificant to one person doesn't mean it isn't huge for the person dreaming it. If you found yourself heading off to college at eighteen with your fees all paid by your parents, the idea of earning a bachelor's degree may not seem like a big deal to you. But if, like Betsy, who came up to me after one of my presentations, you had left school at 15, had three kids by the time you were 22 and spent the next 15 years working odd minimum wage jobs just to raise your kids and make ends meet, then the dream of going to university to earn a degree may seem enormous.

> *"The future belongs to those who believe in the beauty of their dreams."*
> –Eleanor Roosevelt.

Likewise, leaving the security of a weekly paycheck to start your own business may also leave you shaking at the knees. Or, if you have been a professional, working mom juggling the corporate job and the kids since you had your first child, the idea of leaving the workforce to be a stay-at- home mom might absolutely terrify you. Similarly, there are also thousands and thousands of women who have been stay-at-home moms for the better part of a decade or more, who feel completely overwhelmed at the idea of trying to get back into the workforce or even of resuming their studies.

So when it comes to dreaming, size is irrelevant. All that matters is that your dream inspires you, that it makes a difference to who you are in the world, because you are someone who has the courage to have a dream. And even if your dream doesn't inspire anyone else, the fact that you've had the courage to dream it may.

Dreams Evolve

Secondly, dreams evolve as we ourselves grow, discover more about ourselves, experience more of life and expand our horizons. This was very much the case for Darrell Wade, the founder and CEO of Intrepid Travel, who I worked with as a marketing consultant in the late 90's.

A decade earlier in the late 1980's after traveling around Africa, Darrell and his friend Geoff Manchester decided to start Intrepid. They were passionate about people having an authentic travel experience of the culture and people of Asia, whilst also giving back to the communities in which they visited. In 1989, they began running tours in Thailand that gave people an authentic off-the-beaten-track travel experience, similar to the backpacking ones, but without the restrictiveness of the highly structured package tours. Three years later in 1992, they decided to run similar tours in Vietnam. At the time, the only tours people could do in Vietnam were contracted through state-owned tour operators, so it was a risky market to break into, but they figured, what the heck, lets give it a try—lets be Intrepid! That they did, and as the interest in travel to Vietnam began to soar in the early to mid 90's so too did demand for their tours. Since then, the vision Darrell and Geoff have had for Intrepid Travel has expanded exponentially. Intrepid now has nearly 300 people on staff, offering 300 different trips to over 50 different destinations around the world from Egypt to Borneo to Tibet. Along the way, their vision for contributing back to the communities in which they operate has also grown. With the establishment of the Intrepid Foundation in 2002, they are now making a real difference in local communities in health care, education, human rights, child welfare and in environmental and wildlife protection.

So there you go, what began as running a few tours for people to experience a real taste of Thailand has evolved and evolved and evolved and no doubt, will continue to evolve even further in the years ahead. By being open to expanding their vision for Intrepid as new opportunities have come along, Darrell and Geoff have allowed Intrepid to become an organization that is making a huge impact in the lives of people in all corners of the globe—travelers and those in the local communities alike.

Over the years, I've lost count of the number of times my dreams for what I wanted to do when I "grew up" changed as I actually did grow up (and I'm still not quite there yet!) If they hadn't kept evolving, perhaps I'd have ended up working at the local pharmacy near where I grew up helping women choose the right shade of lipstick. As for being a life coach, I'd never heard of coaching until I was in my 30's, so there's no way I could have dreamt of being one before that. In fact in my mid 20's, whilst working for multi-national corporations, my dream job became working in the adventure travel industry, which I eventually did as a marketing consultant with companies like Intrepid and as a freelance travel writer. I guess there are some parallels between this and what I do now. It's just that now I work at helping people embrace a sense of adventure in their everyday lives, for you certainly don't need to set foot in a foreign country in order to step out of your comfort zone. It was in my late 20's whilst living in Papua New Guinea that I first felt pulled in the direction that has brought me to where I am today. I dreamt of becoming a psychologist because I wanted to help people live happier lives. Not really sure exactly where I was headed, I returned to university to study psychology. It was only once I was well into my psychology studies that I came upon coaching as a profession. Voilà! Suddenly my dream took on a completely new form. As for the future, I'm sure my dreams will continue to evolve in ways I cannot imagine right now. Likewise whatever your dream is, however clear or unclear, just know that it is completely okay for you also to change course as you move along and your dreams evolve. After all, dreams are only ever a direction, not a destination.

Dreams Serve More Than Your Ego

Thirdly, dreams serve a larger purpose than just feeding our ego. They exist for far greater reasons than to make us look good to all those we wish to impress. Often people get sidetracked with a vision, which they believe, if it came true, would allow them to live their picture perfect "dream life." This occurs when they confuse the object of a dream with the feeling they want that object to give them. For instance, many people dream about becoming a millionaire (or marrying one), having the body of a super model, being famous, or sitting under a palm tree on a tropical island for the rest of their lives sipping strawberry daiquiris. They believe that if this dream were their reality they would forever experience the feeling of blissful happiness they seek. The problem is that if your dream serves only your ego and no other meaningful purpose, it will lead you down a deep, dark, rabbit hole toward disillusionment

Dreams are only ever a direction, not a destination.

and discontent. Just this time it will be filled with nicer creature comforts, and you will be even more confused about why you are *still* not happy.

All human beings want to feel happy about themselves. We just have different theories about how to achieve it. As hard as some people try to prove otherwise, I've never met or heard of anyone who found *genuine* happiness from doing something that served themselves exclusively. Those who exude a true sense of peace and fulfillment, regardless of their level of worldly success, have all had dreams that served others in some way, shape or form. For instance, if I thought that living in a 10,000 square foot pad on the beach in Malibu, driving a bright red Mercedes coupe *and* looking like Nicole Kidman would guarantee my happiness, then I would be on a sure path to disappointment. The truth of the matter is that being wealthy or famous or skinny or company president or having the cutest husband (or wife) or the greatest tan in the world won't bring you the happiness you want (though it may make you a prime candidate for melanoma). Now I am not saying that there is anything wrong with any of these things per se. Not a bit. I am saying, though, that whilst they can make your life more pleasurable and your ego more inflated, they cannot make you truly happy.

The fact is being rich doesn't guarantee a rich life. Just think about it. Will more of what you have already been focused on for so long really bring you the happiness you want? These things may be the rather pleasant by-product of your dreams, but they will not be the focus of your dream once you've got your ego out the way and connected with your spirit.

The reason dreams will never be just about getting rich or being famous is because there is nothing inherently meaningful about being rich or being famous. It's what you do with your money or your fame that brings meaning. I remember watching a TV interview several years ago, during which Brad Pitt (married to Jennifer Aniston at the time) was asked how he felt about his phenomenal success. He replied, "I know it seems like this is IT, but this is not IT." So there was this famous, wealthy and incredibly hot (well, to me anyway) guy, who most people would think was living the ultimate dream life, and there he was saying, "This is not IT." Why? Because IT is a feeling which comes from serving a bigger purpose than yourself. Being famous or rich are not meaningful goals on their own, unless they are used for some larger purpose. The key therefore isn't to dream of being happy, but to ask yourself *what* you would need to be doing in order to *feel* truly happy. The answer will not be the size of your bank account or your fan club. Richard Gere's advocacy for the rights of the people of Tibet and Bono's campaign for the eradication of third world debt are examples of people who have had the courage to dream of making a difference that is bigger than who they are. In doing so, they are using their celebrity in ways that bring far deeper meaning and purpose to their lives.

Eric was the personification of a poor, rich man. When I met him he was 41 and had been retired for 3 years. He'd made a bunch of money in the IT industry, and when he sold his business for a bundle of cash, he vowed he would never work again. He told me he spent his days reading the paper and getting his golf handicap down. The feeling I got from him was that I was *supposed* to react with envy, but envy was the last emotion I felt. The truth is, I felt sorry for him. As Eric shared his tale of success with me, interspersed with the occasional mention of his car, vacations and fortunes, I began to hear a whole truckload of stories about what a dream life was "supposed" to look like (according to Eric anyway). He was kidding himself that he was living his dream life, because if he had been, I would have felt it in the way that we all do when in the presence of someone who truly loves their life. I didn't. If Eric was living his dream life, he would not have had such a strong need to convince me of it or impress me with it. It would have been there in his eyes, in his voice; it would have radiated from his general "way of being" as I like to call it. My sense was that the only thing Eric felt was lost. He had more money than he'd ever imagined he would, he was living what he *thought* was his dream life, but he was clearly not fired up one iota about his future. The core of Eric's problem was that he was not doing anything meaningful with his new-found wealth and he certainly wasn't giving anything back to the world that had given him so much. It was serving no greater purpose than feeding his ego.

> *The key isn't to dream of being happy, but to ask yourself what you would need to be doing in order to feel truly happy.*

Dreams Don't Have to Be Imminently Achievable

Some people have dreams that may take many years before becoming a reality. Others have dreams they will never be able to achieve in their own lifetime. Nevertheless, these dreams are just as important and valuable as those which you can achieve in the next six months. As I said earlier, there is no statute of limitations restricting how long you've got to achieve your dream. It may be that there is very little you can do right now to make your dream come true any sooner. For instance, if you are waiting until your children leave home to move to the country or buy a smaller house along the coast or are waiting until you and your spouse retire before heading off around the country, it doesn't matter. The very fact that you have a dream will enrich your life right now as you get to imagine how wonderful it will be when that time finally does arrive.

Exercise 4.1: Play "Make Believe" with Your Dream Life

I invite you to step out of your very serious "grown up" shoes for a minute and play a game of make believe with me. I have a magic wand. Yes, really, I do. It even makes this wonderful *brrrrrrring* sound (except when the batteries are spent). Anyway, today I am going to wave it in your direction and grant you the courage to create a dream that really inspires you. No, I'm not going to make your dream come true. That would take all the fun out of it. I am just going to help you have the dream.

So get out your journal and think about what would infuse the most passion, purpose and delight into your life. Write in it what your dream life would actually look like. (Remember, to create something, you must first imagine it.)

Your dream life is one in which you would feel really good about yourself. It does not imply that everything in your life would be perfect and problem-free. (Keep in mind, dreams may actually increase the number of challenges in your life.) But it would have you feeling purposeful, peaceful and grateful.

As you begin to write about your "dream life," do not be hindered by what does or does not make sense. Nor by what is or is not realistic. This is all part of the game of make believe and isn't to be hindered by all the many "buts" or "what ifs?" that will arise. (I'll address those later in this book.) For now, just let your imagination run wild as you embrace the words of Eudora Welty, "All serious daring starts from within." By daring yourself to play this game, you can create a clearer vision of what would inspire you in the future and open up the possibility of it actually coming true. Remember, this is a fun exercise, so just let your pen roll freely to describe your ideal life in as much color and detail as you can muster

If you like, use the following questions to stimulate your thinking.

1. Where would you be living?
2. With whom would you have relationships and what would those relationships be like?
3. What kind of family would you be part of?
4. What would you be doing in your career or professional life?
5. What would you be doing in your community?
6. What worthwhile and meaningful causes would you be championing?
7. What would you do for recreation and relaxation?
8. Who would you be as a person for those who know you?
9. What would your ideal day look like? Describe how you would start, fill and end each day.
10. Write down at least 20 things you would be doing (or planning to do) if you were living your dream life?

Exercise 4.2: Create a Dream Board

If you enjoyed doing the exercise above, then you might also enjoy this one. You will need a few materials—a large piece of card or cork board, scissors, glue or pins, a big pile of magazines, marketing brochures or pamphlets (junk mail is a great source).

Once you've got everything together, put aside at least an hour to select and cut out pictures that really catch your eye. They may represent what you would like to have in your life (or would like more of), what you may have once wanted (perhaps related to your childhood dreams), or maybe just something you like the look of, for whatever reason. In short, choose whatever you fancy! If you are feeling creative, you might also want to draw a picture or write down some words on the card or board that resonate with you. It doesn't have to be a work of art but rather something that speaks to you.

> *"The only place where your dream becomes impossible is in your own thinking."*
> –Robert H. Schuller

Now go through your clippings and decide which ones you would like to put on your dream board (as few or as many as you like). Once you've either pasted them onto your piece of card or pinned them onto cork board, you can strategically place your Dream Board somewhere you will see it everyday such as on the fridge, in your bathroom, your closet, or in your study.

The purpose of this exercise is to tap both your intuition and creativity and produce something that will provide you with a constant reminder of what it is you want to manifest into your life (whether it be a red, sports car or more peace and tranquility). Every time you look at your Dream Board it will remind you of what inspires you most to move your life forward in the direction you want. The images on your dream board will be planted in your subconscious, and as weird and amazing as it sounds, you will begin attracting these things into your life, or just as often, opportunities for bringing them into your life. If you are feeling cynical about this right now and wondering if you can be bothered creating your Dream Board, then think of it this way; what have you got to lose versus what you have to gain? Cynicism will get you nowhere—just do it!

Dare Yourself to Dream Bigger

My dad has this saying that goes, "You may as well do it now 'cause you're a long time dead." As blunt and un-poetic as it is, you can't argue with its underlying truth. So I'd like you to finish the statement below with whatever comes straight into your head (it might be more than one thing). Ideally say this statement out loud adding your own personal ending:

"My life would be more inspiring if I had the dream of..."

As I said earlier, it is a universal law of life that the most you ever get is what you ask for. Having the courage to dare to dream will set the stage for you to ask for more from your life and the people in it than you presently are. By getting clear about what you truly want in your life (and by default, what you don't want), you will be able to transform your life to have more of what you want and less of what you don't.

That you possess the power to live the life you dream of is without question. However, before you can tap into that power and apply it effectively you have to muster up the courage to ask yourself where you could be dreaming bigger in your life. So I ask you again, what is it that you really want in your life? No, I mean, what you really *really* want?

There is something that you, and only you, are called to be doing in the world. There are things that will never be done if you do not do them. It is your responsibility to find the courage to let yourself dream bigger than you have up until now, and then to live that dream so that you will have no regrets when the day comes that you can dream no longer.

For no matter how big or small the dreams you've had in your life up to this point, you can dream so much bigger than you have been doing. Have the courage to dream bigger dreams for yourself and dream yourself to be a bigger person. By connecting with whatever it is that fills you with passion and purpose you will find the courage to step up to the plate in life, play a bigger game, become a bigger person and live a bigger life. In the words of Belva Davis, "Don't be afraid of the space between your dreams and reality. If you can dream it, you can make it so". Amen!

"When you are inspired by some great purpose, some extraordinary project, all your thoughts break their bonds; your mind transcends limitations, your consciousness expands in every direction, and you find yourself in a new, great and wonderful world. Dormant forces, faculties and talents become alive, and you discover yourself to be a greater person by far than you ever dreamed yourself to be."

–Patanjali

Section Two

Courage in Action

The Courage to Be Yourself
The Courage to Speak Up
The Courage to Take Action
The Courage to Persevere
The Courage to Say No

*"Our doubts are our traitors, and make us lose the good
we oft might win by fearing to attempt."*
—William Shakespeare

Chapter 5
The Courage to Be Yourself

*"And the day came when the risk to remain tight in a bud
was more painful than the risk it took to blossom."*

—Anais Nin

It takes a lot more courage to be who you are than who you are not. In a world that pressures for conformity, one of the greatest challenges you ever face is being the one-of-a-kind person you really are. Expressing yourself authentically is a truly courageous act because it requires that you be brave enough to reveal who you truly are—your uniqueness, your insecurities, your beauty, your passions—and risk vulnerability. However, if you don't take the risk to step out from behind the mask that protects you, you run an even greater risk of spending your whole life trying to be a someone you're not, and depriving others of what makes you most attractive to them…yourself!

Why Be You?

Several years ago I attended a personal development seminar in Dallas, where I was fortunate enough to meet an elderly woman named Peg. I recall she was 83 at the time and had lived all her life in far west Texas. Peg's face had deep wrinkles from decades of scorching Texan summers and her shoulders were rounded over to the point that she required a walker to move about. The gentle smile she wore on her face the entire three days (and they were long days) had a contagious effect on everyone, me included. Heck, if Peg wasn't complaining about the arduously long days, then how could we? Near the end of the seminar, the leader asked the group if anyone had anything they wanted to share. Peg raised her frail arm into the air, then slowly stood her aging body to rest on her walker, looked around the room at all of us, and said in her slow west Texan drawl, "In all ma years, I've learned just a coupla things worth matterin'. The one ya'll here should remember is this. *Ya'll be* who ya is, cause ya'll can't be who ya isn't!"

Ultimately, true freedom in life is only possible when you are not shackled to the need for approval from anyone else and are free to express yourself fully, openly and authentically. When you are trying to impress or prove yourself to others in order to gain approval or avoid disapproval, you can neither enjoy true freedom nor ease in the company of others or on your own. The reality is that if you are driven by the need to impress others, no matter how long and how hard you try you will never be able to impress them enough. Yes, of course, you will be rewarded along the way with accolades here and there, but you will never get *enough* accolades, *enough* appreciation, *enough* approval, *enough* admiration! You will forever have to strive, but you will never feel like you've truly arrived. Only by having the courage to be yourself—however flawed or quirky, *extra* ordinary or *un*-ordinary you think yourself to be—can you hope to be truly free from the striving.

The ironic thing is that the less you care what other people think of you, the more you will have to offer the world around you. The reason for this is that when you are caught up trying to conform to others expectations and opinions, you are left with nothing to offer but conformity. Your immediate environment, and the world at large, is not enriched when it gets more of the same which already exists within it, but when it becomes more diverse—in thought, in opinion, in people! You are therefore doing others a disservice when you withhold your uniqueness and fail to reveal who you really are.

Where Are You Not Being Yourself?

Of course, you may feel that you are already yourself and that this chapter simply just does not apply to you. If that is the case, then wonderful! Please pass go, collect $200 and proceed to Chapter 6. However, before you jump ahead, I'd just like you to think about the various different groups of people that you interact within in your life. The reason I do this is because often there are areas of our life where we are simply not conscious of how we are failing to be fully authentic. Sometimes we've gotten so used to acting a certain way among a group of people, that we have become completely oblivious to the fact that who we are for them is different than who we are for the other people in our life. So on that note, I encourage you to do the exercise below and see what appears for you.

Exercise 5.1: Identifying Where You Aren't Being You!

Get out your journal and write down all the different groups of people you interact with or have relationships with in your life. Make the list as long as you like until you have exhausted all the different groups of people that constitute your environment. For instance: your immediate family, your extended family, your friends, people with whom you work, members at your church, your neighbors, parents at your children's school, your college alumni and the list goes on.

Now I'd like you to think about how the people in each of these different groups would perceive you, or put another way, how you "show up" on the radars for people from these different groups. In which groups are you:
- more guarded and cautious?
- more funny?
- more serious?
- more relaxed?
- more open?
- more quiet?
- more friendly?
- more self-conscious?

• more yourself?!

Once you have finished just reflect on where there are inconsistencies in how you are among these groups that would have them perceive you differently. Think about what it is that stops you from being more yourself with the people in these groups.

For instance, I did this exercise recently with a client called Tom who works as a management consultant. Tom shared with me how at home he is very fun loving and likes to joke around a lot, but at work he is quite serious and rarely, if ever, is playful. When I asked him why, he said because earlier in his career and to a lesser extent where he was now, he was concerned that he might not be taken as being the very professional and ambitious person he wanted to be perceived as. Just that in itself showed up an area where Tom was not being fully himself because even though the environment in which he worked may have called for him to be more serious in order to get his job done, the fact that he didn't allow the lighthearted fun loving part of his personality to come out was preventing him from being fully himself. Was it a big deal that he was doing this? No. He was relatively successful in his job. But was it limiting him? Yes. Because by failing to be completely himself at work, he was keeping from those he worked with a very attractive part of his personality that, if expressed at work, would allow him to build stronger friendships without jeopardizing his professional reputation as someone who can get the job done well.

So there you have it; being yourself is something that is relevant to all people right throughout the course of their lives. So in that spirit I hope that you will not "pass go and collect $200", but stay with me as we explore the various forces that are at play in keeping you from fully expressing the marvelously unique and unrepeatable person you are with all people at all times in all places!

Forces That Keep You from Being You

Imagine you are sitting inside an invisible jail cell. There is an open door in the corner through which you can exit the cell. However, you are unable to leave the cell because you aren't even aware that you are in it. All that you know is you cannot move beyond a certain space but you really aren't sure why, and so, like the elephant with the chain around his leg, you accept the experience of life you have now as the only one available to you.

The walls of this cell represent the forces that have been preventing you from expressing yourself fully up until now. The real you is not out there waiting for you to find it, it is in you, waiting for you to express it. Finding the courage to be yourself is not about finding the real you as much as it is about letting go of the unreal you. Only by becoming aware of the various forces that have been keeping you from being yourself can you begin looking for the exit door to freedom and become fully yourself in the world. What follows is an exploration of the walls of your personal cell that have stifled your full and authentic self expression along with some exercises to help you express yourself more openly, authentically and unreservedly.

Fear of Your Own Inadequacy

Even though on some level you may feel inadequate, you are not inadequate in any way. One of the greatest fears we human beings have is that we are inadequate, unworthy and undeserving in some way. These fears create a powerful force that may have kept you up until now from expressing yourself fully—from being who you really are. The only way to get past them is to first connect with them, to acknowledge them as real.

The first step is to ask yourself, "Where do I fear I am inadequate?" Perhaps you fear there is something about you—the *real* you that you don't like others to see—that is lacking or deficient in some way and which, if found out, would expose you to the world as a fraud or cause people to like or respect you less, or worse still, to outright reject you.

Perhaps you were once in a situation you were unable to deal with, or because of your inadequacy, you failed to deal with it as well as you would have liked. Or maybe you once did something—or failed to do something—that made you feel like you have a big flaw in your character or are "less than" adequate in some way. What happened that made you feel this way? What is it that you feel, if you had had more of, would have made all the difference in this situation and in your life today? More brains, more personality, more courage, more honesty, more tenacity...more what?

Often what hinders us from being fully authentic and powerful in who we are is a fear of having to feel the emotions that would arise should our efforts fail to produce the results we seek. In this case, we fear the shame and rejection we'd feel if we were uncovered as the flawed, unlovable, imperfect, selfish, incompetent and inadequate person that we are. Suddenly people would realize they had been duped and we'd have no where else to hide.

Of course, a feeling won't kill us but often we act as though it will. Even our language reflects this irrational belief. For instance, "If he left me I'd just die," or "It would kill me if this didn't work out." Our fears therefore have extraordinary power over us. Only by connecting with them and feeling to the core the emotion that drives them can we undermine their power and be unleashed from their confining grip.

Exercise 5.2: Feeling Your Fear of Inadequacy

This exercise is based on the premise that the only way to get past the fears that stop you from being yourself is to connect with them and feel them fully. To begin take your journal and take yourself somewhere private where you won't be interrupted or distracted. In your journal describe a situation in which you are being fully yourself with a group of people (or even just one person) whose approval you seek, or to put it another way, who you would really dislike to have disapprove of you or reject you.

Picture this situation clearly in your mind's eye: *Where are you? What time of day is it? What are you wearing? Who is there with you? What are they wearing? What are you talking about?*

Now, imagine that you are being very expressive in what you are *doing*, in what you are *saying*, in who you are *being* and even in what you are wearing which causes them to respond in a way that makes you feel their judgment or disapproval. *What do they do or not do? What are they saying or not saying that is upsetting or hurtful for you or just makes you feel uncomfortable?* Describe the feeling on paper and when you are finished put down your pen and feel the sting of their judgment or their rejection. What is going on for you inside your head? What are you saying to yourself? Where is that feeling of being rejected manifesting in your body…your stomach, your chest, your throat? Just sit there and stay with that feeling that you absolutely do *not* want to feel. Take a deep breath and breathe into the spot that you feel it in your body. Stay with it. Keep breathing long deep, slow breaths right into that spot and don't stop until the feeling has loosened its grip.

If you find your mind wandering (a self-defense mechanism to protect you from feeling the discomfort these feeling conjure up in you), bring it back to the scenario again. Just stay there breathing deeply and resist doing anything else until you feel you have really sat with this feeling. You will know you have done this when you bring the picture into your mind and it does not produce the knot in your stomach or whatever sensation that it did previously. This is a sign that its power has diminished. You can now imagine something not going how you would like it to go without it literally tying you up in a knot. Once you are finished with your breathing, pick up your pen again and write in your journal how you would feel if you were no longer afraid of rejection or disapproval from this person or group of people.

If this exercise becomes too difficult for you to do properly by yourself consider engaging a trained professional to help you with it. You may also need to repeat this exercise several times before you are able to get to the real core of your fear (obviously our deepest fears have the most power and so take the greatest effort to overcome). The purpose of this exercise is not to make the fear disappear (there are some fears you may never overcome), rather it is to quash its power to keep you from expressing yourself freely and find the courage to just be who you authentically are—no acting! This exercise can also be helpful in addressing any of the many doubts and fears that arise as you begin to find the courage to take action in the various areas of your life. You can return to it as you move through the following chapters of this book and become more courageous and powerful in every aspect of your life.

People Pleasing and Proving Yourself Worthy

From the moment you were born and let out that first big scream, there have been forces shaping you to be a particular way. The people who surrounded you as an infant had opinions about what would be best for you and who you would need to be to be your best for them. These made up the expectations you *felt* you had to live up to—from *how* you should act to *who* you should be. The underlying message, whether real or imagined, was that if you were not this way you would not be as loved or as lovable as if you were. Now, I am not saying this was the reality of the situation, but rather what you perceived since as children we interpret all sorts of meaning into things that isn't necessary valid. Of course to any adult, the idea of being unloved is scary but to an infant, it is literally a matter of life and death. So it is from our deepest instinctive drive for self-preservation that we have become the person we believe will allow us to enjoy the acceptance and love we want from the world, to please those we care for, to prove ourselves as worthy of their love and admiration and to "survive!"

Through her teen years, Sally just knew she was an undiscovered "popular" person. She thought that if she just starved herself thin, wore her hair just right, used the right makeup, and liked the right singing groups, the "in crowd" would discover her. But try as she might, it just didn't work. She did, however, manage to gain the attention of a handsome young Air Force officer who she found herself married to. Needless to say, Sally figured her efforts to be the person she felt would impress others had paid off handsomely! But as the years rolled by their marriage grew unhappy. After 13 years of marriage her husband filed for divorce. Sally shared with me how she now believes much of this was because her husband came to see that the woman he thought he had married was not really that woman at all but a fraud who had put on a mighty good act. Sally felt deeply rejected and completely devastated and says that, at the time, she felt like "it was the end of the world."

Fast forward ten years to the summer of 1993. Sally was sitting in her family room with her teenage son and his best friend. They were watching *Revenge of the Nerds*—for the fifteenth time. Throughout the movie, she laughed at the nerds' weird clothing and odd behavior, but got really angry when the beautiful "in crowd" people made fun of them and destroyed their fraternity house. Then comes the closing scene, which Sally had now watched many times, and which she just loved but isn't really sure why. It's the night before the big football game. Everyone is at the bonfire and the nerds are being harassed yet again. Then, as the nerds get their revenge and finally become triumphant, it suddenly hit Sally why she loved this scene so much—she's a nerd!

All at once, everything began to make sense for Sally. She realized that her entire life she had been seeking to squash the parts of her personality that weren't conducive to a "popular" person. She'd begun reading science fiction when she was eight but she hid the books so no one would know, because it was not what a "popular" girl would do. Later she began programming computers long before it was popular. She'd enjoyed all sorts of things "nerdy" people did. What she'd never much enjoyed nor been very good at were all the activities and pursuits that the "in crowd" she had so desperately wanted to be part of liked to do.

Suddenly she was able to embrace a huge part of who she was instead of being ashamed of it. She realized it was okay to be a nerd! This insight changed her life as it allowed her to find the courage to simply be who she was. No more pretending, no more trying to be anything more or less or different than the original one-of-a-kind woman she was. With her brand new sense of herself came a brand new horizon of possibilities. She posted an ad on the personals on the Internet and caught the attention of Ray, a professional speaker, who enjoyed the same "nerdy" things she did, like attending science fiction conventions. He wanted to spend the rest of his life with a woman just like Sally and in 1995 they got married.

> *It is impossible to be your authentic self when you are preoccupied with impressing people and having them like you.*

Sally has discovered that letting her authentic self shine through—by coming out from behind the mask she was wearing for so many years—she attracts people who are right for her not only in her personal life, but in her professional life also. Sally now enjoys far more ease, more love and a lot less anguish by simply being the woman that she is, the woman that for so long she did not have the courage to reveal.

Of course, there is nothing inherently wrong with wanting to fit in, to be liked, approved of and "look good" in the eyes of others—or at least in the eyes of those whose opinions we care about. However, if your desire to achieve this comes at the expense of expressing who you are—no smoke and mirrors—then it cuts you off from being your authentic self. Think of it—how can you simply *be you* whilst you are preoccupied with how other people will respond to you, what they will think about you, what they may say about you and whether or not they may like you? You can't!

In Zen Buddhism they speak of living with one's "original face". The Buddhists describe the "original face" as being relaxed, without tension, free of pretension, devoid of hypocrisy or superficiality. Your "original face" is the one that comes when you find the courage to be authentically you with a full alignment between what you feel, what you think, what you do and what you say. Whilst there have been numerous things I've wanted to prove over the years, I remember the time I was least connected to my "original face" was during my first year or two after leaving my parents farm in rural Victoria to move to Melbourne 200 miles away to attend university.

The Degree course I began when I was 18 attracted a very high proportion of students from upper class privileged backgrounds. Most of the students had parents who were doctors and lawyers and tertiary-educated professionals. Most of them had also attended the better private schools in Melbourne leaving only a handful of us who had come from less affluent homes and schools. Desperate to fit in and make friends, I pretty quickly found myself in a frantic scramble to rid myself of my country girl image and replace it with a more sophisticated city girl look. However, instead of just packing away my old clothes, I packed away anything that might blow the cover that I really was "just a farmer's daughter" and tried my hardest to "fit in." Oh, how I tried, but no matter how much I tried, I just couldn't cut it and I felt more and more like a pathetic fraud. The problem was that I was being inauthentic. As my dear friend Anna, who befriended me despite my rough edges was to later say to me, "Margie, Margie, Margie—you can take the girl out of the country, but you can't take the country out of the girl." How right she was.

Eventually I came to see that by withholding those aspects of my personality which were a direct export from my life growing up on a farm I was stifling myself. By letting go the need to pretend that I was a sophisticated city girl, it created the space to embrace the rough-around-the-edges aspects of who I was and for my real personality to blossom—in short, to become more of who I was and less of who I wasn't!

So how about you? What would you be like if you didn't have to prove anything…to anyone…ever again? Are you even aware of what you are trying to prove right now, or of the impression you are making on others?

Often we are completely unaware of the impression we are making on others and the experience they are having of us. Interestingly enough, research has found that two out of three people are dramatically out of touch with how they see themselves compared to how others see them. So, even though we may think that we are being impressive to others, we are often off the mark.

In Australia we have developed a not very original term to describe people who want to impress others with how great they are—we call them "Try Hards." (I told you it wasn't that original.) Try Hards (which is how I would describe myself back when I began university) are people who try *really really* hard to be *very, very* cool, smart, successful, funny sophisticated or whatever they think will leave a positive impression on those they meet—that they will be impressive! But do you really think the Try Hards have any idea what a not-so-favorable impression they are actually making? Of course they don't. They have absolutely no idea how they are being perceived, otherwise they would employ another strategy.

Whilst it's pretty easy to spot a Try Hard a mile away, we often have a pretty tough time identifying where we ourselves may be trying hard to prove something about ourselves to others. Even if you aren't a Try Hard in the Australian definition of the term, you may still have a need to impress upon others a particular quality or qualities (for there can be more than one quality about ourselves we're trying to impress others with). See if anything comes up for you in the exercise below.

Exercise 5.3: What Are You Trying to Prove?

Get out your journal and at the top of it write "Sometimes I feel the need to convey to others my…" Then as you read through the following descriptions see if any of the descriptions apply to you. You will probably recognize people you know (or have met) in the descriptions to some extent, but the greater challenge is to see if you can recognize yourself in any of them. Be honest with yourself and, if you're up for it, ask someone else who you feel would be honest with you to read through this list and see if they feel any descriptions apply to you. Remember, often other people can see in us what we cannot see ourselves.

Your Brilliance—Do you really love having people acknowledge you for how smart and clever you are? Do you often say or do things that will make people aware of your brilliance? Do you go out of your way to make sure as many people as possible are aware of something clever you've accomplished?

Your Modesty—Do you always play down your accomplishments? When people compliment or praise you, do you reply with a self deprecating comment that undermines their compliment? Do you go out of your way to make sure no one would think of you as egotistical (or as we say in Australia "up yourself")? Do you resist saying anything that might be construed by others as bragging or big noting yourself?

Your Super-Humaneness—Do you always try to fit more into a day than most ordinary "human" folk do and feel very proud of how little sleep you can live on? If you're a mother—whether working or at home—do you love it when people call you a "Supermom"? Are you addicted to being busy? Do you like to let other people know how much you've been accomplishing and how you've become a complete master of multitasking? Do you often just casually drop into conversations things that you've been up to, regardless of their relevance to the conversation, in an effort to have people "oooh" and "ahhh" about how amazing you are?

Your Ditziness—Do you like people thinking of you as a someone who is a little silly, naïve, helpless or a bit of a ditz? Do you often carry on about how stupid you are to explain something you did that wasn't smart?

Your Selflessness—Do you always put other's needs ahead of your own? Do you enjoy when people admire you for your selflessness? Do you often talk about how you've been looking after others' with the implication that you've selflessly put other people's needs and wants ahead of your own? Do you feel guilty when you do something just for you? Does the idea of being really selfless and martyr-like appeal to you?

Your Coolness & Relaxed Nature—Do you love everyone knowing how incredibly cool and laid back you are? Do you avoid showing emotion and like to share with people how much you *don't* get stressed about things? Do you sometimes find yourself talking/bragging about things that validate your super cool/relaxed personality? Do you avoid being around people when you are feeling stressed so as not to blow your cover? Do you often pretend to not care about things when you really are feeling worked up?

Your Toughness—Do you like people knowing how tough you are? Do you like to brag about how you scared someone or how someone was really intimidated by you? Do you tend to share with people situations in which you responded aggressively? Do you like the idea that people would know better than to cross you? Do you like the idea that people might be intimidated or scared by you?

Your Status—Do you like people to know how successful and important you are? Do you look for opportunities to drop something in a conversation that makes others aware of your accomplishments, status or family background? If you hold a position of power or authority, do you like people to know about it so they can admire you for it? Do you like to have external signage (e.g., from the easy to read label you have on your clothes, handbag, glasses, car or briefcase) that conveys to the world just how successful, affluent or important you are?

Your Uniqueness—Do you go out of your way to be different to everyone else? Do you often say things just to get people's attention? Do you love the idea that people think of you as a bit alternative or quirky? Do you work very hard at having people know that you are a non-conformist and ensure that everything about your way of being supports this?

Your Friendliness—Do you like to feel popular? Do you always feel the need to be really, *really* friendly? Do you often go out of you way so that other people will see how friendly you are and notice how many friends you have? Do you feel the onus is on you to make conversation when you are at a social gathering where people aren't really mixing well? Do you get easily hurt when you aren't included in things?

Your Sweetness—Do you like people to think of you as being one of the most thoughtful people they know? Do you speak with a sweet voice and find it hard to raise your voice (even when it's appropriate to do so)? Do you often mention in conversation about how you cooked a meal for a sick neighbor, nursed a stray cat back to health or left little notes for your husband/kids in their lunches? Do you go out of your way to be a nice person to earn the "nice person" seal of approval?

So, who did you recognize here? Did something make you think of your boss, your neighbor, your ex, your mother, your mother-in-law, your secretary…your *self*?

At some point in our lives we all want to prove ourselves on some level. If you still feel a need to prove yourself, then let me ask you this: Who would you be like if you did not care what people thought of you? I know for sure that, regardless of your answer, once you begin to express yourself more freely, to speak your truth more openly and to be yourself more fully, your need to prove yourself to others will gradually begin to diminish.

The reality is that as human beings there is always an aspect of ourselves that wants to be admired, appreciated, respected, loved and prized by others. These are not attributes of only the needy or insecure. But even though our need to prove ourselves or please others in some way may never completely vanish, by starting to become more conscious of how much we are allowing this need to drive our words, our actions and who we are being in the world, we can reclaim the power it has had in our lives.

By continually asking yourself the question: *"Who would I be if I did not need to prove myself or impress people right now?"* you can begin to close the gap between who you think you should be and who you really are and create alignment between the person you are on the inside and the person you are on the outside. For whatever the answer is to this question, it will reveal to you the "real" you and beckon you to step out into the world as the wonderfully authentic and genuine person that you have within you to become.

Labels You Stamp on Yourself

As previously discussed, our stories are a big "hodgepodge" of opinions and beliefs about ourselves and our world. None of our stories have a bigger impact on our life than those about the kind of person we are. From these we extract labels that we apply to ourselves. Some labels are seemingly positive in nature, others negative. Some we've come up with ourselves and others our parents gave us before we could even think for ourselves. If we have given authority to the person making the assessment (e.g., a teacher, a parent), then it automatically becomes an unquestionable truth that we label ourselves with and which we then act from—either proving its truthfulness or seeking to hide or make up for the deficiency we believe we have. When we fail to question these labels and treat them with the same factuality we apply to the color of our eyes, they can confine our lives and stifle our potential.

Clinical studies have proven the existence of this phenomenon: how people's labels of themselves impact who they are—both how they perceive themselves and how others perceive them. In one particular study, all the participants were people who were classified as chronically shy to the point of being unable to develop social relationships, much less intimate ones. The researchers asked

Whether you are trying hard not to be one label or to embody another, you are exhausting yourself and failing to be the one-of-a-kind masterpiece you are.

the participants, for a period of one week, to simply pretend that they were confident, outgoing and friendly like the "popular" people they had always held in awe. Their assignment was to pretend that they weren't really shy at all. The amazing result was that at the end of the week, the participants actually

reported that they felt much more confident by simply pretending to be confident.

But what about you? Perhaps you have a story about yourself that has you stamp yourself with labels like outgoing, clever, bright, studious, kind, attractive, diligent, dramatic, thoughtful, funny, likeable, ambitious, witty, organized, friendly, athletic, strong-headed, easy going, capable and determined. Perhaps you have also stamped yourself with labels like technically inept, forgetful, klutzy, ordinary, impatient, stupid, pig-headed, disorganized, plain, shy, slow, vague, thoughtless, detached, aggressive, uptight, lazy, timid or socially inept!

Whatever labels we apply to ourselves, we are each a bit of everything. We each have parts of us that we like and parts of us that we aren't so attracted to (and which we fear will also be unattractive to others). But even with those parts of you that you are not so enamored—those aspects of your personality you'd rather hide or disown—you are still unique and talented and beautiful in your own way. Embrace every aspect of who you are and give up trying to live up to or deny ownership of any particular label—however seemingly good or bad. For whether you are trying hard not to be one label or to embody another, you are exhausting yourself and failing to just be the glorious mix of all the many labels that make you the one-of-a-kind masterpiece that you are.

So it is not that some labels are good and others bad. Rather it is whether or not your labels are serving you in life or whether they are stifling your potential and limiting your self expression. For whilst you certainly are not the labels you place on yourself, you do exist in the reality those labels confine you to. Your labels have the potential to limit the success of your career, the shape of your relationships, the state of your health and the quality of your life in general. By becoming conscious of your personality labels, you can decide whether or not they are holding you back from being able to express your personality fully and authentically…from finding the courage to be yourself!

Rebecca was a 29-year-old IT consultant who was feeling disillusioned with her job, in particular the long hours she worked, and unhappy about life in general. She was interested in coaching because she felt burnt out from her work and wanted to become more confident in creating a rewarding and fun life outside work. In her quiet voice, Rebecca shared with me that she didn't have very many friends and had always suffered from being very shy and awkward around people. Numerous times during our first conversation, she referred to herself as both a "hard worker" and as a "computer geek." My label antennae went up. You see the "hard worker" label that she had on herself, whilst not necessary a bad label, prevented her from ever deciding to call it a day at 6 p.m. and the computer nerd label kept her in a computer nerd, anti-social straightjacket. In fact, Rebecca admitted that working really long hours was a very convenient excuse for not having to have a social life outside work. When we discussed the concept of labels, Rebecca came to see that the only way she could be anything other than a workaholic or a computer nerd was to stop classifying herself as one. Her commitment to dropping the "hard worker" and "computer geek" labels from her lexicon opened the way for her to begin to express the other more fun and social aspects of her personality whilst also establishing the work life balance she really wanted.

Until you are aware of the labels you've placed on yourself, you will be unable to step out from the confines they impose on you.

Ladies, Own Your Beauty!

When I was young, I was much bigger in build than my sister Pauline, who was two years younger than me. From an early age I thought of myself as big, clumsy and a bit of a "plain Jane". As an adult this story about myself left me always trying to be attractive, but no matter how hard I tried I was never able to feel attractive enough. But not only did I have a story about myself that I was plain, I had another story that to even begin to think I was beautiful would mean I was vain, egotistical, and, as we say in Australia, "up myself." Can you see how stifling our stories can be?

When it comes to beauty I know that many women find it difficult to embrace their beauty fully—partially because they have a story about themselves that they are not beautiful (because they don't conform to a narrow social definition of what makes one beautiful) and partially because they think it would be vain and egotistical to do so. I cannot tell you how many women I have met who cannot take a compliment or who spend enormous amounts of energy trying to make themselves beautiful and then still can't take a compliment!

All the labels we have on ourselves in relation to our beauty (or perceived lack thereof) prevent us from owning our beauty, undermine our sense of ease and ultimately stifle how attractive we can be. The most beautiful women I have ever met aren't those with the most stunning or "perfect" physical features. Rather they are those women who radiate ease within themselves and can own their beauty fully—without needing to prove or deny it. If you have a label that hinders you from owning your beauty, then I challenge you to let it go and invite you to own your own unique beauty. Doing so will allow you to radiate far more ease to become even more beautiful!

> *The most beautiful women are those who radiate ease within themselves and can own their beauty fully—without needing to prove or deny it.*

You may not have given much thought to the labels you have on yourself. However, unless you are aware of them you will never be able to step out from the confines they place on you. Identifying your limiting labels and making a conscious decision to rid yourself of them will help you to find the courage to simply be who you are.

Exercise 5.4: Removing Your Limiting Labels

In this exercise I want you to get out your journal and write down at least 15 words that you would use to describe yourself. You may write more if you feel like it. Don't censor what you write, just write down whatever words come into your head, good and "not so good" alike.

Once you've done this, I want you to go through your list and underline any of the words you feel actually limit your ability to do the things you'd like to do.

For instance, when I asked a client of mine to do this, her list looked like this:

Kind, thoughtful, <u>timid</u>, reliable, <u>unassertive</u>, <u>procrastinator</u>, hard working, organized, responsible, friendly, <u>lazy</u>, honest, caring, <u>indecisive</u>, helpful, <u>guarded</u>, <u>cautious</u>, <u>wary</u>, <u>untrusting</u>.

Now rewrite the list of words that describe you, but this time leave out the words which you underlined above. For instance, my client rewrote her list as:

Kind, thoughtful, reliable, hard working, organized, responsible, friendly, honest, caring, helpful.

Rewrite the list a third time, but this time go even further. At the beginning of the list I want you to write "I am…" and insert the positive words you listed above. Then at the end of your list write "and every day I am becoming more…" and insert the opposite words for whatever negative words you underlined above. For instance:

I am kind, thoughtful, reliable, hard working, organized, responsible, friendly, honest, caring, helpful, and every day I am becoming more <u>trusting</u>, <u>open</u>, <u>confident</u>, <u>assertive</u>, <u>action- oriented</u>, <u>decisive</u>, and <u>energetic</u>.

By eliminating the negative labels and replacing them with positive ones, you are transforming the disempowering into the empowering and moving closer toward being the authentic person you aspire to be. Even though you may not always feel more confident, assertive or whatever, the important thing is that you are working toward becoming more this way. It is not easy to suddenly be trusting or decisive or to stop being so cautious and guarded. If it was, we'd all just do it. It is a gradual process: you're slowly moving away from one way of being and moving toward another. Some days you will do better than others at living out the new labels and getting out from underneath the shadow of the old ones. Even if you feel like you're taking two steps forward and one step backward, you will still be making progress.

What "Everybody" Will Think

Another force that often hinders our ability to be fully ourselves is our beliefs about what "everybody" will think of us if we are. The reality is that you don't know *everybody* and even if you are someone who does know a bloody lot of people, they are still likely to represent only a miniscule proportion of the *every bodies* who inhabit planet earth (over six billion on my last count). The real truth is that your "everybody" represents even a smaller proportion of the population than your rolodex. In fact, psychologists have found that our *everybody*—which they refer to as the "generalized other"—is usually a collection of about five or six people. Exactly how many people constitute your *everybody* doesn't matter as much as the fact that you have unconsciously given these people an enormous amount of power in your life.

When it comes to expressing yourself fully and authentically, you give a disproportionate weighting to the opinions of these few people (or to what you assume are their opinions) and, in doing so, give them power to determine how you will express yourself, what you will do or who you will be. Ironically these few people are not necessarily people whose opinions you even particularly respect. They may even be individuals whose approval and admiration you once wanted (e.g., the guy in high school you had a wild crush on) but no longer have anything to do with. In my experience it is parents, other family members and people from the years when we were developing our sense of individuality and personal identity whom tend to rank highest on people's *everybody* list.

Exercise 5.5: Reconfiguring Your "Everybody"

The aim of this exercise is to get your "everybody" working for you rather than against you. In doing so you will reclaim the power you've been giving to an "everybody" that holds you back from being who you want to be, and in its place, create an everybody that fully supports you becoming the self-expressed individual that you not only have the *ability*, but you have the *responsibility*, to become.

Whoever it is that comes to mind for you, the fact is that the "everybody" you speak of is not truly representative of "everybody." Indeed if your "everybody" is stopping you from doing something you'd love, from changing something you don't love or from expressing yourself in a way that you've always yearned to but never had the guts, then you will be well served by reconfiguring your "everybody."

Get out your journal and on a fresh page draw a line down the middle. On the left side, write down the names of those people who come to mind when you think of expressing yourself more fully and authentically and would respond with mild cynicism or outright scorn. Perhaps someone's face is flashing in your head. Maybe it's a parent, an old boyfriend, the girl who was critical of you back in high school, the heart throb who dumped you, your first boss, your current boss, your first (now "ex-") husband, your sister, or your neighbor of ten years. Maybe it's all of them! It could even be someone who is no longer alive. Include in this list those people whom you feel get some pay off by you continuing to behave as you have in the past. If you found yourself relating to any of the labels described earlier in this chapter, who do you think is very attached to you being this way?

On the right side of the page, write down the names of those people you know would really encourage you in being more open, more yourself. Once you have done this, look over the names on the right side of your list and write down the names of any other people you either know, or would like to think of when you think about "everybody." They may even be famous people you have never met but long admired or people you once knew but who are no longer alive (e.g., an encouraging school teacher, someone who had a positive impact on you).

From now on, if you begin to act differently when you find yourself wondering what everybody thinks of you, think about what your newly configured "everybody" will think. These people will be courageous in their own right, self-expressed in their own way, and fully encouraging of you being the same. By doing so, you will find the courage to allow your personality to overcome the intimidation you've experienced from the personalities of others.

Don't Allow Others to Define Who You Will Be

As you let go your need to prove yourself to others and become more authentic, people will begin to see and relate to you "differently." Now when I say "differently" I do so intentionally because not everyone will necessarily like you more. Some people will not like the new, more real you! These people will be the forces that resist your authentic self expression. Why do people sometimes do this? I believe that there are three main reasons.

Firstly, because some people like you just the way you have always been. Like it or not, you have unconsciously trained the people in your environment to see you in a certain way and respond to you in a certain way—a way that is familiar to them. It is a well-worn fact that we humans innately like the familiar, the known and innately dislike the unfamiliar, the new and the different. We are therefore often averse to change in others, even change for the better. So the people around you can't help themselves from wanting things to stay just the way they always have been and that includes you.

> *"To be one's self, and unafraid whether right or wrong, is more admirable than the easy cowardice of surrender to conformity."*
> –Irving Wallace

Secondly, and more importantly, most folks generally like or dislike people based on how those people make them feel about themselves. So, if you start transforming into this fabulously new self-expressed person, not everyone is going to like it because it's going to create discord at some level in those who are not self-expressed. Your changed way of being will unsettle them and challenge their own sense of identity and self-worth. It may even conjure up feelings of jealousy. Of course, they won't see it this way for that would be to openly acknowledge their fear. Some will not understand themselves why they dislike the changes they see in you. Those who possess sufficient self-awareness to realize this may still refuse to acknowledge their feelings, since by doing so, it would be acknowledging their insecurities.

In reaction to the discord they feel, they may criticize you, avoid you or start nitpicking about all the things they don't like about you. Just remember that if people start acting in ways that you can intuit are aimed at making you feel badly—whether through snide remarks, sarcastic innuendos or straight out avoiding your company—that it is not about you…it's about them! Let me repeat myself here because this is a very, *very* important point. It is not about you…it's about them! Now as your life coach, I'd like you to repeat that to yourself three times…

1. *"It's about them, not about me"*
2. *"It's about them, not about me"*
3. *"It's about them, not about me"*

People tend to make disparaging comments because of a concern they have about themselves. So if someone does make a comment to you that you find hurtful or upsetting, ask yourself, "Why do they have a need to say that to me?" Or, if they do something that is hurtful ask yourself, "Why do they have a need to behave in that way?" This will help you realize more fully that it's a concern they have about themselves, triggering an unpleasant emotion, which is driving them to behave in ways that are upsetting to you! I can assure you that people who are self-expressed and who feel truly good about themselves have no need to make comments that hurt or put down others (after all, a superiority complex is really just an inferiority complex in disguise). So whatever you do, don't stop being who you are to make others comfortable. There's no integrity in that.

The third reason not everyone will automatically like you when you are yourself is simply because no one, however authentic, ever receives unanimous approval. The fact is that not everyone loves

Oprah, not everyone loved Princess Diana and, forgive me my lack of wit but—not *Everybody Loves Raymond!* Likewise, not everyone will love you! So just get over yourself because it ain't ever gonna happen, no matter how sugar and spice nice you are, no matter how real you are or hard you try. Worse yet—brace yourself—some people may actually dislike you! So, given this reality, you may as well decide that if people are going to like you then at least have them like the real you. And if they are going to dislike you, then at least have them dislike the real you! The fact is the only person you can ever be a first-rate version of is yourself!

Hey You...the Real You...Come on Out!

The term "coming out" is one I've heard used many times in reference to people who are gay. Most times it has been in the context of how liberating it was for them to do so and how their only regret is that they didn't "come out" sooner. But it is not only those who are hiding their sexuality from the world who can benefit from "coming out"—it is *anyone* who is hiding a part of who they authentically are from the world for fear that there are people in it whom may shun them.

> *"Insist on yourself; never imitate. Every great man is unique."*
> —Ralph Waldo Emerson

Who you are is who you are. You don't need to create the real you and you certainly don't need me or anyone else to tell you how the real you should be. You simply need to let the real you step out from underneath all those masks that have kept you hidden from the rest of the world and even from yourself. As you muster up the courage to express yourself fully and let go of your need to prove yourself to others or hide yourself from others, you will gradually become more comfortable with being you. Here are some ways you can begin to tap into your courage and move toward being yourself with more ease and less angst.

Reveal Yourself One Step at a Time

Expressing yourself in a way that you have not had the courage to do so before is extremely liberating. It can also be terrifying. If revealing yourself in one fell swoop is daunting to you and leaves you with a rock in the pit of your stomach, then consider revealing yourself in small steps. Better that than to retreat behind your mask pretending to be someone you aren't and hiding yourself from the world. For what you will find is that as you gradually begin revealing more of yourself to those around you, you will become more comfortable with it and being "natural" will start to feel more natural.

Diane, a client of mine, sought coaching because she had come to recognize that there was a complete absence of fun in her life. Diane had raised her son on her own, put him through college and, along the way, had become a successful executive with a large telecommunications company. Now, at age fifty-something, Diane wanted to have a bit more excitement in her life, but she just didn't know how to break out of the box in which she had been living for so long. When I met Diane she was dressed in a smart gray suit: very corporate, very minimalistic, very serious and very gray. On approaching me after a presentation I'd done at her company, she was not very comfortable looking me directly in the eye, and though she was a very attractive middle-aged woman, my first impression was that something about her seemed distant and almost cold. I sensed it was a big thing for her to share with me how she felt about her life.

> *"Remember you not only have the right to be an individual, you have the obligation to be one."*
> —Eleanor Roosevelt

After several coaching sessions, I learned that, many years earlier, Diane had decided that to get on in life and in her male-dominated workplace, she needed to tone down her femininity and ramp up her masculinity lest men not take her seriously, or worse, try and hit on her or take advantage of her. As a result, she was someone who people knew not to joke around with. In fact, I got the feeling that most people kept their distance from Diane and found her very hard to warm up to. For Diane, reclaiming the fun-loving part of her persona involved a series of baby steps. After discussing where she could begin, Diane decided to start by adding a bit more color into her wardrobe. She went out and bought a red sweater. The next time we spoke she told me with great delight that a lot of people had commented on how nice it looked on her. She said they had likely never seen her in anything but gray or black. Next, she bought a lipstick that was not the completely neutral shade she usually wore but a little brighter. After that, she got herself some new jewelry and accessories. Diane was beginning to look like a very different woman than the one who had walked up to me following a presentation four months earlier. Within a year of her "coming out" Diane had taken a vacation to Italy, with a new friend she'd met at an Italian cooking class, during which she did numerous things—including flirting with Italian men—that before she would not have conceived of doing. For Diane, learning to express the fun side of herself was, and will continue to be, a series of small steps which all began with a new red sweater.

Act As If

It is interesting to know that research psychologists have found that the reason so many people struggle to make the changes they want to make in how they are living and interacting with others is because they are trapped by the labels they have about themselves—which form their present self-image. The results of their studies have led them to propose that unless we "see" ourselves as we would like to be in the future—and in so doing create a "future self image"—we will find it difficult to become the kind of person we want to be.

Given this information, it makes sense then to create a vision for yourself as being a person who is authentic, unpretentious and none other than "yourself!" It will help you be very clear about who it is you really want to *be*. Once you commit to this, you can take actions to support your vision. The Act As If! approach can be really helpful in doing this. It is a very powerful and effective technique you can use when your confidence isn't as great as you would like it to be and you are still growing into the new unadulterated, more real and authentic you. So, when the road gets somewhat wobbly, try saying to yourself:

- I am going to *"Act As If"* I am someone who doesn't have a need to prove myself to others.
- I am going to *"Act As If"* what others think of me is none of my business.
- I am going to *"Act As If"* I really think I am an absolutely fabulous person.
- I am going to *"Act As If"* I am confident and self-assured in simply being myself!

In the case of Rebecca, the computer geek I mentioned earlier, my assignment to her was to simply "act as if" she was the confident outgoing woman she really wanted to be without a need to prove she was a workaholic or a computer nerd. Over a period of several months of consistent effort (and real "hard work" on her part), Rebecca gradually became far more comfortable with working hours that allowed her to have evenings to herself again. She also began to feel more and more self-assured as she took up, and sought out, more opportunities to meet new people and to expand her social circles. Her conversations were increasingly punctuated with dry, witty humor. Rebecca was learning to really be herself, no longer confined to acting out her personality label. She was more and more comfortable in the company of others and with her future direction. It was a true pleasure to witness such a beautiful transformation as her personality began to blossom.

> *Discovering the depth of your uniqueness and expressing it freely and authentically in the world is not just your responsibility, it is your obligation.*

Affirm Yourself

The extraordinary power of language makes affirmations powerful tools for changing belief systems and subsequently, changing the behavior that flows from our stories and beliefs. Whether you have used affirmations in the past and experienced their effectiveness or dismiss them cynically as "positive thinking cockabalony," this doesn't change the fact that, if practiced regularly, affirmations can be highly effective in shifting negative thinking patterns. Not only can affirmations be used to counter negative self-talk, but they can also implant in your subconscious a positive message that will impact not only how you feel about yourself but will make you more confident and capable of taking the actions you need to take. Since we can only think one thought at any given moment, affirmations are an effective way to help you become more purposeful and deliberate in your thoughts.

Affirmations have a quantum impact at the cellular level. Dr. Deepak Chopra, a renowned expert in quantum physics and spirituality, stated that at the cellular level your cells actually change color when you use positive affirmations. However, to be effective, affirmations must be phrased to reflect what you do want rather than what you don't. And, they must be expressed as though they were already a reality in *present tense*, i.e. you are feeling what you want to feel, doing what you want to do, and being who you want to be.

Exercise 5.6: Creating Affirmation for Authenticity

In your journal write down a few ideas for an affirmation or personal motto that you could adopt and use as you interact with others to let go of your need to prove yourself to others or to please them. There are many affirmations you can choose, so choose the one that resonates with you. Here are a few you can use if you'd like. The important thing is to write them down:

- *"I need prove myself to no one."*
- *"I am beauty, grace and ease."*
- *"I am an authentic person."*
- *"I am whole and perfect just as I am."*
- *"I will be me, and no one else."*
- *"I have nothing to prove."*
- *"I feel at ease with myself at all times and with all people."*
- *"I express myself authentically at all times."*
- *"I have no need to impress anyone."*
- *"I don't need to please anyone."*
- *"Who I am is who I am!"*

When you find an affirmation that really resonates with you, write it down on index cards and place them strategically around your home, car and office so that you will see them throughout your day. At first, you might feel like a bit of a geek doing this, but hey, what do you have to lose? Just get over yourself, stick them up and stick at it for at least a few weeks.

Hallmarks of Authentic People

It is a lot more work to be someone you are not than someone you are. Obviously, authentic people come in all shapes and sizes because authentic people have no need to conform to any set of expectations about how they "should" be. That said, once you begin to be more yourself you will find that you share some common characteristics with others who are also comfortable with who they are.

Openness—when you can be yourself, you have nothing to hide and you feel comfortable sharing openly about yourself. You don't need to put energy into keeping things secret from others. Nor do you feel a need to hide from others those aspects of yourself which you feel aren't so attractive or that you struggle with. You share your humanness, your struggles and your challenges as openly as you share your successes because you are not concerned with impressing others, just with being who you are and sharing what is for you.

Lack of pretension—you don't have to pretend in any way to be someone different than who you are. You have no need to pretend to be "really together," successful, superior, relaxed or any of those traits listed above. You wear no mask and don't engage in superficiality. You are genuine, sincere and, given that you wear your "original face", you cannot be "two-faced."

Attractive—when you are yourself—and not trying to be anyone or anything else—you are your most attractive. The sense of ease you feel with yourself helps put others at ease around you. You can own your beauty, your intelligence and all the idiosyncrasies of your personality without needing to prove or deny any aspect of who you are. Being comfortable in your own skin you radiate freedom, positive energy and love of life to those you encounter and share your natural beauty with the world, not because you are vain, but because you beauty is part of who you are and it gives you joy to share it.

Whether or not you have yet to experience your uniqueness fully, the truth remains the truth—you are unique beyond comparison. Discovering the depth of your uniqueness and expressing it freely in the world is not just your responsibility, it is your obligation. Will it take courage? Yes, sometimes more than others. However, by finding the courage to express who you are authentically you will be able to enjoy the wholeness and freedom that comes from being the same person on the outside as you are on the inside. Nothing is more liberating to the human spirit.

> *"The snow goose need not bathe to make itself white.*
> *Neither need you do anything but be yourself."*
> —Lao-tse

Chapter 6
The Courage to Speak Up

The price we pay for avoiding life's "difficult conversations"
far exceeds the discomfort we feel having them.

Your willingness to find the courage to speak up about the issues that are important to you—whether in the conference room or the bedroom—has a pivotal impact on your ability to achieve what you want in life. The fact is, what you are not saying in your relationships limits your relationships.

Speaking up isn't always easy since it often involves risking emotional discomfort. Every time you express an opinion, raise an issue of concern or ask for what you want, you risk the possibility of confrontation, criticism, rejection, humiliation, appearing too pushy, or at the far end of the spectrum, of being personally or professionally ostracized. Given the risks involved in speaking up, it's little wonder that we often choose not to speak up about the issues that affect our marriage, our careers and our life in general. We stay silent, keep our thoughts to ourselves and avoid all risk of ruffling feathers or rocking the boat. Ultimately, we choose the *certainty* of never resolving an issue because of the *possibility* it may feel uncomfortable emotionally to do so.

It may seem a strange concept to you but the conversations you have with people have tremendous power. As Susan Scott wrote in her book *Fierce Conversations*, "Although no single conversation is guaranteed to change the course of any of your relationships, your career or your life, any single conversation can." Conversations are the lifeblood of your relationships. Only by speaking about the issues that have the potential to undermine your relationships can you effectively resolve them. The unfortunate irony is that the very issues we don't want to speak up about for fear of jeopardizing our relationships are the same issues which lead to the demise of our relationships (or at least, to stifling the amount of joy we experience in them). Likewise, people fail to achieve the professional success they want because of the conversations they *don't have* for fear that they may limit their promotional opportunities. Too often our lack of success is really a result of our unwillingness to make a stand for what we believe in and to ask for what we *really* want.

The fact is, you count and so too do your feelings and opinions. It does not matter whether others always agree with what you think; what matters is having the guts to say what you think. Unless you do you will be unable to create the relationships you want or gain the respect you seek (both from yourself and from others). You will also be unable to exert the influence you could on the opinions of others or on the decisions they make which affect your life. For that reason it is not only your responsibility to speak your truth, it is your obligation. Enormous power comes to you when you find the guts to enter into courageous conversations: power to resolve issues, power to see things from a heightened perspective and, ultimately, power to generate positive and profound changes in your relationships, in your life and in the world.

Starting today I challenge you to begin having conversations that are new to you. I'm not talking about having new kinds of lightweight conversations—there are already more than enough of those going on in the world. I mean *real conversations* that go beyond the surface level, that call on your courage, that convey what you *really* think and address the issues that *really* concern you.

The Costs of Not Speaking Up

Of course, speaking up about the issues that matter most to you is not easy because it means putting yourself "out there" where you may have to face disapproval, criticism or God forbid... confrontation. Sure, taking a stand for anything in life means paying a price one way or another. But failing to take a stand and speak up also has its costs. Only by becoming more aware of how much it is costing you in life when you don't speak up, will you be able to find the courage you need to find your voice, say what you think and ask for what you want.

Your Sense of Wellbeing—Body, Mind & Spirit

Given that integrity is about wholeness and consistency between what you know is the right thing to do and what you are doing, then failing to speak up undermines your sense of integrity and triggers a barrage of internal conflict which can undermine your sense of wellbeing—body, mind and spirit. Remember, without integrity, nothing works!

Now just imagine your arm is extended and you are holding a full glass of water. You could stand there with your arm out holding that glass of water for 10 minutes—no problem at all. After a while, though, your arm would grow tired. The glass of water would not be any heavier, but the act of holding that glass of water would definitely have become more burdensome. The same happens when you fail to speak up and put issues on the table. The issues that cause you to feel angst, resentful, frustrated, stressed, taken for granted, or "all of the above," don't just go away. No siree! Rather, they fester for lack of oxygen, burden you, undermine your integrity and hinder your ability to enjoy self-respect and true peace of mind.

Obviously, the long-term impact of withholding your thoughts and feelings is stress... *unnecessary* stress. Study after study has found that stress can have a profound affect on your health—mental, emotional and physical. Stress raises the levels of cortisol and adrenalin in your body. If it stays at an elevated level for a long time, it lowers your immune system functioning and puts you at risk of all sorts of nasty diseases. In the short term, it affects the quality of your sleep, makes you easy prey for every cold floating round the office, slows your digestive system and, contrary to popular opinion, it also slows your metabolism (i.e., you put on weight—a definite "don't want" for most of us)...and the list goes on!

How People Treat You—You Get What You Tolerate!

One of my favorite sayings is "You get what you tolerate!" This applies to your relationships since failing to speak up about something carries the implication that you are okay with it—that you are prepared to continue tolerating it. As the saying goes, "silence means consent." If you tolerate your boss or colleague making snide or offensive remarks, it will continue. If you tolerate your spouse's continual lack of consideration for your feelings, it will continue. If you tolerate people always turning up an hour late for meetings or social engagements, they will continue to be tardy and waste your time. If you tolerate your child's lack of respect, it will continue. By tolerating a behavior you are in fact teaching that person that it is okay to treat you in that way.

The problem is that when people habitually treat you a certain way, their behavior becomes invisible to them. That may be why your friend doesn't think twice about turning up late; your spouse or colleague is totally unaware that their comments offend you, and your mother has no idea her constant disparaging comments on your life are very hurtful and drive you completely nuts. It is up to you to decide on what you will and, more importantly, what you *will not* tolerate. If you are ready to make a stand for yourself, you need to be firm in your resolve with anyone who isn't treating you as you want to be treated. Ultimately, you must be more committed to living with integrity and self respect—which is diminished when you allow yourself to be treated with *dis*respect—than you are to keeping the peace or playing safe.

Only when you take responsibility for your own happiness do your relationships stand a chance of being whole and completely rewarding. If you choose to let your fear stop you from letting people know how you want to be treated, you are, by default, choosing to continue to sell out on your own happiness. By courageously sharing how you feel, you are not only making a stand for yourself, you are modeling what it is to live with integrity and so inspiring others to also speak up themselves!

Exercise 6.1: Teaching People How to Treat You

In your journal write down any situations you currently face that cause you to feel:

- Unappreciated, taken for granted
- Unrespected
- Resentful
- Misunderstood
- Manipulated, coerced into doing what you don't want to do
- Abused—physically or emotionally
- Put down or less than—like your opinions, your feelings and you don't count

Now with your list in front of you, I want you to read aloud these two affirmations:

1. *"I take full responsibility for being allowed to be treated as I have."*
2. *"From today on, I will take responsibility for speaking up so that I am not treated this way in the future."*

Well done! You reclaim power in who you are being in the world when you take this stand.

The Quality of Your Relationships

It's normal for issues that have the potential to cause conflict to arise in relationships. However, relationships don't break down because people have different opinions; they break down because the people in the relationship fail to have authentic conversations about the issues. Often they keep the airways jammed with superficial conversations so that they don't have to talk about what is really on their mind. Meanwhile, the issues sit there like a big white elephant in the corner of the room while everyone pretends, because they are so busy talking, not to notice it.

What isn't talked out gets acted out.

Sheryl is now divorced after 11 years of marriage to Jack. Together they have joint custody of their 9-year-old son. The reason Sheryl filed for divorce was because she felt that Jack cared more about his career in the IT industry than he did about her. She had given up her career in consulting when their son was born to stay at home and raise him. Initially, Jack kept his work at work but slowly his work began to take up more of their evenings, and by the time their son was four, he worked most weekends. The sad thing is that Sheryl never spoke up about her feelings to Jack. Instead she just pretended that she was fine with his working hard because she felt that it was important to support him in getting ahead in his career. Every now and again she would explode at him about how he didn't spend enough time with their son and would lash out with a barrage of insults about what a hopeless husband he was. But not once did she ever sit down and calmly let him know that she felt like she was playing second fiddle to his work and ask him to spend more time with her and their son. Instead she let her resentment build up and up and eventually one day decided that she wanted a divorce. When she told Jack, he was completely dumbfounded as he had genuinely thought he was doing the right thing working hard to get ahead so that he could provide the most financially stable future for his wife and son.

Sadly, this story is one that sounds all too familiar to many people. Resentment, jealousy, envy, upset, misunderstanding… all left to brew and fester rather than put on the table to work through. I mean, just think about it—how can you have a quality relationship if issues are not discussed and the individuals in the relationship are pretending everything is hunky dory when, underneath, there is a simmering inferno waiting to explode? What isn't talked out ends up being acted out. Do those snide remarks, innuendos, sarcastic jabs and the "silent treatment" ring a bell? And what about the person who walks out on their job or their relationship without notice, or like Sheryl, calls the divorce attorney because that seems easier than talking to her husband? Or the people who psychologically check out of their jobs or their marriages? Sure, they turn up at the office

When you fail to tell the truth to another, you are concealing yourself from them and diminishing the quality of your relationship.

every day, but they aren't fully present. Sure, they get into bed beside their partner each night after staying up as late as possible watching TV, but they're no longer married in spirit.

Sure, it's not always easy to lay your cards on the table and express how you genuinely feel about something. It may even be the hardest thing you've done in your entire life and take more courage than you ever thought you had. Your stomach may be in knots, your hands shaking and you may feel like a golf ball is lodged in your throat. However, unless you find the guts to speak your truth, to be fully authentic—however vulnerable that makes you feel—you will be selling out on those you care for. Even more so, you will be selling out on yourself.

The quality of your conversations determines the quality of your relationships. When you fail to tell the truth to someone, you are concealing yourself from them and diminishing the quality of your relationship. If you are not being honest with someone in order to save or protect the relationship, then you need to take a good hard look at what kind of relationship it is in the first place.

Conversations are the oxygen that keep your relationships alive— whether your closest personal relationships or your work relationships with your boss, colleagues or employees. Every conversation you have has the potential to either erode or build the trust that exists in a relationship. Too often, though, we wrongly assume that we may damage trust by raising issues the other person may not like to discuss or may disagree with. In reality, the opposite is true—conversations centered on real issues provide an opportunity for you to build trust in your relationships.

> *Every conversation has the potential to either build trust in a relationship or erode it.*

People may not always agree with you but at least they know you are being honest with them.

The gap between what you are thinking about (your "private conversations") and what you are prepared to talk about (your "public conversations") correlates closely with the quality of your relationships. Obviously, I'm not proposing that you say everything that is in your mind at the moment you think it. Doing so would obviously cause unnecessary hurt. For instance, what is to be gained by telling your girlfriend that her new dress makes her look fat or telling your spouse that his breath stinks as he gives you a kiss when he arrives home from work in the evening? Nought. (You can communicate that more gently with a bottle of Listerine placed strategically beside the sink later on.) A relationship built on trust, respect and commitment is one where the individuals are committed to expressing themselves fully even when it comes to sensitive matters. Where people in a relationship are committed more to the relationship than they are to being right or playing it safe, their relationship will be all the stronger for it. However, it all hinges on one thing: mustering up the courage to speak up.

Only when people are more committed to their relationship than they are to being right or playing safe can trust deepen and love blossom.

Obviously Sheryl and Jack learnt this lesson the hard way and at a huge personal cost. Had Sheryl spoken up sooner about her feelings and let Jack know the way she wanted their marriage to be, it may have taken a very different and far happier course. Of course, it may have also resulted in them breaking up a lot sooner, but then that also would have been a more positive outcome than spending years in an unfulfilling relationship that ended up with a lot of bitterness and heartbreak all round.

The reality is that speaking your truth may jeopardize the status quo in your relationship. But what kind of relationship do you want to be in anyway? One in which you have to censor your words so as not to offend? One in which you get treated as the doormat? One in which you have to tip toe around the issues that are really on your mind (and your partner's) and do a daily Oscar-winning performance to make sure everyone thinks your life is a picture of domestic bliss? No, of course not! You want real, meaningful, open and mutually respectful relationships where you can be yourself, share your thoughts and feelings and in which the other person can do the same. Does this mean it might put your relationship on a slippery slope? Absolutely!

As difficult as it may be for you to swallow, the cost of not speaking up about the things that matter to you FAR exceeds the discomfort you feel in doing so. For when you withhold what you really think, it makes real love and true affection unavailable in your relationships and undermines the quality of your life.

Professional Success

If you work in an organization, your success depends on the perceived value you bring to your organization. Sure getting more technical or hard skills may be worthwhile but what differentiates those who get ahead from those who don't aren't their hard skills but their ability to speak up and express their opinions in ways that develop relationships, earn respect, build trust and bring alignment around common goals.

These traits ultimately allow people to be more influential and move into leadership positions of greater responsibility and opportunity. If you find yourself sitting in meetings with something to say but are struggling to spit it out, you are not only limiting your career or business opportunities, you are limiting your paycheck!

I have noticed repeatedly that my clients who have the greatest difficulty expressing their opinions are those who value their own opinions the least. If you work in a team, then part of what you have to contribute is your unique perspective. However, if you continually compare what you know and what you don't know with others, it is easy to undervalue and discount what you have to say. Too often, when the opportunity arises for you to put your opinion on the table, you hesitate and say nothing, or mumble out some watered down version of what you *really* wanted to say. In the meantime, someone else speaks up and says the very thing you were going to say and everyone acknowledges their contribution. Sound familiar?

> *You become more highly valued by your organization when you speak up and contribute value to the conversations going on within it.*

Since conversations are essential for your organization to operate effectively, how are those in your organization going to value the contribution you can make if you don't add value to those conversations? They won't! In fact, they might not even know who you are if you don't speak up. It happens. So, speak up even if your stomach is turning upside down with nerves and nagging voices in your head are screaming at you to keep your mouth closed for fear that you will say something stupid or humiliate yourself. Acknowledge the butterflies and the voices, and then just get on with saying whatever you have to say anyway!

If you are in a position where you have to manage others, then speaking up is even more important. One of the big problems in many organizations is the lack of honest feedback employees receive from their managers. Too often, managers are reluctant to give critical feedback to their staff or direct reports because it seems less complicated to ignore the situation and assign the employees to another department so they can become someone else's resource problem. Obviously, this lacks integrity. If you are in such a position, it is important to offer your employees the opportunity to address areas of weakness to develop their skills and abilities. If you don't pinpoint the areas that need improvement, then you are giving them a false sense of their own ability and, most likely, a false sense of their value in the organization. Of course, what they do with your feedback—whether they respond constructively or react destructively—is up to them. You can only do your part. However, failing to speak up not only denies them a valuable opportunity to develop but also denies you just as valuable an opportunity to grow as a leader and as a person.

Kate, who worked as a manager for an energy company, had a recent graduate called Frank working for her. Frank was a very confident, young man, who she felt had a lot of potential in the organization. However, she felt that he was at times too confident in his dealings with other more senior members of the team. In fact, several people had made comments that he was a little too full of himself. Kate felt awkward about raising this with Frank, as she thought he would most likely not take the feedback very well. Given that Frank was only due to spend six months in Kate's department as part of his graduate program training, she felt very tempted to just let the issue go. After all, four months from now Frank would be someone else's problem. But, after talking it through during a coaching session, Kate decided to do what she acknowledged was the "right thing" and raise her concern with Frank. She asked him into her office and began by sharing with him that she felt he was a very bright and talented young man with a lot of potential to do well in their firm. She went on to share with him that he sometimes came across as being somewhat brash, even arrogant with others. She suggested he tone down how he communicated what he had been doing and focus more on listening to what others needed of him to get the project done. How did Frank respond? Whilst he obviously hadn't enjoyed receiving the feedback, he thanked Kate for being so honest with him and said he would "work on it." Over the following few weeks, Kate noticed a difference in how Frank interacted with others and also received feedback that he seemed easier to get along with. When, after four months Frank did move on to his next placement, his behavior had dramatically improved. Before leaving, he went to see Kate in her office to thank her once again for her candor and coaching. By speaking up, Kate made a real difference for Frank, her organization, herself and for her own confidence in having this kind of conversation.

Cost to Your Organization or Business

Given that the organization you work for is comprised of individuals just like you, it makes sense that your organization's effectiveness is intrinsically linked with both the quantity and quality of conversations that take place between the members. You may be only one small cog in the wheels of your company, but every cog has a role to play in allowing the whole organization to operate at an optimal level. The willingness of the people who work in an organization to speak up and engage in quality conversations that build relationships is a key determinant in the organization's productivity. To optimize the synergy and coordination in various parts of your organization requires relationships between those parts; without conversations, even at the lowest most seemingly "junior" levels of the organization, synergy cannot be maximized. Regardless of your position in your organization, you play an important role. Moreover, if you don't speak up about issues that are important to you, your organization isn't doing as well as it could and neither are you!

Peter, who works as a manager in a large financial services organization, prides himself on having a lot of integrity in his work and life. Peter shared with me how he was in a meeting when a colleague undermined the initiative on which he was working. Initially Peter was angry because he felt his colleague should have come to him first about his concerns with this initiative rather than voice them in a large meeting. His initial reaction was to let his colleague know how he felt "in no uncertain terms," and threaten that if he ever did it again Peter would undermine his efforts on his own competing initiatives. Fortunately, he resisted acting on his first reaction and took some time to reflect, given his commitment to conducting himself with integrity, on how else he could respond. He decided to speak with his colleague and say, "You know I was really disappointed when you basically slammed my initiative at the meeting yesterday. I guess I'm wondering what is going on for you that would make you think that doing that would serve a positive outcome. I'd also like to talk about how we might be able to work together here more as a team rather than as competitors and how I can support you in moving the initiatives you are working on forward successfully." His colleague responded to this in a very positive way. He even shared with Peter that he had felt threatened by Peter's initiatives and apologized for his actions—a very different outcome than if Peter had gone with his initial reaction.

Eight Essentials for Speaking Up to Get What You <u>Really</u> Want

Speaking up about often "sensitive" and emotionally charged issues takes courage but to do so effectively also requires some skill. And while no one is born with a mastery of advanced communication skills, like all skills, those required to communicate effectively can be learned. As you muster the courage to speak up, you can hone your communication skills by applying some of the ideas, strategies and techniques provided here.

1. Box Your Ego and Tap Your Heart

To be really effective and powerful in your conversations you must enter into them with the highest intention for yourself, for the other person and for the relationship. You can do this by connecting with your heart to get clarity on what to achieve most from your conversation. For when we connect with another person from a spirit of respect and love, our words are able to reach places they would never be able to otherwise.

However, this isn't always as easy it sounds because it requires that you first contend with your ego. You see your ego, the vain insatiable creature that it is, is much more concerned with making you look good, regardless of the cost on your relationships. It certainly isn't concerned with your sense of integrity; it isn't bothered about whether or not you treat others with respect and it certainly doesn't give a toss about whether you act in ways that foster trust in your relationships. It cares only that you be perceived as a "winner" or, if that doesn't appear to be an option, that you avoid the humiliation of being perceived as a loser. In its efforts to avoid any loss of face and gain the upper hand and protect your pride—should it be at stake—your ego reacts in one of two ways—it fights or takes flight. Put another way, it drives you to 'violence' or 'silence.'

Choosing to "fight" means donning your boxing gloves (metaphorically speaking of course), putting your head down, and charging determinedly into battle intent on coming out the victor. You might argue that this isn't such a bad thing. I mean, what's so wrong with looking good, with being a winner? Well, nothing, so long as it isn't hurting anyone else. However, when your ego is at the helm of your conversations spurring you to win or prove your superiority then, by default, someone else has to lose, be made wrong or be left feeling

No argument is ever won without loss.

inferior in some way. Nothing is ever won without loss. Of course, it can feel awfully nice to sit in the winner's seat, but if you are always having to "win" then others always have to come out worse off resulting in a relationship that will be marred with distrust, fear and resentment.

When this occurs, speaking up is more appropriately called "talking down". Unlike speaking up, talking down does not come from a place of integrity by connecting with your heart. Rather talking down is driven by the ego's need to come out the victor and so carries undertones of self righteousness or superiority. This leaves the other person feeling put down or "less than." So if, in speaking up, you end up simply force feeding your opinion down other people's throats, expressing your opinion in such a way that leaves others feeling unheard or (either implicitly or explicitly) making other people's opinions wrong, then it will pay you to close your mouth for a moment longer than you usually do and reflect on how you could speak up in a way that doesn't leave others feeling talked down to. Whilst you may enjoy the momentary satisfaction of winning the battle, you will most certainly lose the war as you alienate, offend and intimidate others with your forcefulness.

On the other hand, your ego's need to protect itself from humiliation may cause you to flee from any conversation that may involve any hint of confrontation. You put on your smiley mask and pretend everything is okay, you stay silent or withhold relevant information, and just hope against hope that the issue sorts itself out. Unfortunately, this rarely happens. Instead, the issues burrow underground where they fester.

It is therefore paramount to the success of your conversation that you put your ego's need to win or to play safe second to what you know in your heart is right. This not only requires courage, but calls for humility and integrity. So when you seek to get clarity on your highest intention, the answer will most definitely not be about proving that the other person is a first class twit (regardless of what a dimwit you think they have been). Rather it will be to achieve a good outcome for both you and the other person and build trust in your relationship. For instance, your heart will clarify that you want to have a happier more harmonious marriage more than you want your spouse to know they are a lazy, inconsiderate so-and-so for never picking up the towels or emptying the dishwasher. Or, it may be that you want to create a more enjoyable work environment for your team with better systems and higher productivity, rather than point our how your assistant is incompetent and disorganized and should show you more respect.

I remember when my husband Andrew and I got engaged. At the time I'd only been earning a professional salary a short time, and prior to that I'd either been a poor, frugal student at university or an even more frugal backpacker traveling around the world and living on the smell of an oily rag. I was pretty tight with money and still adjusting to my new income and more prosperous reality. Andrew, on the other hand, hadn't been traveling like me and had no issue spending in one evening the equivalent of what I could have lived on in Thailand for a week (heck, make that two!).

Anyway, after we got engaged we decided it would no longer be *his* money or *my* money but *our* money. Suddenly his spending habits, though not irresponsible by "normal" standards, began to upset me. I felt as though he was not appreciating the sacrifice I'd made for so many years to live on as little as possible. My motto had long been to do everything the cheapest possible way. His wasn't. The thing is that I was well aware that I was being unreasonable and a perfect example of a "tight-arse." However, my emotions ran riot over my intellect (as they so often do for we mere mortals). I found myself getting my knickers in a knot when he would order the most expensive menu item, take his car to the official dealer for service rather than some discount repair shop like I did, and…I could go on, but the list of "offenses" gets steadily more petty.

I would try to keep my upset to myself since I felt I really didn't have a good argument for why he should spend differently. But internalizing my upset only resulted with me getting my knickers into a bigger knot and often giving Andrew the silent treatment, because I was terrified that if I opened my mouth, out would erupt a litany of frivolous charges amidst a downpour of hysterical tears and that would just be far *far* too humiliating.

Then one day after going to the ATM and seeing I had far more money in my account than I'd ever had in my entire life (i.e., I was a "thousandaire"), it suddenly hit me how much my silence was undermining our relationship. Sure, it was illogical my getting upset with the way Andrew spent his money—no, *our* money—*however,* unless I spoke up and shared my struggle with this issue, it would only fester more, driving a real wedge in our relationship and in my sanity. So eating humble pie, I mustered up all my courage and shared with him my "fiscal hang up." I even went as far as asking him to help me as I tried to resolve this issue (i.e. unload my "baggage"). As always, he was very loving in his response and said he would do his best to be sensitive to how I felt. Being the very rational and thoughtful man he is, he also offered to do a spreadsheet of our finances so I could see just how irrational I was being.

Now I won't say that speaking up about this issue solved the problem immediately. Sometimes we still need to sit down and talk through our different feelings and opinions about how we should manage our finances and spend our money. The important thing though is that we did begin to talk then about the issues that threatened to undermine our relationship and we have never stopped. Had I let my pride get in the way (or had Andrew), who knows, maybe our marriage might have ended in another divorce statistic. Short of that, I am sure it would have resulted in a lot more tension and conflict. But by being committed to putting our feelings on the table—even my irrational humiliating ones—it paved the way for the strong, open and harmonious partnership we enjoy today.

2. Walk a Mile in Their Shoes

Of course, the reason it's important to speak up is that you have something on your mind you really want to share. However, communication is not defined by what is being *said* but by what is being *heard*. For this reason, it is vital that you gain a good appreciation of how the other person will listen—interpret, process or assign meaning—to what you have to say before you can influence or persuade him or her effectively. By really trying to put yourself in the other person's shoes, and understanding why they see and feel things as they do, you will come to better understand why they behave as they do.

> *"Courage is what it takes to stand up and speak; courage is also what it takes to sit down and listen."*
> –Winston Churchill

Real listening is concerned with gaining a deeper understanding of the person's story about themselves, about you and about whatever issue it is you wish to speak to them about. This requires giving up your certainty that you already know exactly what they think. After all, if you really did understand them perfectly, then you wouldn't have the conflict in the first place! Remember, however different their story may be from yours, it is just as valid for them as yours is to you. Instead of rejecting their stories as you listen to them, try to put yourself in their shoes. Ask yourself how you would feel about the situation if you'd walked a mile in their shoes?

Diversity is an asset, not a liability. There is much to be gained by opening your mind to observing a situation or person from a different perspective. Indeed doing so can *only* serve to enhance your own perspective and enrich your human experience. Given the increasingly globalized world in which we all live, this extends to appreciating how the cultural and social background others come from may be affecting how they observe things and how they may interpret what you do and say yourself.

Interestingly, the word conversation comes from the same Latin origin as "conversion". Whilst we may not end up with a conversion of our opinion through listening, we may well have a conversion in our heart in how we feel toward the person we are listening to. When you really put yourself into someone else's world, respect for who they are moves from being an obligation to an outcome. Genuine listening enhances trust—regardless of whether or not there is consensus of opinion. In doing so it helps to move the other person toward being more receptive and less defensive and to reciprocate with genuine listening themselves.

> *Communication is not defined by what is being said but by what is being heard.*

Following are some different ways you can improve the quality of your listening and your understanding of the way the world looks to the person you wish to communicate with:

- *Take responsibility for how you have been listening to others in the past.* If you've been ineffective at resolving a specific issue (or having a fruitful conversation about any issue!) then take responsibility for the results of your communication with them rather than simply blaming your lack of success on them. Give up being self righteous, a martyr, or making the other person wrong. Instead, take it upon yourself to gain a better understanding of the way the world looks to the person you are dealing with in an open-minded and non-judgmental way.

- *Listen with the intent to understand, rather than to reply.* Too often, we kid ourselves that we are listening when we are really just taking the opportunity, whilst the other person speaks, to reload for our next "shot." Real listening is being present for that person and paying full attention to what they are saying (not to what you want to say when they finally pause to breathe) rather than being pre-occupied with what you want to tell them.
- *Listen beyond their words to their concerns.* Even though you may be doing your best to make them trust you, sometimes people are still uncomfortable sharing what they *really* think (saying what they really think is foreign territory for many people). Listen *beyond what they are actually saying* to what they are trying to communicate, aren't willing to or are simply unable to verbalize. People always speak from a concern on some level about something so as Peter F. Drucker, a leadership expert said, "The most important thing in communication is to hear what isn't being said." So ask yourself, "What do they want me to know that they aren't comfortable saying?" If you have a hunch about something they aren't saying, share it. (e.g., "I know you say you don't really care about whether we do this or not, but I get the feeling that maybe you feel upset that I didn't ask your opinion about it beforehand?")
- *Speak only to deepen your understanding.* Never speak if it will be at the expense of making the person feel you're not really listening to what he or she is saying.
- *Build on the pool of facts* so if the person leaves out an important piece of information, mention it. The more factual information you both share about an issue, the more likely you will be able to move to a shared understanding of an issue.
- *Agree* whenever the person says something you also agree with (e.g., "You're absolutely right. It has been a difficult time and the pressures of the move have taken a toll.")

- *Reflect* back verbally what you think the person is saying (e.g., "Let me check that I understand what you mean or how you feel..." or "Correct me if I've got this wrong, but you feel like I haven't been as supportive of you as you think I should have been.")
- *Don't fill in the silence* with questions or comments if the person pauses between thoughts or becomes silent. Silence can lead to the real treasure. Just allow the silence to be since the reason for it is that the person is trying to process his or her thoughts. The more emotional the conversation, the more valuable the silence becomes in helping lead the conversation to the heart of the issue.
- *Never criticize* regardless of how much you might feel like doing so. Likewise don't interject with your conflicting opinions. Just hear the person out. Remember the point of listening is to understand so whether or not you agree with what they are saying is not the point.

3. Don't Get Stuck In Your Stories

As important as it is to listen to someone else's story about an issue, so is your willingness to examine the stories you have about it. Given that I dedicated an entire chapter to this very point, I hope you are now more willing than before to acknowledge there is more than one way to view any particular set of circumstances. Your stories can roadblock fruitful communication. Why? Because insisting that something is a certain way leaves no room for it to be any other way. Therefore, unless you are vigilant about the stories you may have—about yourself, about the other person and about the issue you wish to discuss—those stories will undermine your ability to communicate and manage the situation effectively and achieve what you want most. In particular reflect on whether any of these stories may be at play for you.

- *Victim Stories*: Be wary of where you may be painting yourself as the poor helpless victim in the situation since it is extremely unlikely that you had

Your stories can roadblock fruitful communication.

nothing to do with the situation in which you find yourself. Instead, take a good hard look at how you have contributed to your situation. An example of victimhood comes from a client called Claire whose husband had taken up golf. He had already worked long hours during the week, often getting home from work after the kids were in bed and so when, at the urging of a buddy, he began playing golf every Saturday (which took up a large chunk of the day) Claire became increasingly resentful. She felt like the helpless mother and wife left at home and that there was nothing she could do about it. Eventually, in a huge showdown, she exploded into a hysterical mess accusing her husband of being incredibly selfish. Seeing how upset she was he cut back his golf to every second week and made an effort to get home early enough to see the kids at least two nights each week. The point here is that had she not become so attached to her "poor me" story in the first place they could have come to this agreement months earlier and spared everyone a lot of grief.

- *Scoundrel Stories:* Be equally vigilant about casting someone as a the scoundrel at whose feet you lay all the blame. If there is someone like you in your story that personifies the devil himself, then it might be a clue to pay closer attention to your story. Ask yourself, "Why would a reasonable person have done this?" For instance, another friend of mine was recently telling me about her sister in law. "That woman is such a cow," she told me. "I swear she hasn't got a nice word to say about anyone and is hell bent on making my life a misery." Comments like this were creating a reality for my friend that left absolutely no space open to actually have a good relationship with her sister-in-law. Only by letting go her villain story about her sister-in-law would she stand any chance of being able to have an authentic, open and fruitful conversation with her about their relationship and from there, begin building a new and more harmonious one.

Elizabeth was a single 37-year-old woman who engaged me to coach her because she said her boss, who was located in another city and who had never actually met her, "had it in" for her. On learning more about the situation, I discovered that Elizabeth had a long history of employment crises, with different bosses and with different companies. When I challenged Elizabeth about whether her boss genuinely felt she was not doing her job well (given that she'd been away sick a lot and, as she confessed to me, had not been very focused at work due to her personal issues) she responded by defending her work and saying he should be more understanding. I could see that these stories were blocking her ability to have an effective conversation with her boss about the issues. In fact, she had had several conversations with her boss but none of them had gone well, as she had consistently felt he was not being sufficiently understanding of her situation. Elizabeth decided to suspend the coaching sessions with me as her financial situation was precarious. When I followed up with her several months later, she told me that the situation had gotten worse. They had tried to fire her but she had threatened with legal action and was now on a long-term disability leave due to the various health ailments she had suffered due to the stress her boss had put her through. It saddens me but my prediction is that Elizabeth will continue to find plenty of evidence to support her victim stories, and these will continue to prevent her from engaging in fruitful conversations, which will limit both her professional and personal success. I might add here that Elizabeth was not on speaking terms with her mother because of something her mother had done several years earlier nor had she ever had a long- term relationship. See a pattern here?

4. Be Body-Wise

Have you ever noticed how when you meet some people they can make you feel either immediately relaxed and comfortable and when you meet others they cause you quickly feel tense and on guard without them ever even saying a word? The reason this happens is because as human beings, our *way of being* speaks more loudly than our *words*. Likewise, your non-verbal communication can completely undermine your verbal communication if you are not mindful of it. The way you hold yourself impacts not only how confidently you can say what you want to say, but also how what you say will fall on the ears of the listener. If you speak up about something and your non-verbal message is screaming, "I'm such a loser, I don't blame you for treating me like dirt," or, "I don't care what you think, all I know is that you are a complete idiot," you won't be effective in influencing the other person the way you truly want to. Here are some ways that can help you be more body wise.

- *Become aware of your posture and non-verbal language.* Practice saying what you want to say in front of the mirror and watch your body language. What is it saying? Do you resemble a bulldog poised for attack or a doormat waiting to be trodden all over? If you are slumped back in your chair trying to disappear into the seat, your words will not be very convincing. Likewise, if you look as though you're about to devour the person you're speaking to you're also not going to have a fruitful conversation. Whilst you might like to feel certain that you have the right opinion about an issue, shift your posture from one of certainty to one of curiosity.

- *Practice Being Centered:* Pretend there is a string coming out through the center of your head that is pulling you up tall and upright. Not only will this help to shift your posture, but it will help you feel much more grounded, confident and at ease.

- *Act As If:* This technique, which I introduced in Chapter 5, is very helpful when it comes to speaking up. So even if you don't feel particularly confident at speaking up, "Act As If" you were. Think of someone you really admire (even if no longer alive) who is self-assured and able to express themselves confidently and then ask yourself how that person would act in your shoes. How would they stand or sit when they spoke up? What would their gestures and facial expressions be? Whom would they speak to and what would they say? By modeling yourself on that person's behavior, it can help you to step forward with more clarity and with greater self-assurance.

Brenda, a former client of mine, constantly struggled to speak up at meetings. Brenda worked for a commercial construction company and was the only woman manager. When she attended meetings, she told me that she felt intimidated by the men and although she had worked at the company as long as most of them, she was often timid about voicing her opinions during meetings. I suggested that Brenda center her posture by pretending there was a string through the centre of her head pulling her up tall. I also suggested that she think about how she would hold herself if she possessed the confidence that she wished she did. Brenda shared with me that Marianne, a vice president at the company she'd previously worked for, was someone she admired tremendously and would love to emulate. Just two days later, Brenda called me unexpectedly, her voice brimming with excitement. "It works Margie. It really works!" She went on to tell me she had been cynical about my "Act As If" idea but figured she had nothing to lose. That morning, while attending her weekly project planning meeting, she found herself in that usual predicament of wanting to say something but too scared to speak up. So she straightened her posture and pretended she was feeling as self-assured as Marianne would. "Next thing you know, I'm sitting there telling everyone how I feel we need to

Your way of being speaks more loudly than your words.

reconsider how we are moving forward on one of the projects and why, and I'm sounding like I've been running the place for the last five years. Honestly, it was amazing. I think all the guys were stunned too but not half as much as I was." The best part of this story is not that Brenda spoke up at that meeting and in doing so, changed the outcome of the decisions being made, but that it allowed her to experience her own greatness and realize that her opinion was important. She has since been promoted to a more senior position.

5. Don't Leave Emotions at the Door—Manage Them!
You may have heard people say, "Check your emotions at the door," in reference to an issue that may be sensitive or emotional. The obvious implication of this is that you can enter into a conversation without bringing your emotions into it. However, as nice as it would

be to sometimes take time off from our forever-changing emotions, the reality is that emotions are central to the human condition and, as such, you cannot *not* experience emotion. We humans are innately emotional creatures—in fact we emote before we can even reason. In his groundbreaking book, *Emotional Intelligence*, Daniel Goleman wrote, "We have feeling about everything we do, think about, imagine, remember. Thought and feeling are inextricably linked together."

Every emotion you have predisposes you to an action of some sort (for example, anger disposes you to inflict pain on someone and fear to avoid it or protect yourself) and so unless you are in tune with your emotional state, your emotions may undermine your efforts to speak up in an effective way. It is therefore important not to discount either your emotions or those of the person you are seeking to communicate with and to learn to manage the emotions going on in the conversation—yours and theirs—effectively. Only by doing so can you think clearly and respond successfully to other people's emotions or pursue productive and fruitful dialogue with them.

> *Emotions are central to the human condition. Unless you learn to manage them, they will undermine your communication and sabotage the results you want to achieve.*

I'd like to share with you two distinctions you may find helpful in dealing with your emotions:

Responding vs *Reacting*—Reacting to an emotion is a gut level response and usually produces a result that does not resolve an issue or build trust in the relationship. Responding, on the other hand, is a thoughtful response to an emotion, which serves to strengthen the relationship and address the issue effectively. Reacting to anger with anger only worsens the situation, often exponentially. If someone is getting furious and their adrenalin levels are rocketing up, respond by being curious and patient as they level out again. Perhaps even suggest having a break from the conversation: a "time out" for cooling down. Given that speaking up about the issues that matter to you may well invoke an emotional response from the other person, it will pay you well to be prepared to deal with the emotions effectively as they arise—yours and theirs!

Anger vs *Aggression*—There is a distinct difference between feeling angry and acting aggressively. Anger is an emotion; aggression is a reaction to anger. We can feel anger without acting aggressively by choosing to respond to our anger in a constructive rather than destructive manner. If you begin feeling as if you want to explode, don't continue the conversation. Tell the other person you will resume talking when you are ready. Your anger may well cause you to say things that cause a lot of hurt, and damage the trust in your relationship. Remember, having the courage to speak up doesn't mean spilling your guts and slaying the other person with your words. Sometimes acting with courage means choosing to walk away from a situation when part of you would rather stay and fight. Courage comes in many guises. When you can model the change you want to see in others, the words you speak have much more impact and power.

If you find yourself beginning to feel upset, you need to take responsibility for shifting your emotional state. Here are a few ways to help you and others remain emotionally calm in the midst of a sensitive conversation:

- *Linguistic Reconstruction* helps you quickly reframe your "private conversations" (or self-talk) about an event and disentangle the facts from the emotion you've attached to them. This enables you to be more responsive, and less reactionary, to the emotions you feel. This is best done by writing it down, but even simply reconstructing a situation that is causing you to feel emotionally volatile verbally can be helpful. First, make a statement of fact. Next, make a statement about how that fact will impact you. Finally, make another statement or two about how that will make you feel. Here is an example of how it can be used:

  1. *Statement of fact*—My boss has asked me if I will work this weekend to finish up a report due to management on Monday, and I've already worked late every night this week.

  2. *How fact impacts me*—This means I will not be able to spend time with my family or play tennis as I had planned.

3. *How I feel about fact*—I feel resentful that he has asked me to work this overtime and angry that he did not plan better which would have avoided this situation

4. *How I feel about fact*—I feel upset that I won't be able to play tennis because I was looking forward to it.

- *Conscious Breathing* helps you alter your emotional state by being conscious of your breath and focusing on taking longer, slower and deeper inhalations than you would otherwise. This is an effective technique because it is rooted in the body's physiological response to stress. When you begin to feel angry, your body sends blood to the vital organs of the heart and, as it does so, there is literally less oxygen reaching your brain. That old saying about not being able to think clearly when you're mad is literally true because your brain is deprived of the very stuff that makes it function well. Taking long deep breaths (you may wish to count to ten on each inhalation and exhalation), helps you get that much-needed oxygen back up to the brain. At the same time, it calms you and helps to restore your clarity of thought. If you have the opportunity to get away to a quiet place, meditation can also be extremely powerful in moving out of your negative emotional state.

- *Exercise* is a well-known antidote to stress. Physical exercise literally burns up the excess adrenalin and cortisol that anger and stress produce in your body.

- *Music* directly accesses the limbic system, which is the part of the brain that receives the sensory input and attaches an emotion to it. As you may well have experienced yourself over the years, music can dramatically shift your emotional mood. (I only have to hum Lionel Ritchie's "Dancing On the Ceiling," and my mood feels brighter!)

- *Going Outdoors* is also a great way to shift your emotional state. Ideally, head out to a park, the beach or the mountains since Mother Nature has a way of infusing your spirit with whatever it needs at that moment. Unfortunately, this is not always an option and that's okay. Simply getting outside and going for a walk around the block can do the trick. The change of space to outdoors can help you shift your emotional space and envision new ways of handling an issue that stumped you while your were feeling upset.

This simple technique proved highly effective for a client named Sue. When I visited Sue in her office, I found that she was stressed out about everything, to the point of being unable to function properly. She dissolved into tears when I asked her how she was doing. She was upset about a whole range of different issues and so emotionally overwhelmed that she felt paralyzed, unable to do anything, much less have effective conversations with people to address various pending issues. I suggested taking a walk outside together in the parklands right behind her office building. As we walked, I got Sue to stand tall and center herself (remember that string through the top of your head) and just focus on taking deep breaths and filling her lungs with oxygen. After approximately 30 minutes, Sue's emotional state improved dramatically as did her demeanor. She began to feel more at ease and see how she could resume her work and start addressing various work tasks for which she was responsible. Getting outdoors had a huge impact on her ability to manage her emotions and get on with having the necessary conversations, some of them sensitive ones, to effectively address the issues on her plate.

6. Share What You REALLY Want to Say

If you have something you *really* want to say, then chances are that there is someone who *really* needs to hear it. Following are some guidelines to help you speak your truth in ways that will serve the highest intention for everyone.

- *Stay mindful of your highest intention.* Speaking up is not about manipulating, convincing, forcing, coercing, defending, dominating or martyring yourself. Therefore, always be conscious of whether what is coming out of your mouth honors you (and so has integrity) or not. If you are in the right emotional space when you speak up, your words will be more likely to land in the right space in the ears of the listener enabling you to address your concerns. So, as you begin to speak, remember what it is that you want most to achieve from the conversation and resist the urge to prove your rightness (or their wrongness) or superiority (or their lack of it)! Even though you may not respect the other person's opinion or behavior, at least respect their dignity.

- *Keep it Real.* Speaking up effectively involves much more than just saying what you want to say articulately, strategically, eloquently or intelligently. It requires you to express your thoughts authentically, in all their rawness— that you be real. If you feel awkward, nervous or uncomfortable, just say so. For example:
  - o *"I've been putting off this conversation with you because I feel so uncomfortable about talking to you about it, but it's important so..."*
  - o *"I'm feeling really awkward about having this conversation with you, so I'd appreciate it if you'd be patient with me as I try to share with you what's on my mind."*
- *Begin with Facts First.* Begin by stating what is indisputable. For example:
  - o "You've been working at least one full day every weekend now for the last *two months*."
  - o "You failed to submit the weekly report to me on time twice in the last month, and you made a major mistake on the daily sales sheet three times." You might ask the person if he or she agrees or disagrees with you. It's important you both clearly understand what the facts are.
- *Proceed with caution* when sharing your "story"—opinions, beliefs, perceptions—about those facts by using language that allows for other possibilities. I say this because you are guaranteed to offend someone when you present your opinions as though they were the "truth." Sharing your opinion with caution will help make the person listening to you less defensive. For example:
  - o "I'm getting the feeling you'd rather be at work on weekends

than at home with me," rather than, "You obviously aren't as committed to our relationship as I am."

o "I'm wondering if you are still committed to fulfilling your responsibilities in your current job," rather than, "The fact is you are obviously incompetent at doing your job."

- *Use "I" statements.* When you are describing how you feel use "I" statements rather than "You" statements. This opens up the conversation rather than shutting it down when you use the accusing "you did," "you said," "you forgot." For example:

o "When you making disparaging remarks about my work/cooking/weight, etc., I feel as though you don't value my contribution or care about my feelings."

o When you are repeatedly late for work, I feel that you are not committed to your job here." If appropriate, ask how the person would feel if they were in your shoes.

- *Avoid speaking in absolutes and over generalizing.* For instance, "You *never* show me any appreciation!" "You *always* mess up the reports." "It's impossible to get anything done around here." When you say things like this, you automatically raise the defense of the person you are speaking to which does little to help resolve the situation.

- *Stay future focused.* Keep your conversation focused on what you want your conversation to achieve, rather than on the past and what should or shouldn't have happened. Instead of what *should* have been (past) focus on what *could* be (future). For example:

o "Given what you have on at work, what can we do so that we get to spend enough time together?"

o "What can I do to help you get these reports done on time and correctly?"

o "I'd really appreciate your help in working through the obvious problems we have with our procedures here in the office. Would you be up for helping me do that?"

- *Don't fill the silence.* I mentioned the importance of this in the section on listening, but I mention it again because silence is such a valuable element of communication (that also requires courage), for in the space that silence creates you can get to the core of what the conversation really needs to be about.

- *Invite Speculation.* Finally, you might find it helpful to invite speculation about how to achieve your mutual goal or intention. For example, you could ask questions like:
  o "What do you feel would be the ideal solution to this problem?"
  o "If we could create the ideal relationship, what would it be like for you?"
  o "What do you need from me for us to move forward?"

7. Make Powerful Requests To Get What You REALLY Want

Not only is it important to find the courage to speak up about the issues that concern you, but also to muster up the courage to ask for what you want...what you *really* want. After all, you can't have what you truly want by just wanting it. You must first be prepared to ask for it.

If you are busy in a demanding career and possibly juggling family and other commitments as well, then there are going to be plenty of people making requests of you. Whenever you have a lot of requests being made of you, you need to be making plenty yourself. Too often when people find themselves feeling resentful or being stretched beyond capacity, it is because they are not making as many requests as they could be.

The only way to make powerful requests is to have the courage to ask for what you want (as distinct from what you think you might get!). After all if you don't ask, you can't get. None of this, "Umm...I'm just wondering if maybe you wouldn't mind doing this for me sometime...if you get the time." That is no request! Nor is just making a statement like "Gee, this house is in a real mess." Instead, ask for what you really want and specify when you want it. Don't pussy foot about with your request. Be direct. For example:

The most you ever get from life is what you are willing to ask for.

- *"Would you please make an effort to get home in time to see the kids at least twice a week?"*
- *"Could you please get that report with all the regional sales figures back to me by midday Friday?"*
- *"I would like to attend a professional development course sometime this financial year. Will you support me on this?"*
- *"Would you be able to take on these three new clients starting the first of next month?"*
- *"I would like to get engaged in the next 6 months. Would you be open to that?"*

Likewise, don't let yourself be dragged into what I call a "Slippery Promise." Ensure your commitments have integrity and hold water, which means that there are explicit conditions of satisfaction so that both you and the person who is responding to you understand the exact nature of the commitment they are making. You are at threat at finding yourself entering a Slippery Promise when someone responds to your request with a reply like, "That should be okay," or "I think I will be able to do that." Either it *is* okay or it *is not* okay. Either that person can do something or they can't.

Sometimes people intentionally make their commitments vague because this allows them to weasel out of them afterward. But if there is no clear *what* and *when*, then down the track you will likely end up frustrated, disappointed or angry and in the midst of a conversation that goes something like this: "Yes, I thought that was probably going to be okay but something else came up and I wasn't able to do it after all. Sorry about that." Or, "I said I'd look into it when I had the time but I've been pretty busy." Whatever you do, don't let people off the hook with a vague slippery reply to your requests. If someone replies to a request of yours with something like, "That shouldn't be a problem," have the courage to ask the person, "When will you know for sure?" or "Can you get back to me by midday tomorrow with a definitive answer?"

Often what stops people from being direct in their requests is the fear of getting a negative response. For instance, what if you ask your boss for a raise and he says no? Well, if he's going to say no then surely it's better to know that you have no chance of a pay rise than to sit there growing increasingly resentful and forever wondering, "What if I asked?"

That said, if someone does say "no" to your request, then don't make a "no" mean anything more than it does. It's more than likely a rejection of your request, not you. Don't confuse the two! Whilst you will have to accept that their answer is no (for now at least), the most important thing is to leave the door open to establish room for compromise. For example:

- *"Well what professional development will you consider supporting for me?"*
- *"Can we discuss my salary again in 6 months time?"*
- *"Do you ever want to get married?"*

A "no" today does not mean a "no" tomorrow or next week or next year. But even if their "no" did result in your worst case scenario, then at least you would know where you stand. Surely that is a better position to be in than living in blind hope that sometime you will get what you want.

Exercise 6.2: Mastering Powerful Requests

Whether you feel like you have more on your plate that you can handle or you're simply someone who struggles to ask anyone for anything, take a minute to think about what requests you could be making that would help bring more of what you want into your life.

In your journal write down your answers to these questions:

1. What is someone doing that you would like them to stop doing or do differently?
2. What need do you have that is not being filled? Who can help to fulfill it?
3. Is there something you don't enjoy doing that you could be delegating or outsourcing to someone else?
4. Write down a request you could be making of someone specifying exactly what would you like them to do and when? For example:

   o "Son, can you please put your laundry away before

dinnertime?"

> o "Susan, could you please take on the monthly sales analysis and prepare a summary report for me by the 15th of each month?"

> o "Boss, I would like to discuss opportunities for me to move into a position of greater responsibility. Can we schedule a meeting sometime this month?"

8. Go Easy on Yourself...Seek Progress, Not Perfection

Denise came to me for coaching for several reasons. One of the main reasons was that she felt like the man she had been married to for over 20 years had become a stranger. Apart from discussing their two children and general domestic issues, she and her husband, Tom, didn't talk at all. Denise said she felt a growing distance and tension between them that neither of them wanted to acknowledge, much less talk about. She was beginning to wonder if she still wanted to be married even though the idea of being single terrified her. When I initially suggested to Denise that she talk to Tom about how she felt, she was completely against it saying that they just didn't have "those kinds of conversations, and besides, I'm hopeless at talking about my feelings and so is Tom." After several coaching sessions Denise began to come around to the idea that maybe she could have one of "those kinds of conversations." With butterflies running rampant, she mustered up all her courage to have a conversation with her husband about how she felt, about their marriage and their future. Before she did though, she wrote down a few notes about the key things she wanted to say. She also practiced how she would begin the conversation, which to her was even more difficult that sharing what she wanted to say. Of course, the day she asked her husband to go for a walk with her so they could talk, she still felt extremely nervous. However, she told me that once she began to open up with him he did likewise, and they had the most meaningful conversation they had had in many years (even decades!). Ultimately, Denise and Tom decided to get marriage counseling through a service associated with their church. When I last heard from Denise, she said the relationship had greatly improved and was headed in the right direction. She and

Tom were now aware of the importance of saying what was on their minds, and though it wasn't always easy to do so, they were both becoming more comfortable and confident in speaking up in ways that nurtured the trust in their relationship.

Don't wait to feel masterful before you begin the conversations that are undermining your happiness, limiting your success and causing you either low grade or high grade angst. Becoming an effective communicator requires ongoing commitment and practice. Begin right now by taking a big deep breath and, as you exhale, decide that the time has arrived for you to begin speaking up and putting your thoughts and opinions on the table—however clumsily!

Before you launch into a conversation that you feel nervous about, invest some time up front to prepare yourself as Denise did. It will be well worth your while. Here are a few suggestions:

- *Write* down some notes about the key things you want to convey or exactly what it is you want to ask for. This will help you remain more articulate should nerves kick in when you're in the thick of a conversation.
- Tap the power of *visualization* by picturing yourself sitting in the conference room, contributing fully to the conversation. Picture yourself being able to express your feelings with your husband or friend or asking your boss for the pay increase that you feel is long overdue.
- *Rehearse* your talk either in front of the mirror, in the shower or with someone close to you who can be your pretend conversational partner. This prep work will pay off when your knees begin to shake during the actual conversation.

So what are you not speaking up about? Exercise 6.1 may have helped you in identifying situations in which you feel like you have been treated with less dignity than you would like. But there are also many times in our lives when it's not a case of someone treating us poorly, but rather, that issues arise which we fail to resolve through conversation and simply live in hope that with time, our "upset" will abate. If nothing in particular comes to mind, I'd like you to think about those people in your life that you have had close relationships with over the years (even if not now)—your parents, your brothers, sisters, children, spouse, friends or colleagues. What issues, however old or seemingly trivial, are keeping you from having the warm, intimate and joyful relationships with them that you would like?

Often life's most important conversations are also the most difficult. No matter how uncomfortable you feel, you are capable of speaking up about anything to anyone at anytime. Finding the courage to speak up about the issues that matter most to you will be well worth your while for the price you pay for failing to speak your truth far exceeds the discomfort of doing so. Begin wherever you are. Your conversations may not always go as you hoped, but they will always provide valuable experience and lessons in how to speak up more effectively in the future—*if you look for them*! So don't waste your time and energy beating yourself up if your conversation takes an unexpected detour. Just stay committed to giving voice to that which concerns you and doing better next time.

The quality of your conversations determines the quality of your relationships.

By consistently conducting yourself in ways that honor the dignity of every person (and yes, that includes your own), you will be able to speak up in ways that deepen the trust and respect in all of your relationships. When it comes to speaking up, you are capable of more than you think you are. Given that you have a mouth from which you can speak and a heart from which you can draw courage, then you have everything you need right now to begin to speak up and create the changes you want in your career, relationships and life. So what are you waiting for? Get talking!

Chapter 7
The Courage to Take Action

> *"Yesterday is gone. Tomorrow has not yet come. We have only today. Let us begin."*
>
> —Mother Teresa

Life rewards action. Nothing great has ever been accomplished without it. Nothing ever will be. However, stepping into action and making the changes you want in your life takes courage. Don't worry if you feel like you've already hit your limit when it comes to bravery. Just hang in there and trust me when I tell you that you truly do have all the courage you need to make the changes and take the chances to create the kind of life you *really* want.

Just imagine how you will feel one year, five years or twenty years from now if you have failed to take any action and made zilcho changes to address those parts of your life which don't score a big 10/10. My guess is not too good. Why? Because it's impossible to feel really great when regret and "what ifs?" hang over you like a big dark cloud. Is that how you want to feel? I doubt it. But now just imagine how you will feel if you could look back on the intervening period and think to yourself, "I'm really proud of myself for finding the courage to take action despite the obstacles that I had to face and the fear I had to overcome. It sure wasn't always easy but I did it anyway".

> *"Delay is increasingly expensive."*
>
> —Thomas J. Leonard

Lights, Camera...Action!

So before we go any further into this chapter, let me ask you three simple questions.

Firstly, are you committed to your happiness and success in life? Secondly, is there an aspect of your life right now in which you don't feel completely happy, fulfilled and successful? And thirdly, are you ready to take the actions you need to take to experience the happiness and success you want?

I am hoping your answer to all three questions was a firm resounding "YES!" Great! You have just declared that you are ready to call on your courage and step boldly into action (despite how "unbrave" you are actually feeling inside). If you didn't answer with a resounding "YES!" then don't hang up your hat in "I just haven't got the guts" resignation. You do have the guts, we just haven't drilled down far enough through those layers of story, fear and self-doubt to access it...yet!

Beware of the "Action Traps"

If it were easy to just get into, and stay in, purposeful and effective action toward your goals everyone would be doing it. The reality is, it's not. In fact, there are many different traps you can get caught up in without even being aware of it. When you fall *into* action traps, you fall *out* of action. You procrastinate, you "catastrophize," (i.e. come up with the worst possible case scenarios you can imagine), you go around in circles. You tell yourself that now just isn't the right time, that you need more money, more experience, more guts...and somehow you always seem to find yourself back at the same familiar place you started from. In the end you resign yourself to the idea that it makes more sense to stick with the status quo than it does to go gallivanting about trying things that offer no guarantee of success.

The only way to get out of a trap is to first know you're in it. Once you come to recognize the traps, you'll be able to free yourself from them. Once you're out of them, you will be able to make the changes and take the chances you need to take to achieve what you want. So let's take a close look at what these action traps are.

Procrastination

The word procrastination derives from the Latin *pro* meaning forward, and *cras* meaning tomorrow. When we procrastinate, we put off doing something today and move it forward until tomorrow.

"I'm going to look for a new job, rewrite my CV, join a gym, resume my studies, get my pilots license, change jobs, save more money, register with a dating service, learn guitar, start a small business, go on a safari, get out the toolbox and fix the hinges on the front door, start a herb garden, lose 30 pounds, write a book, do what I really want to do with my life…"

"When?" I ask.

"Someday…maybe tomorrow, or next week or next year. Not now though. I'm too busy right now with so much other stuff going on and besides, I just don't think the time is quite right."

Of course, the catch 22 for the habitual procrastinator is that tomorrow never comes and the time is never "quite right." The problem with falling into this trap is that whilst we gain some comfort from the temporary respite of taking no action, we end up paying a lofty price for living forever in the tomorrow.

Back in my student days I worked at a bar with a woman called Marni who was about 27 at the time. We'd often chat about what we were doing in our life. Most of Marni's conversations consisted of how she was going to apply to go back to university and study interior design. Well, if I heard it once, I heard it a million times. Yet, when I'd ask at which university she wanted to study, she always had some reason why she'd not done anything about it: she'd been too busy working extra shifts, her mother had been sick, her boyfriend thought they should go traveling around Australia, her cat had been run over and she'd been too grief-stricken to do anything. There was always some excuse. When I left that job a year later, Marni was no closer to even getting an application form than she was when we met. Talk about procrastinating!

"You can't build the future in the future."

Unfortunately for Marni and for all people who've fallen into the trap of procrastination, they usually don't step very far into action—if at all—before they are presented with another opportunity to excuse themselves, and bang, they're back on their butts convincing themselves that the status quo isn't such a bad place. ("I mean my job may be boring but at least I have one and it puts the food on the table." "I know I'm overweight but hell, I'm not as fat as that guy on *60 Minutes* last night" Excuses, excuses, excuses—yada, yada, yada.) Left untended procrastination can be incapacitating for, as Benjamin Franklin once said, "He that is good for making excuses is seldom good for anything else." A tad harsh perhaps, but you get the point.

If you feel that this even remotely describes you, then I'm guessing that procrastination has shown up in more than just one area of your life and during more than just one period of your life. Are there several different things that you find yourself procrastinating about or has there been just one thing you've procrastinated about for a long, *l---o---n---g* time?

If you would like to remain in the job you find so boring, in a relationship that drains you or to keep living a sedentary existence where the most exciting thing on your horizon is tonight's rerun of Seinfeld, then go right ahead. Just be conscious that it's 100% your choice—and not because the economy is in a downturn, your boss doesn't appreciate you enough or you have no opportunities of meeting new people where you live. Only once you become aware that you (and only you) are the root cause of your procrastination, then you will be able to break out from the inertia and step into action.

During a coaching training seminar I attended in Dallas in 2002, I remember Thomas Leonard, sometimes referred to as the father of modern day coaching, saying that, "Delay is increasingly expensive." Take a moment to remember something you hesitated to do because you were scared of things not working out well or failing, though deep inside you knew you really wanted to do it. For instance:
- Leaving a job you didn't like
- Starting a business
- Taking advantage of an opportunity
- Getting into a relationship
- Ending a relationship

- Confronting someone about unacceptable behavior
- Terminating an employee
- Investing in real estate
- Starting a family

Whatever decision it was you delayed making, reflect on what it cost you—financially, emotionally, physically, mentally (with stress and anxiety), and professionally (through reduced performance and productivity). I can assure you that unless you find the courage, as the Nike slogan says, to "Just Do It!" you will pay an increasingly expensive price somewhere in the future. On the other hand, when you choose to be decisive and move forward deliberately, you will enjoy the rewards that go to those who take the world on with gusto.

Exercise 7.1: Escaping the Procrastination Trap

Before you can rise above the quagmire of excuses that is procrastination you first need to identify which aspects of your life you are "putting off until tomorrow." Get out your journal and write down anything that you have you found yourself continually putting off in relation to:
- your relationships
- your job or business
- your health, weight or wellbeing
- the physical state of your home (something you've been meaning to fix or update, but you just haven't gotten to)
- your finances
- your social life

Now, write down how you would feel 12 months from now if you take action on these items or issues. The exercises that follow in this chapter and the next will provide you with an opportunity to create a plan for stepping into action on the items and issues you listed.

Catastrophizing

Another trap that people often fall into is a game called "catastrophizing." Though I've made up this word, clinical studies have found that we have inherited emotional and cognitive mechanisms that have us hard-wired to overestimate rather than underestimate certain types of risk because, given our instinct for survival, we have learnt that it is better to be overly cautious than

> "I am an old man and have known a great many troubles but, most of them never happened."
> –Mark Twain

to not be cautious enough. So when you catastrophize, it means that your imagination has a field day conjuring up as many dreadful images as it can about what might happen if things don't work out accordingly to plan. Suddenly you are paralyzed from action as terrifying images race about your head. You see yourself on the front page of the paper with the headline "Loser!" placed above your picture. Perhaps you see yourself living on the street, pushing a shopping cart along and scavenging for food from trash cans, as your children, dressed in rags, sit nearby, forlorn and ashamed of their parents' downfall.

Okay, okay, okay…maybe these images are a little more dramatic and catastrophic than those plaguing you. For you, catastrophizing might simply be a vision of you walking into your ex-boss's office to humbly ask for your old job back. Maybe it's a group of people (whose opinion you value) gathered around a dinner table, talking disparagingly about your failure—"I mean, how on earth did she ever think she was ever going to make a success of it? She must have been deluding herself." For me it was, "Who did she think she was writing a book? What a joke." It doesn't really matter what your worst case scenario is, what matters is how it impacts you. If it's paralyzing you from taking any action, then it's keeping you stuck somewhere you don't want to be.

If you find yourself being trapped by catastrophic images, the first and most important thing is to acknowledge that these situations are real for you. Don't be ashamed of being absolutely terrified of public humiliation, of losing your money or having to eat humble pie. Your fear is real. Second, you need to decide how probable it is that your worst-case scenario would actually occur. More often than not it's extremely unrealistic. In fact, studies show that more than 90% of what we worry about never materializes. So, most likely what you catastrophize about will never actually happen. But, for the sake of the exercise, let's just say that things don't work out well. You quit your job and move out of state to work for a new company and it goes under for reasons you had no way of predicting. Suddenly you're out of a job, with no money coming in and paying out plenty for your mortgage, car payment, health insurance, school loans and the list goes on. Do you head straight to the local grocery store and borrow a shopping cart to begin your life on the streets? As if! No, you do what you need to do to find some work until you sort out your life. Yes, you handle it the best way you can. The truth is that whatever happens, you will be able to handle it—catastrophe or no catastrophe.

Lisa, a 28-year-old publicist, loved the idea of traveling through Africa ever since she was a young girl. She wanted to experience the diversity and richness of the people, cultures and nature of the African continent. Ideally, she wanted to spend about six months traveling and take a break from her demanding career a consulting firm. She knew she would be able to afford it as she had been putting money aside for some time for mortgage payments on her apartment and to finance the trip. However, she was stuck in the catastrophizing trap with two key worst-case scenarios running through her head. The first was that her employer would not give her the time off to go overseas. This would mean resigning and not having a job when she returned. Furthermore, Lisa worked in an industry where jobs weren't always easy to come by. The prospect of being unemployed indefinitely, which would look bad on her resume, terrified her. The second scenario was that if her company did agree to give her a leave of absence, it would still not provide her with the opportunities for promotion and career advancement it may have otherwise, because it would now regard her as not being serious about her career. Going to Africa meant imperiling her career progress, or worse still, being permanently unemployed. Just thinking about this sent shudders down her spine.

In reality, taking time off to travel to Africa didn't necessarily mean she would be overlooked for promotions or relegated to the bottom of the "to interview" pile. In fact, her travel experience could actually make her a more attractive employee, as she would gain confidence and become more assertive. However, how could she know unless she first went to her boss and asked? To help her with her fears, I asked Lisa to do the following exercise.

Exercise 7.2: Disempowering the Catastrophic

The intention of this exercise is to put your biggest fears onto paper and in doing so shed enough light on them that they no long have such a paralyzing impact on you.

> *"Our doubts are traitors and make us lose the good we oft might win by fearing to attempt."*
> —Shakespeare, *"Measure for Measure"*

The very process of writing is often very therapeutic. The process of transferring the anxieties that sit in the pit of your stomach onto paper allows you to take a step back from them and see them more clearly, more objectively and more rationally. Indeed writing down your fears—however terrifying and catastrophic they may be—can liberate you from their grip.

1. Write down the goal or dream that you would like to achieve.
2. Write down what you fear might happen if you chose to take action toward your goal. Describe your ultimate "catastrophic" situation in as much detail as you can muster (e.g., my business will fail, I will be left homeless, I will look like the town fool, etc.)
3. Write down what you would do if it began to appear that things were not going as you had intended (e.g., downsize your home or car, get a second job, cut down your expenses, etc.).

4. Using the Law of Averages (LOA), write down the likelihood of your "worst-case scenario" actually coming to fruition. Rate it on a score of 10—with 10/10 being extremely likely and 1/10 being extremely unlikely.

After Lisa got herself out of the catastrophizing trap she had fallen into, she went to her boss and asked if the company would give her a six-month leave of absence. The answer was no. Her boss explained that if the company approved her request then it would have to give it to everyone and, "...next thing you know, Lisa, we'll have everyone lined up asking for six months off. We just can't run our business like that. I'm sorry." After much thought, Lisa decided to resign anyway, and off she went. When she returned, she made it a full time job to find a full-time job. It took her a whole three weeks to land an interview with a larger publicity company that did a lot of work with clients based in South America. She got the job. That was two years ago. She now earns more money than she would have had she stayed with her former employer. On top of that, she absolutely loves her work and occasionally travels on business to South America, where she gets to do some local exploring and savor the foreign cultures she enjoys so much.

> *Whatever happens, you can handle it!*

The "If It's Meant To Be, It's Meant to Be" Cop-Out

Some people fall into a trap of adopting an "If it's meant to be, it's meant to be" philosophy. Though this sentiment can be reassuring at times, it is not an excuse for passively watching life pass by, especially when you have the ability to do otherwise. Opportunity does not come to those who are lucky. It comes to those who go seek it out. Just ask my cousin Allison who found her ideal partner after systematically working her way through a list of potential "candidates" through an online dating service. Had she adopted the "if it's meant to be, it's meant to be" approach, she'd likely not be happily married with a beautiful young daughter today.

You see some things need a chance "to be" and only by taking action can you create the opportunity you need to create the reality you want. If you are single and would really love to not be single, then don't sit at home watching television hoping that Mr. Right is going to turn up at your front door disguised as the pizza delivery man. It may be one long wait. If it's meant to be that you enjoy great prosperity, great health, wonderful friendships, a rewarding career, a loving relationship or whatever else you dream of in life, then it will only "be" if you proactively take action to make it happen.

Fear of "Stuffing Up"

It is important to understand that once you find the courage to step into action you will also risk making a mistake or, as I have always liked to say, "stuffing up!" It would be comforting to know that whatever actions you took, they would all produce the results you wanted. Obviously, there are things you can do to maximize the possibility of that outcome. You can do your "homework" and research your options to make an educated decision. You can ask people for advice. You can create a spreadsheet and analyze the numbers. You can consult your financial consultant, your attorney, your realtor, your mother or your fortune teller. But at some point you are going to have to make a choice and take some action, and when you do, you will risk making a mistake!

But what are mistakes anyway? The *mis* in mistake comes from the Latin for *wrong* and so the word mistake literally translates as to "*take wrongly*". When you make a choice to take one course of action over another and your choice fails to produce to results you were hoping for (i.e., you got it wrong), you have made a mistake.

If you're like a lot of people you may be feeling pretty apprehensive about that possibility. I mean, who likes to "stuff up"? You procrastinate, you make up excuses about why you can't do anything "just now" and, in the end, you choose to sit in limbo land a bit longer because you are so scared of messing up. Unfortunately, any achievement worth your time and energy doesn't come with a guarantee of instant success. That's

Only by having the courage to make a wrong choice can you make a right one.

why it takes courage. But only by having the courage to take a risk now and then can you ever hope to have what you want most in your life. When you don't muster up the guts to make a mistake you forfeit all possibility of realizing the *results* you'd really like to experience in your life. Remember, the longer you wait to do so, the more it will be costing you.

Whilst you may never relish the experience of making a mistake you can choose to embrace the learning opportunity each mistake provides. Ultimately you can leverage your mistakes to strengthen your muscles for life. When you don't risk mistakes, you sell yourself short. You stagnate, your "life muscles" wither and, as they do, they deprive you of ever getting to experience how strong, resilient and capable you actually are. Nothing truly great would ever have been achieved had people not been willing to risk the possibility of making a mistake. Nothing ever will be. Ask any person who has accomplished something worthwhile about their mistakes—and they will be able to recount more mistakes than you will have time to listen to.

Patricia was a client of mine who had just finished taking her bar exam and was looking for work as an attorney. A perfectionist by nature, she'd studied hard and had done very well academically resulting in employment options with four different big law firms. Now you would think that would be a good thing...but being the perfectionist that she was, Pat was terrified of choosing the wrong one. Would a big firm offer more long-term opportunity or a small firm provide greater mentorship and diversity of experience? These were just some of the questions she was trying to answer. In fact, when she came to me, she was close to jeopardizing at least one of her employment options, as they had already extended the deadline for her to respond to their offer. Yes, it sounds crazy, but she was so scared of making a mistake with choosing who to work for that she was close to limiting her choices altogether.

> *"It had long since come to my attention that people of accomplishment rarely sat back and let things happen to them. They went out and happened to things."*
> —Leonard da Vinci

I pointed out to Patricia that only by having the courage to make a wrong choice could she make the right choice. And, even if she did decide at a later date that it had not been the best choice, she would still have gained truly valuable experience along the way after all. She needed to simply make a choice based on the information she had about the different firms and let go the idea that she had to make a perfect decision. Indeed, as anyone who has ever worked for any sort of organization knows, no organization—including a prestigious law firm—is perfect. Sometimes only by learning what doesn't work for us can we discover what does.

So let go of having to achieve a perfect score when it comes to making the right decision every time. Be okay that sometimes you are going to make a wrong move. Accept that you will make misjudgments now and then. Give yourself permission to not get things 100% right 100% of the time. Of course I am not advocating reckless abandon since failing to do your homework before making a choice is irresponsible. However, I am suggesting that once you have decided what you want to do that you take action toward it.

Action Strategies

Like I said at the beginning of this chapter, nothing changes if nothing changes. So, let's get down to business and look at some strategies that will help you a) take action, and b) stay in action to make the changes you want to make in your life! Some of the following strategies will resonate with you more than others. However, don't discard any of these without first applying them— you may be surprised at how effective they are.

Write It Down

A very important first "action" step is to write down what you want for yourself and get your arms around your dream enough for you to be able to step into action toward it. Whilst an idea or dream is only in your head, it is still intangible. You begin making it real by writing down what you want to achieve in ways that are measurable.

As we said in Chapter 4, it doesn't matter what you dream of— after all, your dream is not about a *destination* you are supposed to arrive at but rather a *direction* you will begin to travel. However, unless you give your dream parameters, your dream will be doomed to failure before you ever begin taking action to achieve it. For instance, I often hear people say that they want to make a difference in the world. But what is "making a difference?" Who are they going to make a difference for? What sort of difference are they going to make? How big a difference are they talking about? How will they ever know if they have accomplished their goal and made a difference?

> *"Most folks tiptoe gently through life only to make it safely to death."*
> —Eleanor Roosevelt

Take Bono for instance. He is a man obviously very committed to making a difference in the world. To accomplish this, he has put parameters on his dream and defined it by saying he wants to end Third World debt. So as you write down what it is you want to achieve or change in your life begin to think about what would have to occur for you to feel that you had achieved your vision.

The clearer you are about what you want to do, the less ambiguous you will be about what you don't want. I recently coached a woman who wanted to leave her university administrative job she had long grown tired of and move to Colorado to pursue her passion for bookbinding. When she contacted me, she had been offered an administrative position at a university in Colorado and was considering taking it. After doing this exercise and writing down on paper what she really aspired to do, she realized with great clarity that she really didn't want to move to Colorado only to do the same work she'd been doing for nearly 20 years. As I have said before, if you don't know where you want to go, any road will take you. Writing down what you want will help to you see the road you should take.

Break It Down—Identify Your First Steps

It's human nature to want a welldefined path to travel before setting out your journey. The problem is that there is no *www. mapquest.com* to log onto instantaneously provide you with a mile by mile description of how to get to your destination (if you even have a clear destination). But as much as the uncertainty of what lies ahead can at times be unsettling, it's this very same uncertainty that makes life exciting. Just imagine for a minute how incredibly boring your life would be if you knew every single thing you had to do to and how to do it!

Those who are most successful at living their dreams master the art of shifting their sights from the big canvas to the immediate actions they need to take. The steps you need to take will appear as you get closer to each step. So once you've identified which staircase you want to climb, which goals you would like to achieve, start climbing. Action, *any* action, no matter how small, is very important since it is only through action that you can begin to build positive momentum. Large planes use up to 60% of their fuel just to get off the ground so be prepared for the fact that in the beginning it will take a considerable more amount of effort to create momentum than once you're up and running. Taking that first step is a huge milestone. As Horace once said, "He has the deed half done who has made a beginning."

If you don't know what the first step is, then finding out what the first step *is* is the first step!!! Maybe you just need to make a few telephone calls or perhaps do some research on the Internet and send a few emails to find out more information. No one is born knowing how to start a business, apply for college, run for local council, train for a marathon or anything else for that matter. Everyone has to learn. And so do you.

Rena wanted to transition from her full-time job in marketing with a large telecommunications company to working independently as an interior designer. She came to me because she was in a rut and didn't know how to get moving. She felt completely overwhelmed by the idea of starting her own business, and not knowing where to begin, she just kept procrastinating. Rena knew there were hundreds, even thousands, of steps separating her from her goal. During our coaching sessions, we talked about what made her feel so overwhelmed. One of the key things that emerged was that she liked to work from definite lists, just as she did in her work. Rena liked the certainty of knowing exactly what the steps were and in what

> *"Take the first step in faith. You don't have to see the whole staircase, just take the first step"*
> –Dr. Martin Luther King Jr.

order she would take them. Though she had a very detailed business plan, she felt frustrated that she didn't know exactly what the long term future held and therefore couldn't plan concrete actions and strategies beyond the short term (12 to 24 months). I asked Rena if nine years from now, she would know what she needed to do to grow her business in the next 12 to 24 months. "Of course," she replied and I could see from her expression that the penny had dropped. She'd got my point. Simply put, you don't have to know exactly what you need to be doing five years from now, one year or even six months from now to begin taking action to accomplish your goal. The steps you need to take will become clearer as the time to take them draws nearer.

If you've ever climbed a mountain, you will understand this point entirely. Whilst living in Papua New Guinea, a group of friends and I decided to climb the highest mountain in the country, Mt. Wilhelm, which is 14,880 feet (4,508 meters) high. The logistics for even getting to base camp were overwhelming initially as PNG is an undeveloped country in many ways, with only a basic infrastructure. The road networks are poor to non-existent in some of the more remote areas including where Mt Wilhelm was located. From the airport in Mt. Hagen, we'd sat in the back of small pickup trucks and traveled up the narrow, unsealed roads past small villages to the point from which we had to hike to the base camp. Even the hike up to base camp was grueling and altitude sickness hit some of my fellow trekkers really hard. From base camp we could see the summit of Mt Wilhelm and, fortunately, we had a couple of wonderful guides to help us reach the summit. We began the climb from base camp to the summit at 1:00 a.m. so we'd be at the peak at sunrise. The hike up was extremely difficult. At times, I could see the next few hundred yards ahead of me, and at other times, as we ascended into the clouds, we literally couldn't see more than two steps ahead. Of our party of 14 only five of us made the summit. The others dropped out due to altitude sickness (including a fellow who was from the military and whose fitness level far exceeded my own). I remember looking at them longingly, as they turned around and began to descend. But I pressed on, convinced that surely we'd be there soon. Seven hours after setting out we reached the summit, though we had missed the sunrise due to bad weather. I remember feeling an enormous sense of accomplishment sitting on the top, though I didn't sit there for long as the cold wind quickly ripped through us when we stopped moving. Of course, we also knew that we had to climb all the way back down which took another 5 hours.

One thing I know for sure from that hike (and from others I've done over the years) is that when embarking on the journey to climb to the summit, it is okay not knowing the size and shape of every step that lies ahead. This is what makes it such an adventure in the first place! Who knows, had I known every grueling step of the journey before I embarked upon it, I may well have felt too overwhelmed to have ever set out.

Rest assured that whatever mountain you aspire to climb, the next step you need to take to reach the summit will unfold before you by the time you are ready to take it. Don't waste your energy or your precious time wondering what lies around the next corner and whether or not you will have the courage to make it the whole way. Relish the excitement and adventure that comes from not knowing what lies ahead. As George Conrad said, "Courage is only an accumulation of small steps." Focus on the step immediately in front of you—it's the only one that ever matters.

> *"As you go the way of life, you will see a great chasm. Jump. It is not as wide as you think."*
>
> —American Indian Wisdom.

Exercise 7.3: Clarifying Your Goal

If you haven't already done so, get out your journal and write down a goal that you would love to accomplish. The key purpose of this is to be able to get enough clarity on what you want to enable you to identify the first few action steps necessary to achieve this.

Some examples:

- I want to utilize my IT skills in the non-profit sector, in a leadership role.
- I want to go to Africa. I would like to spend at least two months traveling around the continent and visiting different countries including Kenya, South Africa and Malawi.
- I want to lose weight and feel good about myself. I would like

to lose 15 pounds to fit into size 8 clothes and look good in a pair of jeans.

- I want to learn how to make jewelry and sell it at home parties and local fairs.
- I want to meet a professional guy, get married and have a family. I'd like him to be someone who is clever, kind, committed, thoughtful, funny and able to express himself well. I would like him to be someone who values family and wants to be a great father.

Then break it down into the first few steps you will need to take to achieve it. Put a completion date beside each step. For example: Contact an employment agency—end of week; Contact realtor—end of next week; Join a gym—end of day!

Schedule Your First Steps

If you are like most people I know, you are busy. However, it is very easy to find oneself frantically busy, yet achieving little of significant value or meaning. If your calendar is booked solid with activities, how realistic is it that one day you will find yourself with lots of free time on your hands and nothing else to do but start taking action toward those long-held goals and dreams? Not very! The reality is that you will probably only get around to doing it if you schedule it!

> *"Be not afraid of going slowly, be afraid of standing still."*
> —Chinese Proverb

The other benefit of scheduling your actions is that it helps keep you moving forward even when you don't feel like it. I mean if you had to wait until you were "in the mood" to pick up the phone and make a few calls, you might be waiting a long time. So, by scheduling what you need to do helps you get it done, whether or not your feel like it. Funny enough though, often when you just get on with doing something, the feeling you want to have catches up with you. For instance, if I had to be feeling energetic before I went to the gym, I'd never have walked into one. But by making the commitment to get to the gym, I find that by the time I'm finished there, I really am feeling energetic. How you feel is so variable, so just schedule what you know you have to do and get on with it whether you're in the mood or not!

Exercise 7.4: Schedule Your Action

Get out your planner, calendar or whatever you use to manage your time and write in when you will begin taking action on the first few steps you have identified.

Ideally, schedule a time when you can focus on whatever you need to do—when no one and nothing can interrupt you. You may choose to put aside an hour a day, an hour a week or a day a week. You may also like to write down a deadline—by when you will have accomplished a specific task. There is no right and wrong time of day or amount of time—it is what will work best for you given your other commitments. The only thing that really counts is that you have made a commitment to doing *some specific thing,* by *some specific time,* which leaves you stepping boldly into action.

Reshape Your Private Conversations

As we've discussed before, your thoughts and words—through the "private" conversations you have with yourself and the "public" conversations you have with others —have created your reality and have enormous power in their ability to get you into action or pull you out of it back into the pit of procrastination, resignation and ordinariness. So be very mindful of your conversations as they have the ability to pull the rug out from under your feet *if* you let them.

Take responsibility for the conversations people have around you.

Daring to take action something that will pull you out of your comfort zone automatically triggers fear. And so the pattern that most of us fall into when we dare to dream is that about a millisecond after we've connected with a vision of what we really want to do, our self-deflating ego roars onto the scene to invalidate us, to invalidate our dream and to stop us in our tracks with put down comments to ourselves like:

• "Oh don't be so bloody ridiculous; who am I kidding that I

can ever do that?"
- "I've tried this before and failed. Why bother again?"
- "Who the hell do I think I am to be trying to do this? I mean I've never tried to do anything remotely like this before."
- "People will think I'm deluding myself to want to be trying to do this."
- "I really don't know that I have what it takes. Am I crazy?"

Sound familiar? It's part of the human condition— to live with that "Small Poppy Committee" in your head that is hell-bent on keeping you playing safe and living small (well at least smaller than you are capable of!).

This is precisely what happened to me when I decided that I would like to speak to groups rather than only coach individual clients one-on-one. The initial thought of speaking was exciting to me, but the post-initial thought that followed a millisecond later had me feeling nauseous with a lump in my throat. I mean, "Who am I to speak to people? What the hell do I know anyway? I haven't even spoken in public (beyond my wedding) in my entire life. I'm kidding myself."

The incessant little voices of my Small Poppy Committee ran around in my head whenever I thought about taking a step in the direction of speaking. They still do, usually about a minute before I'm due to walk on stage. Fortunately, I have gotten better at beating them back into submission for that is exactly what I had to do to take the initial steps toward becoming a speaker. Say, "Yep, I heard ya. Now shut up!" and then just get on with it.

So, if you find yourself being pulled down into a quagmire of negative thinking and self-deprecation, start first by simply noticing what you are saying to yourself. "Aaahhh…there is my Small Poppy Committee (or gremlin, or whatever name you want to give it) trying to keep me playing safe and small again." Get clear that this voice in your head is not coming from the sacred part of you that longs for you to step out more boldly into the world and into the fullness of who you. Rather, this voice is that of your ego trying to protect you from risk and keep you in the same place you've been up until now. So knowing that, simply acknowledge it. Thank it for its comments and then tell it to shut up! But, of course it isn't going to just shut up because you tell it to. Unfortunately that is not the way of the ego which is determined to just keep going and going and going until it has worn you down. That's why you need to be just as determined to push back. The way you do this is by starting up your own conversation, using positive self-affirming language. For instance:

- When you find yourself thinking "I can't do x," start to say, "I haven't done x before, but I am going to learn."
- When you find yourself thinking, "I'm just hopeless at y," start to say "I am going to work at becoming better at y."
- When you find yourself thinking, "Who am I to do this? Why me?" start to say, "Who am I not to do this? Why not me?!"
- When you find yourself thinking, "It's just impossible to do z," start to say, "I know there is a way to do z. I just haven't found it yet...but I will!"
- Instead of saying "If only I'd..." say, "Next time I will..."

Curb Your Complaining Conversations!

Obviously, the conversations you verbalize with others (your "public conversations") can also undermine your ability to take the actions you need to take to make the changes and take the chances to achieve what you want. Complaining conversations are a chief culprit, so I encourage you to adopt for yourself the motto: *Don't complain about something unless it is to someone who can do something about it.* You see, whatever payoff you get from whining about something, it isn't near enough to make up for how much it costs you. Take a moment to think about what conversations have you had in the last day in which you have been negative and held no higher purpose than to vent? Whilst complaining doesn't help fix your problems it can undermine your ability to face them and take the courageous actions you need to address them.

But it's not just about giving up complaining. It's about any sort of negative conversation you have with someone in which you paint yourself and your future with a negativity, resignation or helplessness. Your words really do have an extra-ordinary power over your emotional, mental and even physical state. Why? Because your subconscious cannot discern between what is real and not real. If it hears you say something negative, then that is what it takes on as "the truth." If you say something like, "I'm never going to be able to work through these issues with my partner," then that is the reality you will likely live into. But if you rephrase your language to say, "I've had a difficult time communicating with my partner in the past. However, I know that we will find a way to work through our issues in the future," you are leaving open a whole lot more possibility and empowering, rather than disempowering, your ability to resolve the issues you face together.

Even your physical strength is impacted by the words that come out of your mouth. Here is a little experiment you can do yourself (with the help of someone else) to experience just how true this is. Close your eyes and say to yourself several times a positive statement such as, "I am strong and powerful," "I can do anything I choose to," or, "I feel great about myself and my future." Now extend your arm at right angles to your body and ask someone to try to lower it with their outstretched hand. Now close your eyes again, but this time repeat to yourself a negative statement such as, "I am weak and powerless," or, "I am unworthy," or, "There is no hope in my future." Then hold your arm out again, and ask your friend again to try to push it down. The person will likely be able to bring it down very quickly and with little effort. Notice the difference? What is impressive about this exercise is that you don't even have to fully believe the words you're saying to keep your arm firmly outstretched, and become physically stronger. That's because the words you speak affect your physical strength by conveying a message to your subconscious.

"Birds of a Feather..."—Choose Your Company Wisely

I hate to tell you this but you are responsible for more than just the conversations that go on in your head, or which come out of your mouth. You are also responsible for the conversations you tolerate others having around you. As you've probably experienced already in your life, when you are around people who are having positive conversations (regardless or not of whether you are participating in them) you feel differently (i.e. better) than when you are in the presence of people engaging in negative conversations. The fact is when you hang out with toxic people you end up intoxicated! Not in the traditional sense of the word, but the impact it can have on you is similar. Naysayers and cynics can undermine your efforts to step into and stay in action. Their negative emotions, moods and conversations will infect you—it's impossible for them not to! You, therefore, need to consider the kind of people you are hanging out with because negative people, and the negative stories they have about themselves and life, can impact your predisposition to take action and quickly have you sliding down the slippery slope of resignation to join them in their narrow and cynical world.

The fact is if you hang out with people who are trapped in narrow conversations, you will be hard pressed to see anything but the same limited view of life that you always have and harder pressed still to take the actions required to expand it! That's why people who don't want to confront issues in themselves choose to stay in small superficial conversations with other likeminded people who will not only validate them but who will fail to challenge them to getting off their butt and taking responsibility for actually doing something about their woes. In those mundane often complaining and generally shallow conversations they can remain safe, secure…small. As the saying goes, "Birds of a feather, flock together."

> *"Free spirits have always encountered violent opposition from mediocre minds."*
> —Albert Einstein

Of course, it is not always possible to outright disentangle yourself from relationships which fail to support and empower you. However, you still have a few different ways you can deal with their negativity. Obviously, you can try to minimize how much you see of them. As you grow stronger within yourself, you will likely grow apart from some people. So be it. Sometimes, though, you have no say about whether or not these people are part of your life, so you might ask them to refrain from having the type of conversations with you about certain issues, which they have traditionally been very negative about (e.g., their job, their spouse, their mother-in-law, politics, etc). Of course, this can take guts, but as I like to say, "You get what you tolerate." Given that when you sit and listen to their negative talk, you are in essence implicitly supporting it (silence speaks consent), you need to ask yourself, "Am I acting with integrity by not speaking up about how I feel about their comments or opinions?"

You could just say something along the lines of, "I know you see things differently to me and you have every right to your opinion. However I find it draining when you talk about xyz and so would prefer we didn't speak about this anymore." Another way to help dam the flow of negativity that can sometimes pour forth like Niagara Falls in the spring is to ask, "Why do you have a need to be so negative about this?" or, "What positive purpose are you trying to achieve by complaining about this?" It may not dam the flow permanently, but it will at least give you a moment of respite as they pause to consider their answer. Who knows, you may even make them present to their own narrow conversation and open up the possibility for them to broaden it. At the very least, you will be communicating to them that you are no longer willing to tolerate participating in conversations of this nature.

You are always making a difference in the world either by your action or your inaction.

Go Public!

Another strategy which I cannot recommend highly enough to keep you in action is simply to share your goals with people; to go public! Declaring to others what it is you want to achieve makes your goal become more real. Suddenly you and *someone else* know the goal you hold so dear. Yikes!! Now, I am not saying you need to share it with someone to make your life more miserable, should you, for some reason fail to achieve the goal in the time you wanted. Not at all! I'm recommending this because it will increase your chances to succeed. There is nothing like a good friend who has been through your ups and downs, your wins and losses, to lean on for support when things don't go according to plan. It is all the more joyful to be surrounded by people who celebrate your wins along the way.

Going public with your goals takes a little more courage and makes your commitment more real. However, by openly sharing with others—people you know well and those you know less well— what you want to achieve, this leads to even greater accountability. Dr. Kurt Lewin, named by many as the father of social psychology, found that subjects who made a public commitment to doing something were more likely to stay the course than when they kept their aspirations to themselves. Social pressure is something that can at times be a negative force in our lives, but in this case, you have the opportunity to get social pressure working in your favor.

Sonia had two school-aged children and worked part time in reception at a medical center. She sought coaching because she wanted to start her own small business designing and producing personal stationery such as invitations, birth announcements and birthday cards, but she had been stuck procrastinating about it for over a year and wanted some help getting started. She confided in me that she hadn't shared this with any of her friends or work colleagues because she felt awkward about it and feared they might think this was a foolish idea given her lack of experience.

I assigned Sonia the following assignment: over a two-week period, she was to share what she aspired to do with her stationary business with at least a dozen people—a mix of people she knew well and those she didn't know as well. At our next session at the end of the two weeks, Sonia reported back how everyone had responded enthusiastically to her idea and a few people, including some she hardly knew, told her they would like her to provide them with stationery once her business was up and running. She admitted that sharing her goal with these people had initially felt quite scary and that she had been nervous, but the more she talked about it the less awkward she felt, and the more real the whole idea became. In fact, it turned out that some of these people ended up becoming her biggest supporters and were instrumental in helping her to get her business off the ground by promoting her services through word of mouth.

Whatever it is you would like to accomplish or even just change in your life, in the beginning you may feel a little awkward in sharing your aspirations. Many people do. However, as you become more practiced in letting people know what you want, you will gradually become more and more confident and comfortable doing so.

Spring Clean Your Physical Environment

Spring cleaning your physical environment is renewing. It also frees up space in your life for more rewarding and meaningful pursuits. Whether it be it your house, your car or your office, spring cleaning your environment is one of the most significant ways to create a physical environment that inspires you (rather than slows you down). Before undertaking a new activity or project, I encourage you to take action and clean up the "not so new" in your environment. You know, the pile of old newspapers, the pile of bills, the laundry, your closet and the clothes in it you never wear, the repairs to your car, the two-year-old food in the back of your fridge, the overdue library books, the even more overdue tax return...even the 6-month-old emails in your inbox!

Nurture Your Spirit

Sure life would be a heck of a lot simpler if we were all like Mr. Spock, the Star Trek Vulcan who never got himself in a funk and didn't have to contend with moods and emotions. Then again, emotions are what give life its richness. However, unless we look after ourselves properly, our emotions have the ability to really drag us down and, with that, out of action.

So not only is it important to pay attention to your physical environment but also to your spiritual and emotional environment. That is, surround yourself with things that help center, uplift and inspire you (which comes from the Latin *spirit within*) and allow you to keep the blues at bay. Read great books (I've listed many on the resources page of my website, but you don't necessarily have to buy them—you can get wonderful books and audio books from your local library), go to seminars where speakers can empower and inspire you further, watch uplifting TV programs and as I've said already, surround yourself with like-minded people. Make time in your schedule to do whatever it is that will help you really feel good about yourself.

In Chapter 6, we explored how to manage emotions in the

context of effectively engaging in conversations about "emotional issues." The fact is you emote before you reason—this means you have no choice but to experience emotion. So, it's pointless to beat yourself up when you find yourself in a less than "uplifted" mood. Even the most upbeat, positive people in the world sometimes get into a funk (my humble self included!). The good news is that we humans have the power to choose how we respond to our emotions and to shift our response. So, as soon as you become aware you are feeling less than happy and centered and are descending the slippery slope of pessimism into the vat of negative emotion—despair, anger, resignation, depression, anguish, resentment or worry—take some time out from whatever you are doing and do something about it. (Some practices to keep you in good spirits are covered further in Chapter 11.)

Stay Vigilant of Your "Everybody"

I cannot caution you strongly enough about giving other people the power to decide what you will or will not do in your life. Too often, the people that make up our "everybody" are the doomsayers and naysayers who are living small lives themselves. "Small Poppy People" living Small Poppy Lives. Not only that, often we don't even know what they really think and instead just conjure up something negative that paralyzes us from action. So if you are going to listen to the opinion of other people, then at least be sure that the opinions are from people who really and truly have their life on course and are living the kind of life that inspires you. Whatever you do, don't take life advice from someone whose made a mess of theirs (or at least failed to make a success of it)! As I suggested back in Chapter 5, reconfigure your "everybody" to represent people whom you really admire and respect rather than people you simply wish would more readily approve of you.

Mitigate Risk

In *The Art of War*, Sun Tzu discusses the importance of mitigating the risk and preparing for the possibility of things not going as planned. Sure, you may not be going into war, but it is still important that you do your homework. Research the market, get the skills or training you need, restructure your finances, prepare a plan, make a budget, seek advice from those who've gone ahead and take whatever precautions you need, so that if things don't work out exactly as planned, you will not be caught off guard.

Although it is important not to let fear stop you from stepping in to action, that does not imply throwing caution to the wind and taking irresponsible actions that have the potential to cause harm to you or others. I, therefore, disagree with the advice of some people, who subscribe to the rationale that if there is nothing to fall back on you will have no choice but to make it work; that it is better to "throw all your eggs into the one basket." Of course, if that approach is one which resonates with you and you are young, single and have nothing to lose but your pride, then, by all means, go right ahead. However, if you do have other responsibilities—family, mortgage, etc.—it may be wise to have a back-up plan should things not go according to plan. After all, there is a distinct difference between being gutsy and being reckless.

> *There is a distinct difference between being gutsy and being reckless.*

Over the next few decades there are going to be many wonderful things done in the world. Whether in the realm of business, politics, science, arts or humanities, a lot of people will make great accomplishments and leave their own unique mark on the world. What will distinguish these people from those who achieve little and make no mark is not luck, opportunity, privilege but action. Why not be one of them? In the words of Peter Drucker, "The best way to predict the future is to create it." You have all the courage you need to do what it takes to create the future you want...one step at a time.

> *"Whatever you can do or dream you can, begin it. Boldness has genius, power and magic in it. Begin it now."*
> –Goethe

Chapter 8
The Courage to Persevere

> "Nothing in the world can take the place of
> persistence. Talent will not; nothing is more common
> than unsuccessful men with talent. Genius will not;
> unrewarded genius is almost a proverb. Education will
> not; the world is full of educated derelicts. Persistence
> and determination alone are omnipotent. The slogan
> Press on has solved and always will solve the problems
> of the human race."
>
> —Calvin Coolidge

It would be nice to think that all it takes to successfully accomplish your goals and dreams is to find the guts to take that first big bold step into the unknown, after which it would be a down hill run to the finish line. Yes, as I say, that would be nice. The reality is though that between where you are now and where you want to get to, you will have to contend with innumerable obstacles (internal and external), setbacks and the odd wrong turn.

But of course if you could accomplish your goals without any hassles, hurdles or hiccups then your goals would really not be that much fun to accomplish after all. You see it is in overcoming the challenges that will arise as you begin to head toward your goals and dreams that will make your eventual success truly meaningful. A goal would hardly be worth pursuing if it didn't present at least a few meaty challenges that called on you to dig a little deeper into yourself to meet them and still have enough resolve left in your piggy bank to push on afterward. The fact is, nothing great has ever been accomplished without a lot of falling down and getting back up and nothing ever will be.

Born the third of 14 children into a working class family in Joliet, Illinois, Rudy Ruettiger dreamt of attending the esteemed University of Notre Dame. Though the odds were stacked high against him— his family had little money and he struggled academically—Rudy never lost sight of his dream. After a tremendous about of hard work and determination, his efforts paid off when he was accepted into a smaller college close to Notre Dame where he was finally diagnosed with dyslexia. Undeterred, he persisted and studied for two years to get the high grades he needed to get into Notre Dame. Three times he was rejected before finally being admitted into the university. He then continued to work hard and developed a new dream, of playing football for the "Fighting Irish", Notre Dame's famous football team. Again the odds were stacked high against him; he was only 5'6" and not a strong athlete. But again he persevered by doing whatever it took to realize his dream including spending two seasons as the team scout with no guarantee that he would ever actually get onto the field. Inspired by his enthusiasm and perseverance, on the last home game of the last season his team mates and coach gave him the opportunity he had been dreaming of—to "suit up" for the Fighting Irish. In the last 27 seconds of the game, he made Notre Dame history as he sacked the quarterback in the only play in the only game of his college football career becoming the only player in the school's long prestigious football history to be carried off the field on his teammates' shoulders.

If this story sounds familiar, it is because a movie was later made about Rudy's courage and perseverance. I highly recommend that you watch the movie *Rudy* for it will inspire you to find the courage to persevere in your own dreams, regardless of the obstacles you face. In the words of Rudy Ruettiger, "Do what you really want to do. Don't let the words of others hold you back. Take a step towards your dream. As you move closer to your dream, new opportunities will open up for you that you never imagined possible. Along the way, the journey will be full of struggle, but I learned that the greater the struggle, the greater the victory! As you go for your dream, you will inspire others to live their own."

Too often we take for granted the resolve and determination of those who have already succeeded in accomplishing something of significance. We assume that they must have had something extra or known something more that we don't. But that isn't true. They had no more nor less courage than you. What they did have was a passion so strong for what they were doing that they felt compelled to keep persevering regardless of the size or the number of hurdles they had to jump. You too can make your own dreams a reality and accomplish something truly extraordinary through hard work, passion and perseverance. But just be prepared, because the higher you set your sights, the more obstacles you will encounter along the way and the greater the courage you will have to find to stay the course.

I'd like to play a game of make believe here. Just imagine that you are back in the year 1897 and that you and your brother are working as bicycle mechanics in a little shop on West Third Street in Dayton, Ohio. You have this idea that you can build a craft that man can fly. You and your brother get to work on your "project" moving to an unpopulated stretch of North Carolina coast in a little place called Kitty Hawk that has vast stretches of sand, few trees and good weather for trying out the latest version of your flying machine.

No one before has ever built a machine that actually flies (without gravity immediately taking over). Many other men, far better educated in physics and aeronautics than yourself or your brother, say it is an unequivocal impossibility. "After all," they argue, "if God had intended man to fly he'd have given us wings!" But you aren't buying that "story" and remain passionate about your dream and committed to achieving it. Countless times you come within a hair's breath of death as you try out your new designs which take you hundreds of hours of hard work to build. But still you don't give up. Rather you incorporate lessons from your last crash to modify your designs and rebuild again. And thank goodness you don't give up because one day in late 1903, after more failed attempts than you care to count, you get your craft into the air and fly it further than man has ever done before. From that day the course of history changes forever.

Of course, we are all thankful today that Orville and Wilbur Wright didn't "chuck it in" and return to their bicycle store in Ohio after their umpteenth failure. No doubt had they done so, they would likely have spent the rest of their lives in a state of downhearted resignation, occasionally looking into the skies and forever tormenting themselves with the question, "What if we'd kept trying?" Indeed those who persist in the face of setbacks and obstacles never have to be hounded by the incessant and disparaging little voice at the back of their head asking, "What if I hadn't given up? What if I had searched out another approach? What if I had persevered?"

If you have set your sights on something that truly inspires

> *However much you'd like to curse your challenges, instead regard them simply as invitations for courage.*

you, then you can bet that there are going to be times when you come up against walls that *seem* daunting, intimidating or outright un-scaleable. There are going to be times you will feel kicked in the gut by a setback, overwhelmed by the challenges that lay ahead and disheartened with yourself—"maybe I don't really have what it takes?"

But as much as you may want to curse your challenges, instead regard them simply as just invitations for courage. And when you feel your courage to persevere is waning, take time out from your toiling (and cursing) to reconnect with the dream that inspired you to take action in the first place. What was the thing about your dream that grabbed hold of your heart so fiercely in the beginning? Find that "thing," connect with it and recommit to it.

However intimidating the obstacles you face, just imagine the solid stone walls around the Robben Island Prison complex where Nelson Mandela spent much of his 27 years of imprisonment. Being a human like the rest of us there were many times Mandela felt daunted and disheartened. But he never became disconnected or disillusioned with what it was that he felt so passionate about—ending the injustice of apartheid in South Africa. By staying connected to the vision that inspired him so deeply, when he was released from prison at age 71, on February 11, 1990, he still had the courage, the passion and the determination to go on and accomplish his life's greatest work. The fact is that your life's greatest work lies ahead of you so long as you are willing to dig deep and find within you the courage to persist when the going gets tough. You're tougher and more resilient than you know yourself to be. Truly.

Tapping the Determination to Persevere

Acknowledge Your Fears for What They Are (and What They're Not!)

In his first inaugural address to the nation on March 4th, 1933 President Franklin Delano Roosevelt said, "First of all, let me assert my firm belief that the only thing we have to fear is fear itself— nameless, unreasoning, unjustified terror which paralyzes needed efforts to convert retreat into advance."

Sometimes our intellectual understanding of why it makes sense to do something is undermined by an emotional resistance on some level to which we aren't fully present. I mean you likely get why it's so important to push on in the face of obstacles, setbacks and mistakes, BUT when you find yourself sitting on your duff (again) after your latest rejection, mess up or setback, the idea of dusting yourself off, getting back up and pressing on can be anything but appealing. What you really feel like doing is throwing in the towel, burning your "how to" and "self help" books and retreating to the familiar safety (however dull) of the life you have been living up until now.

The reality is that it can be disappointing and painful when things don't work out as you want them to. This pain triggers your instinctive desire for self preservation giving rise to your fear—fear that if you keep going in the same direction (a path that offers no guarantee of success and a very real possibility of failure) you will have to contend with more of the same ahead.

As I said earlier in this book, a little bit of fear here and there can be a good thing, so it would be foolish to wish all your fear away. Without fear you would likely have done even more dumb and reckless things in your younger years than you already did. Heck, if human beings as a species had no fear, we would have been eaten by saber tooth tigers back in our cave dwelling days. So it is important to acknowledge that your fear is seeking to fulfill a positive purpose—to keep you safe and protect you from pain so that you can "survive" life. However, you also need to acknowledge the "potential" power your fears have from keeping you from realizing your unique potential and living the life you truly want to live. You see, when you let your fears get "the better of you" what it really means is that the "best of you" doesn't get a chance to be expressed in the world. Sure, you may be surviving, but you can't be thriving unless you reclaim the power that your fears, doubts and insecurities have been wielding in your life.

The bottom line is that fear has the power to stop you from tapping the courage you need to persevere and stay the course toward your goals and dreams. Indeed, fear stops people from reaching for the stars in their lives way before any external obstacle has the chance to do so. They spend their lives so scared of messing up or looking bad, that they end up not really living life at all. Rather than being scared to death of what might happen if you try and fail, be afraid that you may one day arrive at death, look back at your life and realize you never really lived. Now that is something to be feared!

> *Fear stops people from reaching for the stars in their lives way before any external obstacle has the chance to do so.*

Perhaps right now as you read this you feel inspired about making a change or taking some chances, but you've hit a few bumps in the road before and you are now feeling pretty anxious about what may be lurking around the next corner. Join the club! As I discussed in Chapter 7 when I introduced the concept of "catastrophizing," the irony is that what you fear is usually far, *far* worse in your imagination that it ever would be in reality. And so, as you move forward toward your goals and aspirations, your fear of failing will continue to rise up and attempt to pull you back into a state of resigned inaction. When you experience this fear and all the self doubts that accompany it, know that you are not weak or gutless, inadequate or pathetic. Not a bit. Rather, *you are human.* Acknowledge your doubts, your misgivings, your fears of blowing it, but most of all, acknowledge your humanness. Then, look into your heart, reconnect with your deepest aspirations and, more than you fear failing to succeed, fear the "What ifs" and regrets that will torment you if you fail to persevere.

Staying the Course

Distinguish You from Your Results

If failure is something that truly terrifies you, then it is important to make a big distinction between who *you* are from the *results* you have produced—whether they be due to "mistakes" (discussed in Chapter 7) on your part or setbacks that have been outside the realm of your control.

Wind back the clock a few decades to the time you were celebrating your first birthday and you did a lot of falling over. As you got up from the floor and began to take your first few steps, you continually came crashing down onto the ground. At this point, you did not make a snap decision that it was far too humiliating to be falling over all the time and so much more dignified to simply stay crawling around on the floor, secure, closer to the ground and out of risk of falling. You didn't over analyze and you didn't try to attribute meaning to things that didn't exist. When you fell over, you simply fell over. If it hurt, you cried. Then, without any self-chastisement you got back up and tried again, and if at first you didn't succeed, you tried and tried again. Simple.

> *"Just as a gem cannot be polished without friction, so a man or woman cannot grow in greatness without trials."*
> —Chinese Proverb

As the normal progression of life would have it, as you grew into adulthood you became increasingly aware of the risks associated with trying new things. You also became far quicker to attach a negative meaning to your "mishaps." As we discussed in Chapter 4, there is often a huge difference between the facts of what happened and what we make them mean (a.k.a "your stories"). Too often we collapse the two together and lose sight of the fact that what happened may mean something completely different to the meaning we have assigned to it. This is what so often occurs when we make a mistake. We make a decision or take an action that doesn't produce the result we sought and then we attach a disempowering meaning to it.

Just think back to something that didn't go so well for you (whether yesterday or when you were 8 years old) see if you can recall the pronouncements you made about yourself and the situation in the aftermath.

- *"I am completely hopeless."*
- *"I will never be able to succeed at this."*
- *"I am such a failure."*
- *"I'm such a loser."*
- *"I should have known better."*
- *"I should never have tried."*
- *"I made a complete fool of myself."*

It is vital that you learn to distinguish who you are from the results you produce and not to equate the lack of desired results with your own self-worth or ability to produce different results in the future. Regardless of how resistant you are to this idea, I challenge you to consider the fact that no one is a failure. Sure, sometimes people fail to attain the results they have sought but this doesn't render them a failure as a person. So, confine the "failure" label to your efforts on a particular occasion for no matter how things may turn out, you have never been a failure and nor will you ever be one.

Napoleon Hill said, "Every adversity, every failure and every heart break carries with it the seed of an equivalent or greater benefit." Your failures teach you to deal more effectively with the challenges of the future and provide you with valuable lessons on how to succeed—not only at your current endeavor but in every area of life. Thomas Edison conducted over 1,200 failed experiments before he did one that didn't result in failure. Had he not been prepared to make mistakes and persist time and time again when his experiments failed to produce the result he was after, we would all be sitting around by candlelight every night (which, come to think of it, might not be so bad). After each failed attempt, he could have decided that he was a madman for even thinking that it would be possible to create electricity. No one would have blamed him for packing up his laboratory and calling it quits. In fact, most people thought he was a madman for continuing day after day after day. But instead of deciding that he was a failure because his attempts had failed, he decided not to try to create electricity by the same method the next time. With each unsuccessful attempt, he was able to narrow down ways in which it would work. His experiment may have been a failure, but he wasn't and he would continue on until he was able to produce the results that he sought. As Edison once said, "Our greatest weakness lies in giving up. The most certain way to succeed is always to try just one more time."

Watch Your Pride

Sometimes our pride can get in the way of our happiness, undermining our willingness to "get back on the horse." We get so caught up with doing whatever we can to keep up appearances that we disconnect and shun whatever aspirations may require jeopardizing our social standing. "What will people say?" keeps us playing safe, stuck and unwilling to try anything that could

Don't give other people's opinions the power to dictate what you will do or who you will become in your life.

risk a judgmental stare, a critical comment or, God forbid, social rejection. If what others might think of you is stopping you from taking a risk, then it's vital that you realize that what others think of you has nothing—absolutely zilch-zero-nada—to do with who you really are.

Those people who are already living life on their own terms will be far less likely to criticize you than those who aren't. Just ask yourself why they need to judge, criticize or ridicule you in the first place? Often, it is to make them feel better about whom *they* are. Don't let other people's opinions dictate what you will or will not do in your life or what you will or will not become. If you are going to begin playing a bigger game in life, then that will mean making changes and taking chances. Will you make a mistake now and then? Sure you will, but pity those who don't have the guts to do the same themselves—don't fear them.

Quit Comparing Yourself

I once heard it said that comparing yourself makes you either vain or bitter. The fact is when you fall into the trap of having to compare yourself to others in order to feel good about yourself, you will never really feel good about yourself. No matter how big your house, slim your waist, flashy your car or long the letters are after your name, there will always be someone you come across who leaves you feeling deficient in one way or another. Yes, always!

The habit of comparing yourself with others is particularly debilitating when it comes to the realm of persisting in learning a skill that many around you already possess. The fact that you may be unskilled at something is not the problem at all, for we all have the ability to learn new skills throughout the course of our lives. The problem arises when you compare your skill level with those who have much more skill and then decide it would be too humiliating or embarrassing for you to attempt to become skilled yourself.

Consider how many adults who have never learnt to swim as children never try to learn as adults. Often the reason is that they believe it will be humiliating to be a novice swimmer with no more skill than a three-year-old. Likewise, many people who have never learnt to drive in their early adulthood never seek to learn later on even when doing so could be liberating to their quality of life. They figure they're too old to learn, or it would be just too undignified for them to fumble at the wheel, even though doing so is a natural part of the learning process.

If you take a step back and think about it, the notion that you should automatically be good at something without first having to make your fair share of mistakes is absurd. Yet, for whatever reason, we somehow unconsciously buy into this idea. As children we naturally experiment and are open to trying all and everything. Only when we begin to succumb to the "grown up" notion that failing, making a mistake, of exhibiting incompetence is a "bad" thing, do we begin to withdraw from the ranks of the eager learners. As hard as it may be to swallow, even Lance Armstrong once needed training wheels! Thankfully, he had enough passion for cycling that even a close encounter with cancer did not stop him from pressing on and ultimately becoming the greatest cyclist in the world.

Before anyone acquires a skill that becomes second nature to them, they have to pass through four stages of mastery. These are

- *Unconscious Incompetence*—You don't know that you are incompetent: e.g., a two-year-old doesn't realize that he is not competent at driving a car.
- *Conscious Incompetence*—You are aware that you are not competent: e.g., the thirteen-year-old knows that he doesn't have the ability to drive a car. If he tries he will make lots of mistakes and will almost certainly have an accident.
- *Conscious Competence*—You are learning the skill but have to be very conscious of what you're doing to do it competently. You still can make the odd mistake and move back and forth between being competent and incompetent: e.g., the new 17-year-old driver can now drive, but has to be very focused on what he's doing or else will make a mistake.
- *Unconscious Competence*—You have mastered a skill to the point that you don't have to think about what you're doing in order to do it, and you rarely, if ever, make a mistake: e.g., As an experienced driver you don't ever really think about what you're doing as you drive around the street. You rarely make a mistake and you can drive around competently.

Of course, some people have a natural aptitude in a particular skill and can quickly move through the various stages of learning to master that skill. However, it is completely unrealistic and illogical to think that you should quickly be able to master something as competently as someone who has spent years refining their skill and ability—whether it be cooking, learning guitar, driving a car or running a small business. If you have been struggling to find the courage to learn something that you know will involve making plenty of mistakes, you need to quit comparing yourself, give up the disparaging remarks about yourself and instead realize that you are simply not practiced in a particular skill. Focus your energy instead on mastering whatever it is that inspires you.

Recruit a Support Team

One of my favorite scenes from one of my all time favorite movies, *The Wizard of Oz*, goes like this:

Cowardly Lion: *All right, I'll go in there for Dorothy. Wicked Witch or no Wicked Witch, guards or no guards, I'll tear them apart. I may not come out alive, but I'm going in there. There's only one thing I want you fellows to do.*

Tin Man: *What's that?*

Cowardly Lion: *Talk me out of it.*

The people in your life play an essential role in helping you move forward in the face of your own fears (your own "wicked witch") rather than go hide behind the nearest tree, as the Lion was tempted to do. The fact is that you do not live in a vacuum. Trying to achieve your goals in isolation is not only not much fun, but it can be extremely difficult particularly when the going gets tough and you find yourself falling into a rut of resignation.

If you've ever done Weight Watchers you will know that they build into their program a strong system of accountability and support. The success of their programs speaks for itself and attests to the importance of having other people around you supporting you in achieving your goals. Regardless of your goal, whether it be to drop 10 pounds or start a business, it is really important to find people who will be able to support, encourage and hold you accountable. For as intrinsically motivated and pumped up as you may be about achieving a goal, you can't stay pumped up forever. No one can. There are going to be days when you just can't be bothered; when you're feeling disheartened or demoralized and you just want to give up. On these days, when your intrinsic motivation system is running on empty, you're going to need an external source of motivation to keep you moving forward. By surrounding yourself with people who believe in *you*, you create an environment which makes it that much easier to persevere, and ultimately, to succeed.

When we are exposed to people who think bigger about themselves and about the world it pulls us forward into thinking bigger and being bigger ourselves. People who are passionate ignite our passion. People who are "up to something" in their own life broaden

People who are passionate ignite our passion.

the horizons for what we see as possible for ourselves and support us in staying "up to something" in our life—however tough the going gets. So you will find it much easier to find the courage to persevere when you are regularly having conversations with people where larger possibilities are being discussed (if not with people directly, you can also achieve this indirectly through reading about people's ideas in books—like this one!).

Exercise 8.1: Recruiting Your Support Team

This exercise is intended to assist you in getting started toward establishing a Support Team that will help you be more determined, more persistent and more courageous than if you were going it alone. So get out your journal and answer the following questions:

Who could you ask to be a member of your Support Team?

Write down as many names as you can think of. They could be people who are a few steps ahead of you on whatever path it is you want to travel, or they could be people who just always seem to be really positive, determined and courageous in what they are doing and how they are living their life. Some you may already be good friends with, others you may not know very well at all. Perhaps you hardly know any people who you think would be really supportive. If that's the case then you need to get "out there" and meet them because "happening" kind of people are not sitting home every night watching TV!

Who will you ask to help support you in accomplishing your goals and pursuing your dreams? When?

It's up to you how many people you "recruit," but I suggest at least two and ideally three or more. That said, if you only have one person then begin with them and then work at finding another so you aren't totally dependent on them to cheer you on.

When will you have a conversation with them to ask for their support?

Schedule a time to talk to them. Let them know how you'd like them to support you. Maybe there is a goal they would like to achieve and you could create a buddy system to keep each other in action mode. If you don't regularly see or speak with them in person, then schedule a weekly or monthly phone call or a time for coffee to catch up.

Getting Back Up after a Fall

We often hear the saying, "Hindsight is a wonderful thing" used in the context of regret—"Ahhh, if only I'd known then what I know now, I'd never have made the choices I did." Unfortunately, the way the world works is that we have to step out and give something a try before we can arm ourselves with the benefit of hindsight. Beating yourself up after the fact, when things haven't gone the way you had hoped or expected, will only leave you feeling drained and disempowered. It may also prevent you from seeing opportunities to take action and move forward from this point on.

You cannot know how resourceful, strong, capable and gutsy you are if you've never confronted circumstances that have challenged you to be so!

Sure, rising again after a fall takes great courage but it provides a wonderful opportunity to really grow your muscles for life, discover strengths you never knew you had, and experience a deeper dimension of yourself. You cannot know how resourceful, strong, capable and gutsy you are if you've never confronted circumstances that have challenged you to be so!

If you are living your life courageously then you are also going to have your fair share of falls—certainly a lot more of them than someone who isn't. It goes with the territory. How you choose to respond each time you fall and experience a setback will determine how effective your future actions will be. The key is never to give your mistakes or your challenges more power over your future than they deserve. Whenever things don't turn out the way you were hoping, you can either choose to process them as "failures", or as temporary setbacks providing you

> "Our greatest glory
> consists not in never
> falling, but in rising
> every time we fall."
> —Oliver Goldsmith,
> Irish Playwright

with a rich opportunity to learn, gain insight and foresight and to grow stronger muscles for the changes and challenges that lie ahead. Your willingness to see an obstacle or a mistake in judgment for what it is—no more, no less—and to adjust your future actions accordingly is what will set you apart from so many others around you.

Exercise 8.2: Turning Hindsight into Foresight—Making the Most of Your Setbacks

Many times whilst growing up I heard, "It's not stupid to make a mistake. It's only stupid to make the same mistake twice." The best way to make sure you don't make the same mistake twice is to reflect on the choices you made that produced the result you didn't want, and learn from them.

Anytime you feel that you have made a "wrong turn" and landed somewhere you didn't want to land—whether in your career, relationships, finances or any area of your life—then I encourage you to get out your journal and actually write down your answers to these questions:

1. What did I do that produced this result?
2. What did I not do that would have led to a better result?
3. What factors did I not give sufficient consideration to that would have changed the choices I made and actions I took?

4. What might have been a better approach to have moved forward?
5. How can I apply what I have learned to help me deal more effectively with current and future challenges?

Caren was a client who sought coaching after failing to set up her own small home-based business that specialized in organizing children's birthday parties. She'd invested a lot of time and money into her venture, but after 18 months had had very little growth or income and was feeling despondent personally and professionally. During our first session, we talked through the things that she had done. Initially, she was fairly defensive about her actions and felt like she'd done all the right things and that her business should have been flourishing by now. I then asked Caren to tell me why she felt it wasn't. After a lot of digging and exploring we came up with several things that she could have done to attract more clients and several others she could have done to retain the clients she had. She'd done neither and had assumed that if she did a really good job with the cooking that the business would grow on its own. She was able to shift her perspective and realize she wasn't a failure, but that her marketing strategy had been ineffective. She knew if she wanted to grow her business to the size she aspired to she would have to change her assumptions and employ some marketing strategies that she hadn't previously. She felt very tentative about this, not wanting to invest any more into what she had begun to view as a hopeless venture.

"It didn't work last time, why should it work this time?" Caren said. I replied that this time she knew a whole lot more about how to run her business (apart from how to bake great cakes) than she did 18 months earlier. She had a much better understanding of the market and a better feel for what worked and, just as importantly, what didn't. The mistakes she'd made had all been part of her learning process that would allow her to grow her business as she had planned to do 18 months earlier. Within two years, Caren's business had completely turned around. Demand had grown exponentially to the point that she had to take on several employees to help her meet the demand for her services.

It's when things don't work out the way you've hoped that your courage is put to the greatest test. Indeed sometimes courage calls for you to keep persisting and to try again when you'd much rather throw in the proverbial towel. Unfortunately, the way life works is that you often have to knock on many doors before you find the one you can enter. Then again, who the heck ever said that every door should open for you anyway? Who says you shouldn't come across the odd bump in the road here and there and every so often find yourself facing a mountain in your path? No one! It's from all the falling down and having to get your weary self back up again that you get the greatest sense of accomplishment.

Don't ever forget that courage is not an absence of fear, but moving forward in spite of your fears, your misgivings and your self doubts! You may still feel a churning sensation in the pit of your stomach, tightness in your chest or a lump in your throat at the very thought of how you will feel if things don't work out the way you want them to. No matter! This is what it is to be human. Don't fall for the romantic and unrealistic notion that you should always feel ready to jump back on the horse without a care in the world about the possibility that you may fall off again. Courage expresses itself in many ways and often not in hero form. In the words of Mary Anne Radmacher, "Courage doesn't always roar. Sometimes courage is the little voice at the end of the day saying, "I'll try again tomorrow.""

I am sure that there are areas in your life in which you have not been as persistent as you could have been. Perhaps some cause you to feel regret. If so, let it go. Instead make a decision to not give up so easily in the future. Today is a new day and the very first day of the rest of your life, so which areas of your life do you want to be more persistent in from this day forward? If you just cast your life forward one year from now, what is one thing you would love to accomplish over the next 12 months? If you are struggling with an answer to that question then consider it another way, what is it that you would love to accomplish if you had no fear of failing?

Really think about that for a minute. If you had no fear of failing then you would have no trouble stepping into action and persisting with it because you would remain feeling powerful in the face of whatever obstacles you came up against or whatever setbacks you experienced. If fear was simply an emotion you acknowledged rather than an emotion you succumbed to, just imagine what extraordinary accomplishments you could achieve! It's mind boggling!

You are uniquely positioned to do something truly extraordinary if you are willing to persist. After all, if you don't do it, who will? And if not now, then when? Spending your life in a perpetual mode of "risk avoidance" gives you Buckley's chance (Aussie lingo for "no chance") of ever being able to enjoy the rich sense of fulfillment that comes from putting yourself fully 100% out there in your life. We only become brave by doing brave acts and so it is that you are capable of far more than you think you are—both in the size of the risks that you are taking in your life and in your ability to deal with the challenges they pose.

People who are playing small, tip-toeing their way timidly through lives of mediocrity, experience few setbacks since logic would dictate that you cannot be *set back* unless you are first endeavoring to move forward. Your willingness to find the guts to persevere will set you apart from the ordinary and allow you to become and to accomplish the *extra-ordinary.*

This is what, at its core, courage is all about—feeling your fear fully and yet still putting down this book and taking whatever action is required to advance in the direction of your dreams. The rewards that await you when you do will be worth every ounce of perspiration. For you will come to find in yourself strength and determination you would never have known otherwise. That, my friend, makes it worth persevering!

Chapter 9
The Courage to Say No

We are not only responsible for what we say yes to in life, but also what we say no to.

Today more than ever we need courage to say "no," because today, more than ever, we have so many things we can say yes to. We live in an unprecedented era of choice—from the type of milk we buy to which TV channel we watch to which contraception we use to where we vacation to which career we pursue. There are so many choices we take for granted today that our parents, much less our grandparents, never had. Life was simpler then. Milk was milk. If you were a woman, you became a teacher or a nurse, and when you had children, you stayed home. The term "house husband" had yet to be coined.

But hand in hand with the higher quality of life we enjoy comes increased responsibility to make wise choices. Though some choices don't matter much, other choices matter greatly—choices that impact who you are being in the world and what you are doing each day with your time, your energy and your talents. The challenge is determining which choices you really want to say *Yes!* so that you can find the guts to say *No!* to the rest. You see, you have the time and energy you need to pursue the goals and dreams that inspire you, but you will only find them when you find the courage to say no.

Why No Can Be So Hard

The innate desire in all human beings to seek pleasure and avoid pain can make it bloody tough going to say no. Why? Because it will require giving up an opportunity to enjoy the immediate gratification, the pleasure, that a yes will bring—at least in the short term which is where most people's sights are generally focused. With a yes you get a hit of immediate people pleasing gratification that comes with being regarded as a team player, agreeable, helpful, likeable, dependable, enthusiastic, eager, willing, participative, sociable, indispensable... and the list goes on! I don't know about you, but I sure like to be thought of that way. Who doesn't?!

Of course, there is nothing inherently wrong with human desire except for when the occasion arises that our deepest fulfillment and happiness would ultimately be better served by saying no, and we can't bring ourselves to forfeit the immediate pleasure or take on the immediate pain that comes with saying yes. Little wonder the yes slips off your tongue before you even have time to fully process what you are committing yourself to!

The higher the stakes and the bigger the consequences of your choices, the more difficult again it is to muster up the guts to say no since it costs you even more to do so. That is, the more discomfort you may have to endure and the more pleasure you may have to forego—in security, in the comfort of the familiar and in that which gratifies your ego but not your spirit. Whether it be to change career, forego a business opportunity or end a relationship, what you have to give up in immediate pleasure, can make it very challenging to say no and requires you to dig even deeper to find the courage you need to do what is right for you.

No Is Not a Dirty Word: How Not Saying It Can Cost You!

If you've been treating no as though it was a dirty word and failing to say it to the things that are not aligned with your deepest values and greatest aspirations, then it has probably had a profound effect on your life...profoundly negative! It's therefore important for you to appreciate just how dearly it is costing you when you fail to be vigilant about what you say yes to, either explicitly or implicitly. By implicitly I am referring to those occasions when you never verbally say yes, but find yourself committed anyway because you never said no! Not finding the guts to say no can land you with a calendar overflowing with commitments to people and activities that don't truly enrich your life and leave you feeling stressed, uninspired, run down, unfulfilled, resigned, exhausted and incapable of enjoying your life fully. Only by getting present to the *why* behind the "no" will you be able to find the courage you need when the moment arrives for you to make a stand for what you want to say Yes! to in your life. So as you read through the following few pages think about how your reluctance to say no is impacting you.

Inability to Accomplish Great Things

There will never be a shortage of good things to do with your time each day. Whilst they may bring you a nice measure of admiration, appreciation and perhaps even a good deal of compensation, they will not necessarily provide you with a truly *great* sense of fulfillment or be deeply meaningful to you. In fact, they may even lead you down a path to discontentment and disillusionment. Many people spend their entire lives working hard day in day out only to arrive in the twilight of their lives and find themselves at a destination they never wanted. It is as though they were on a train heading 100 miles per hour and they either never lifted up their head long enough to notice they were on the wrong train, or they did make that realization, but it just seemed too hard to jump off. Besides, everyone else on their train seemed to think it was a pretty good train to be on.

> "He who lets the small things bind him, leaves the great undone behind him."
> –Unknown.

Sometimes accomplishing something truly great—whatever "great" is for you—requires taking a brave leap off the good train you're riding to find an ever better one. It takes guts to say no to the good to make room for the great, but no more guts than what you have. My friend Andy Larkey demonstrated exactly this kind of boldness. Living in Sydney, Australia, Andy had a very successful and prosperous career working for a large retail company. He and his wife Sue had three young children, and his life was going along really well. But Andy had always had a lot of entrepreneurial ideas about things he felt would be great to manufacture and market. The problem was that with his full-time job, he did not have the time to focus on getting any of his ideas from his head onto the retail shelf. He felt frustrated about this situation and wrestled with the idea of leaving his corporate job, with all its perks, promise of advancement and high-profile positions. Ultimately, he made the bold decision to resign from his job and focus on one of his product ideas, a vitamin enriched drink for dogs. To many people, Andy was completely nuts. I mean what kind of guy—with a wife and three children—quits his secure top-paying corporate job to try his hand at marketing a dog drink? Within two years of leaving the security of his six figure salary, Andy had succeeded in getting his dog drink onto store shelves in Australia, the U.S.A. and Japan. Had Andy never had the courage to say no to something very good, he would never have been able to have accomplished something even better.

And do you remember Darrell Wade who co-founded the adventure company Intrepid? Upon returning to Australia after his year traveling through Africa, his former boss offered him a job with a salary that took him seven years to match going his own way with Intrepid. If Darrell had been happy to settle for the "good" job, he'd have never created the extraordinary company he did with his business partner.

Good is always the enemy of great. This is why finding the courage to forego something that is good is a prerequisite to achieve something truly great. Christine provides another great example of this in action. In her early 40's Christine was feeling frustrated and dissatisfied with her life even though she felt blessed to have a loving and successful husband and three healthy children. Christine was committed to being a great mom, wife and active member of her community, but said she felt like "something" was missing. Though she wasn't sure what this "something" was, she felt guilty for feeling this way since she had no good reason for being discontented with her very comfortable life. After some probing (and doing the Dream Board exercise in Chapter 4), it emerged Christine had always wanted to write children's stories (she had been a kindergarten teacher prior to having her first child). The problem was that she had too many commitments to do anything about it. She explained to me how all this came to pass. When her son was first born she got very involved in the local early childhood association and ended up becoming a key member on their board. Then along came a second child and, eventually, a third. By this time, she was on the committee of two different PTOs, involved in the community outreach program at her local YMCA, still active in the church pre-school her six-year-old had left the year before, and actively involved in her church. She struggled with what she should do because all these things were "really worthwhile" activities she felt she should support, and she felt very guilty at pulling out of any one of them. Yes, even the church pre-school her youngest child no longer attended! "After all," she added, "you can't have or do too much of a good thing can you?" Rather than agree I responded, "Could all of these good things be filling up your calendar to the point that you aren't able to spend time on really great things that truly inspire you?" This opened up a dialogue that led Christine to gradually shift her perspective. She decided too many good things could become a "not so good" thing if they were keeping her so busy that she was unable to create the space to think about what would allow her to feel truly fulfilled and to pursue that instead. She came up with a goal of writing and publishing her first children's book in one year. During our following coaching session, we explored *what* Christine could say no to in order to make time to focus on her writing whilst also spending more quality time really being present with her husband and children (as distinct from distracted and pre-occupied with "to do" lists).

That was 2 years ago, and as I write Christine is now working on her second children's book which will be part of a series. Not only is there no longer anything "missing"' in her life, but she is also enjoying a far richer relationship with her husband and children. Relationships with those who mean the most to you are often the first casualty when we over-use yes. Those people who you really want to have the best of you—in terms of time, attention, energy, intimacy, affection—too often get the worst of you—tiredness, impatience, crabbiness and an inability to be present to them long enough to understand the issues going on in their life.

The reality is that achieving something great requires focus. In all my travels around the globe, I have yet to meet someone who has accomplished anything truly great—whether in business, sports, academia, politics, humanitarian work or in raising wonderful children—without dedicating a lot of time and energy toward that particular endeavor and foregoing opportunities along the way to do many other "good" things. Of course it may not have required 100% of their focus 100% of the time, but it did require more than 1% of their focus 1% of the time. For instance, they were not trying to raise their family, run a business, train for a marathon, campaign for political office, coach their son's soccer team, write a book, finish their MBA, and train for their pilot's license whilst maintaining a busy social life. Do I exaggerate here? Well, of course, I do, but only slightly. I regularly meet people who, when they tell me what they are doing proceed to reel off a list of things as long as their arm which leaves me feeling not only exhausted, but wondering how they can still remember their name. It is this lack of "no" power that led me to write this chapter. Most of them are saying yes to so many things, often "good" things, that they are physically, emotionally and mentally incapable of a) doing any of them particularly well, b) enjoying any of them much at all, or c) doing any one fabulous "light their lights up" *great* thing!

In my own life I find that I have to regularly say no to things which I'd quite like to say yes simply because if I don't, I will not be able to accomplish the things that inspire me most deeply (such as writing this book!). I don't enjoy saying no—whether it is to join a friend for coffee (because I know it will eat away a good part of my morning), to take up tennis or golf (which will take up even more of my time), or to take on a new client who has contacted me to coach them. Of course, sometimes it is more difficult to say no than at other times, but I am getting more comfortable with it as I've learned from hard experience that when I say yes to something that isn't aligned with my greatest priorities—largely centered around my family and my work—I end up with this awful gnawing feeling inside me. I know it is the voice of my true self giving me a nudge, because my yes has brought disharmony between my values and actions and taken me off the path of integrity.

People in the "helping professions" have perhaps the toughest time when it comes to saying no. Whether people in the medical profession or those working in social welfare for under-resourced government and not-for-profit agencies, they know that if they decline a request to help someone that the consequences can be very serious to the point of life and death. Not surprisingly, those in the position to help often end up completely burnt out and incapable of helping anyone at all. It is for this very reason that they have even more responsibility to say no on occasion.

Marsha, a pediatrician in her early thirties, had two partners in a busy suburban pediatric medical practice. Marsha loved her work but increasingly found the demands taking over her life. Families of children she cared for didn't hesitate to call her at home night or day to ask for advice on a sick child. After several years of very long hours and too little rest, Marsha became chronically exhausted and developed pneumonia. In her busyness to look after everyone else, she failed to get enough rest. By the time she did finally pay attention to herself, she ended up so sick that she had to be hospitalized for a week and take another two weeks off work to recuperate (doctor's orders!). It was at this point she contacted me for coaching.

During our initial conversation Marsha shared how hard she found it to pull back at work, to delegate and to create boundaries with her patients and their families. However during our conversation she began to realize that if she ever wanted to have the full life she dreamed of (which consisted of having children herself), she had to make some changes. She decided to recruit an additional partner for the practice, cut back her schedule and introduce a new policy for after-hours attention that included a fee for this service. Sure, she was no longer earning as much as she had in the past and a few families got their nose a bit out of joint, but her scare with pneumonia had been her wakeup call. If she kept going the way she was she would end up even more seriously ill and of little use to anyone!

Ultimately, you can't give away what you don't have, so if you are someone who wants to be great at helping other people, you must first learn how to say no and look after yourself first!

Lack of Personal Boundaries

Marsha is a good example of someone whose unwillingness to say no led to a complete breakdown in personal boundaries. But it doesn't only happen to doctors, it happens to anyone who likes to help others or who simply finds it easier (and often less hassle) to put other people's needs ahead of their own. The problem is that when this behavior goes on for an extended period of time, people grow accustomed to your being at their beck and call 24/7. If you have been disregarding your own needs for a long time, you may well have unwittingly taught others to take you for granted. They may have become completely oblivious to the fact that you have any needs (as you may have become yourself). But no longer!

If you've been living with a lack of personal boundaries, then the time has arrived to start living life on your terms rather than on everyone else's. You don't have to slowly wean off all those who have grown dependent on you. Rather you can make the decision right now to draw a new line in the sand and reestablish your boundaries by simply saying, "I know I have done this for you in the past, but I'm no longer willing to do so. I hope you will understand."

Believe it or not, making a stand for yourself is not an act of selfishness, but an act of love, for in doing so you are empowering others to make a stand for themselves. It could be the most helpful thing you've done for a long time!

Lack of Life Balance

Failing to say no regularly enough can also cost you in your ability to enjoy a healthy sense of balance and inner wellbeing. As your life begins to move out of balance, your stress level can quickly sky rocket with the unfortunate effect of throwing you even further off balance. This can dramatically affect your overall sense of wellbeing—body, mind and spirit. You misplace your keys; you forget appointments and small silly things trigger you to "lose it."

Your energy wanes, your relationships suffer, you require more coffee to get through your day, you sleep less well and you catch every damned cold that comes within a 10 mile radius of you. Aahhh… the joys of an unbalanced life.

Rena, a human resources manager, was working on average 60 hours a week when I began working with her. She also had two young children who she often didn't see for days at a time since she left for work before they got up and returned home after they'd gone to bed. She said she felt like she was constantly on the brink of bursting into tears and wondered if I could help her "get it together." Early in our conversation, Rena confessed that she was "hopeless" at saying no to people. Being in a service provider role, she said she felt it was really important that people know they could come to her for support at work and that she be highly responsive to them. After talking some more, it emerged that Rena never said no to anyone for anything in any area of her life (with the exception of her husband and children). Given how free she was with saying yes, it was little wonder that she was completely strung out and heading fast toward completely falling off the rails. By helping Rena become aware of the cost she was paying and would continue to pay if she kept saying yes to everything that came her way, she became willing to do the work required to find the courage to start saying no more often.

Though we hear a lot of talk about having a perfectly balanced life, the truth is that the nature of balance is so dynamic it makes perfect balance illusive. Think of the circus performer up on the tightrope with the long balance beam in his arms that is moving slowly up and down on each side. Somewhere between the top and bottom of each alternating movement he momentarily strikes perfect balance. But no sooner does he achieve perfect balance than he's moving away from it again, ready to adjust his beam the

By aligning what you commit to with what you're most committed to, balance will naturally work itself out.

other way…and on it goes. So it is in your life. Nothing stays the same for very long. You are always either moving toward or away from balance. Whenever you think you've got it worked out (if you ever do), something happens and poof—you get a promotion, your spouse takes a job that requires more travel or relocation, your child takes up a new sport, a parent gets sick, a colleague quits leaving you their workload—and you're moving away from balance again.

Just as life is ever changing so too are the things you need to be saying no to if you want to enjoy a balanced life. By aligning what you commit to with what you're *most* committed to balance will work itself out. Finding the courage to say no can restore your sense of balance so you can move forward more purposefully and effectively and take on your everyday challenges with less stress and more ease.

Courage Blockers That Keep You from Saying No

Two key courage blockers that can prevent you from finding the courage to say no are:

1. Lack of clarity about what you want to say yes to
2. "Shoulding" on yourself

1. Lack of clarity about what you want to say YES to.

If you think about it from a logical perspective, there are 24 hours in the day and, every time you say yes to one thing you are, by default, leaving less time and energy available for other things. If you haven't got clarity about what you want to say yes to, then, without

> *The greatest challenge to finding the courage to say no is first being clear about what it is you most want to say yes to.*

ever consciously deciding to, you can find yourself. Becoming clear about what it is you are *most* passionate and value *most* dearly will provide you with a compass to guide your choices and commitments.

Exercise 9.1: Prioritize on Paper

One technique to help you get clear on what you are most committed to is simply to write it down. In your journal write down what you *most* want to have in your life in each of the following areas. If nothing comes to mind in any of these areas, then just skip them. After all, this is about what you want, not what you think you *should* want.

- Health and Wellbeing
- Financial Position and Future Security
- Life Balance
- Family Life /Children
- Relationship with Spouse
- Social life
- Recreation/Travel
- Career or Business Success/Work Satisfaction
- Spirituality
- Direction of Your Future
- Community
- Education/Skill Set

2. "Shoulding" on Yourself

Dr. Fritz Perls, a renowned psychologist and the founder of Gestalt Therapy, first coined the term living a "shouldie life" to describe people whose key decision making criteria was based on what they felt they *should* do (reflecting the real or perceived opinions of those in their environment) rather than what they really *wanted* to do. Since "shoulds" are pervasive courage inhibitors and can stifle your no before it ever gets out your mouth, the key is to pay attention to your private conversations and when you hear a "should" rear its people-pleasing, approval-seeking head, dong it back into its box (metaphorically speaking that is). Alternately, if that sounds a tad too violent for you, then say what you are thinking aloud, but instead of saying *should* replace it with the word *could*. Doing this will shift how you feel about whatever commitment it is you are struggling with as the word "could" carries with it the implication that neither one option nor another is better or worse—they are just different ways you can choose to go.

Don't should on yourself and don't let others should on you.

Just like Christine who had a lot of "shoulds" driving all her commitments, sometimes I too find myself beginning to fall into the

"Should Trap." For instance, one of my children's teachers sent an email out to all the parents asking for volunteers for a school event that would take up a half day. Now, being involved at my children's school is important to me so my initial thought was that I *should* volunteer (particularly after my neighbor had just come by and shared with me how she is at the school nearly everyday helping out with something). However, before I hit "reply," I did this exercise saying to myself aloud, "I *could* volunteer for this event or I *could* spend that morning working on my book." Doing this immediately lifted a cloud of guilt about being a slack mum and allowed me the freedom to spend that time on something I wanted to do even more. Saying it out loud also helped me to realize how silly it was to think that being a good mother should mean *always* saying yes when asked to volunteer and to find the courage to say no on this occasion. One of my favorite phrases that I like to say to myself whenever I hear myself uttering that "sh" word is, "Don't *should* on yourself and don't let others *should* on you either!"

Exercise 9.2: Escaping the "Should Trap"

1. In your journal, write down all the "shoulds" that come into your head that are preventing you from taking the action needed to pursue your goals. *Here are* a few "shoulds" I've heard from people in just the last week alone:

- *"I really should join the schools fundraising committee."*
- *"I really should join my family business like everyone expects."*
- *"I really should go back to work after the baby is born."*
- *"I really should stay at this company because the money is really good and the job's secure."*
- *"I really should invite over the neighbors over for dinner on the weekend."*

As you read each of these "shoulds," ask yourself, "Who says so?" What great authority says you should do any of these things?

2. Now rewrite each of the statements you've just written but replace the word *should* with *could*, and then finish the statement with another option that you could also take.

For instance:

- *I could join the school fundraising committee, or I could spend that time with my family.*

- *I could join my family's business, or I could pursue a career in environmental law.*
- *I could go back to work after the baby's born, or I could take an extra six months off and then look into going back to work on a part-time basis.*
- *I could have the neighbors over for dinner this Saturday, or I could have a quiet evening at home with my family, watch a movie and order take-away.*

3. Now that you've taken the "should" out of your private conversation, instead of asking yourself, "What *should I* do?" ask yourself, "What do I really *want* to do?"

For instance, "I could join my family business or I could decide to go off and pursue a career in environmental law. What I *really want* to do is…"

Opportunities for Saying No

Throughout your life you are faced with countless choices providing you with the opportunity to say no—whether explicitly through your words or implicitly through your actions. The biggest choices you face in life—those that challenge your integrity at the deepest level—often require less in the way of words than they do in action. These choices—whether ethical, moral or otherwise—call on you to reflect deeply on what it is you value most in your life—in your career, your relationships, your family, your community or your lifestyle in general.

It is not my intention in this book to advise you on the best way to say no in relation to the big decisions you may be facing—whether how to proceed with leaving your job or ending a relationship. There are many highly talented and experienced professionals with expertise in such matters. However, I can tell you that you have within you the wisdom you need to figure it out (which may include seeking professional guidance), and the courage to make that bold leap from the speeding train you are on to one that may well take you in a very different direction.

However, when it comes to the everyday choices I do have some suggestions and strategies that can help you manage your commitments more effectively and become more competent and confident in responding with a gracious no when it serves you best to do so. But given that no is only one of four ways you can respond to any request or offer it's important to first ask yourself the following questions:

1. Is it aligned with the things that are *most* important to me and will it take me closer *toward* or further *away* from what I value *most* in my life?
2. Do I have the time available to fulfill this commitment?
3. What impact will making this commitment have on my other commitments? What will I not be able to do because I'm doing this instead?

By answering these questions as honestly as you can you will know whether or not you need to find the courage to say no or whether you'd be better off responding another way.

Three Alternatives to No

1. "Yes!"—A Wonderful Word When Your Reasons Are Right

Saying yes to one thing (and by default no to another) is serving you only if you do so for the right reasons. Right reasons stem from a commitment to living with integrity and doing what you are most committed to; wrong reasons are ones which are driven by a fear of discomfort, be it failing to please others or leaving the security of your comfort zone. So, if after getting really clear on your priorities and answering the questions above honestly, you still want to say yes, then great—go for it!

However, as a matter of integrity only say yes when you know you have the necessary resources to fulfill your commitment (i.e., time, energy, money, skill or whatever is required). If you are continually saying yes to things and then either not getting them done properly or on time (or at all!), then you run the risk of becoming someone people will regard as unreliable whilst diminishing your own sense of integrity in the process. Therefore, before you say yes to something, be sure you know exactly *what* you are saying yes to and *when* you have to show up or have it done by. If there is a gap in assumptions of what has to be done and when it has to be done it creates fertile ground for unmet expectations that often result in broken trust, tension, disappointment and conflict.

So often clients will share with me a frustration with a colleague who they describe as "unreliable." Often when we explore the situation we find that the real problem is a lack of clear understanding about exactly what was supposed to be done and exactly when it was supposed to be done by. That is, there are no clear and mutually understood conditions of satisfaction.

Recently, I asked my seven year old daughter to clean her room. She came back to me a half hour later and told me she'd done as I'd asked. A while later I was passing by her room and noticed a pile of toys jammed under her bed and some dirty clothes lying on the floor near her dirty clothes basket. When I asked her about this she responded by saying "but I put all my clean clothes away". For her, tidying her room meant putting away her clean clothes, pushing her toys under her bed and throwing her dirty clothes in the corner. For me, well…something else. Only by sitting down with her and showing her what I meant by a tidy room will she ever be able to fulfill my request to my satisfaction.

Just think yourself when you last felt frustrated with someone and ask yourself where might there have been a lack of shared understanding about exactly what it was you expected from them, *or* what they expected from you. Where might you or they have made an incorrect assumption about *what* needed to be done, or *how* it needed to be done or *when* it needed to be done?

2. Negotiate

A second option you have when someone asks something of you is to negotiate. Negotiation is the best option when, having given thought to what your priorities are, you want to make a commitment (to help, participate, get together, contribute or whatever) to something but you are either a) not prepared, or b) not able to fulfill the commitment on the terms indicated or implied in the request or offer. When this situation arises you can *negotiate* on:

    a) the "what"—what you are committing to do (e.g., "I can't organize all the catering, but I'd be happy to look after beverages." "I won't be able to write the whole newsletter, but I would be happy to write a column.")

    b) the "when"—when you can do it, or by when it has to be done (e.g., "I can't do the report by Monday, but I can complete it by Friday." "I won't be able to help out all day, but I could do the morning.")

    c) a combination of the "what" and "when" (e.g., "I can't get over this weekend to help you with your entire business plan, but I can come over one evening early next week to help with the financials." "I can't take over your eight clients by the end of next week, but I can take on four by the end of the month.")

Obviously, in a situation where differing levels of authority are involved, you may not be in a position to negotiate (e.g., Your boss wants you to have a report done by Friday. Period!) However, you can at least negotiate on other commitments you may have (e.g. "Sure I can get the report done by Friday, but it will mean having to put back one of the other projects I was working on until early next week.") At the very least, you can let them know what the impact will be on you to take on this additional commitment (e.g. "Sure, I can get this done by Friday, but it will mean working until midnight the rest of the week to do so.")

3. Offer to Reply Later

Sometimes the best option is to offer to get back to someone with your reply at a later time or date. Responding with something like, "You know, I'm not sure if I can do that, but I will get back to you later today and let you know," can be useful in two ways:

- It gives you time to assess your ability to fulfill the commitment (that is, you may need to check your diary and see how much else you or those you can delegate to have on during that period).
- If you really want to say no but feel pressured to respond with

a yes on the spot, it can also buy you the time you need to muster up your courage and rehearse your gracious but firm no before getting back to them.

Rena, the overworked, overstressed and out-of-balance, working mom I introduced to you earlier, found this technique particularly helpful as she began to tighten up on her commitments. Having been a habitual "yes person" as long as she could remember, she found it really difficult in the beginning saying no to the many requests and offers that came her way. So what she did whenever her resolve was weak was to offer to get back to the person at a set time with her answer. As she became more comfortable saying no she began to rely on this strategy less. It was helpful in the beginning, because it gave her an opportunity to find the resolve she needed to say no in a gracious but firm way.

Putting No to Work

No is the fourth way that you can respond to an offer or request. Often we veer away from no because, although it's just a little word, it can have a lot of punch and we're afraid our no, however gently we try to deliver it, will not land well on those we say it to. Many people find saying no the most difficult response of all because they don't want to hurt or damage their relationship with the other person. They don't want to disappoint the other person, convey that they don't value the relationship as much as the other person does or limit future opportunities. And even if they don't care about the relationship that much, they still don't want to cause offense or hurt.

Since no is usually not the response the other person is looking for, you need to give real thought up front (and perhaps even some time to practice and rehearse) to how you will go about delivering it. You may have heard people say that we should never feel the need to explain ourselves if we don't want to do something someone asks of us (with the exception of a boss or a client), and should feel just fine responding with a simple "No thank you." Of course, whilst I believe that you don't necessarily need to *justify* your no, *explaining* your no is a very different thing. Why? Because explaining why you are saying no helps to take care of the other person in ways that a straight out no does not.

Using "However" to Distinguish the Person from the Commitment

One way to help you say no more graciously and comfortably is by using the word "however" to distinguish between the person making the request or offer and the thing they are making the request or offer about. In short, you can say no to what is being asked of you without saying no to the person.

Naomi was 27 when she came to me for coaching (as a birthday gift from her mother), because she wanted to return to college to get her Masters degree. After a few sessions, she had stepped into action and begun organizing her life around a return to full-time study. Six months later, Naomi gave me a call because she had a problem she was "stuck" about and wondered if I could help. A girlfriend of hers, Steff, wanted Naomi to join her for a girls weekend in Cancun and was giving her a hard time about her reluctance to commit to joining them. Naomi felt pressured to say yes because she valued the friendship and didn't want to disappoint Steff. However, she knew that her workload between study and her part-time job would be intense during the period her friend wanted her to go away and that her budget wouldn't extend as far as it used to. Using the word "however," Naomi was able to respond to Steff in such a way that let her know how much she valued the friendship whilst still saying no to the trip away:

"Steff, I really value our friendship and would truly love to go away with you to Mexico, as I always have such a wonderful time when we do things together. However, I am going to be flat out with my study and work commitments and on top of that, I simply don't have the discretionary money I used to have prior to going back to study to afford this trip."

I recently ran a work-life-balance workshop for a group of women business owners in which I spoke about the importance of saying no. Afterward, a woman called Patty came up to me to share a difficult situation she was facing. The lady who had been cleaning Patty's house every week for several years had invited her to her daughter's birthday party. Since Patty and she had developed a friendly relationship over that time, Patty knew it would mean a lot to her cleaning lady for her to attend. The problem was that after a long week in the office, Patty really did not want to spend half a day of her precious weekend crossing town to attend the birthday party. But she also didn't want to offend her housekeeper. Using the "however" approach, I suggested to Patty that she could respond to her housekeeper with something like this:

"I am so flattered that you would like me to come to your home to celebrate your daughter's birthday. You are such a wonderful housekeeper, and I really appreciate all the great work you do in my home each week. But, after a long week at work running my business, I really look forward to taking it easy on the weekend and doing as little as possible. So as much as I would like to come to share your daughter's celebration, I would like even more to stay home and tend to the things around the house I haven't had time to look after all week. I hope you understand and would certainly like to get a small gift for your daughter. What do you think she would like?"

> *"I don't know the key to success. But the key to failure is trying to please everyone."*
> —Bill Cosby

You will note that I haven't actually used the word however in this response. Instead I have used the phrase, "so as much as I would like to...". It really doesn't matter quite how you phrase your response as much as that you distinguish between the person and the request, offer or invitation they've made of you that you are declining.

Even if you really don't care for the relationship you have with the other person, you can still care about the person's dignity. Even a simple, "Thank you, but I'm unable to accept," or "Thank you, but that is not something I wish to do," is better than a flat out "No!"

Be Authentic & Offer an Alternative

If you are still struggling with how to say no to people who you fear will be disappointed in you or might think less of you, consider sharing your thoughts with them, in a kind way, that reflects your respect for them. You can also offer someone an alternative to what they are suggesting that will work better for you. In Naomi's example above, she was able to finish by saying, "But I would still really enjoy doing something with you a little closer to home. How about going to a movie together then out for dinner?"

Here are some other examples of ways you can implicitly say no, but which still show you care about the relationship:

- *"I'm flattered that you would like me to do that with/for you, but I won't be able to fit it in over the next week/month. Call me back in a month and I will see if I have time then."*
- *"I'm sorry that I won't be able to help you do x but if you like I could help you with…instead of…if that would still work for you."*
- *"Thanks for thinking of me. I know you really love this stuff and I feel kind of bad about this but it's just not my thing. Why don't we try to catch up for a coffee sometime soon though?"*

Dealing with the Fallout of No

Sometimes, despite your best efforts your response to people will leave them feeling disappointed, offended, resentful, jealous… even angry. When this happens, it is really important to keep in mind why you said no and not to beat up on yourself for being an awful person and causing them to feel badly. Often when people find themselves feeling disappointed or hurt by someone it's because they have had an expectation about how others are supposed to behave (e.g., "They should want to do this with me.") that is simply unreasonable or unrealistic. Their expectations have set them up for disappointment. But just as you have to take responsibility for how you respond when you find yourself feeling disappointed, so too must others. You can do your best to manage expectations and minimize offense, but you cannot be responsible for some else's thwarted expectations or disappointment. Perhaps they need to reflect on how realistic and fair their expectations were of you. At the end of the day, it can be quite unpleasant to think that you may cause someone to feel badly, but committing to something you aren't really committed to just to avoid disappointing someone may well be undermining your own sense of integrity. It can also be a sure recipe for later feeling resentful yourself.

I can't tell you how many people I have met who have shared with me how they had serious doubts about getting married but, because they didn't want to hurt their fiancé or deal with the ensuing fallout with family and friends, went ahead and walked down the aisle only to regret it profoundly for years (sometimes decades) to come. There's no doubt there would have been hurt and suffering had they called off their wedding (some have shared how they tried but, as the fallout began to escalate they caved in putting it down to "pre-wedding jitters"), but the hurt and suffering that was experienced in the years that followed was beyond anything they could ever have imagined at the time. The point: "No" can be extremely difficult. "No" can cause others hurt and angst and suffering. But sometimes not saying "no"—not changing direction —can cause infinitely more. Trust your gut. Don't ignore your instincts. Don't cave. Don't sell yourself out. As Shakespeare said, "To thine own self be true!"

When You Slip Up

When you do slip up and find a 'yes' escaping out of your mouth when inside your head a voice is screaming "NO!", try not to beat up on yourself with, "You bloody fool! Why didn't you say no for goodness sake? You gutless wonder!" This serves no positive purpose. So cut yourself some slack and realize that you are a fallible human being, one of many millions on the planet who have done the exact same thing. Alas, in life it happens to the best of us—including even yours truly who coaches people on how to say no!

After forgiving yourself for being human, what you do next depends on exactly how seriously you slipped. If

> *"Have the courage to say no. Have the courage to face the truth. Do the right thing because it is right. These are the magic keys to living your life with integrity."*
>
> −W. Clement Stone

it's just a minor slip up and you feel it's important to keep your promise and you can keep your promise (i.e., you have the time and ability), then don't whine about it, but take responsibility for your yes and get on with it in good spirit. You might also consider asking someone else to help you meet your commitments since if others are making a lot of requests of you, you need to be making a lot yourself. It can never hurt to ask. After all, they can only say no!

If on the other hand, your slip up has really violated the set of values you have for yourself, then you may be best served to "uncommit" yourself. This was the predicament that Amy found herself in. Amy owned a database management business and employed about fifteen full-time and several part-time employees. An active member of the local Chamber of Commerce, Amy was married to Damian, an accountant with whom she had two children who were involved in numerous sporting and extra-curricular activities. After meeting me at a Chamber luncheon, she asked me if I could help her manage her time more efficiently as she wasn't getting to spend as much time with her family as she wanted and there were a lot of things she wanted to do with her business that she wasn't getting around to. When we met for our first coaching session two weeks later, I was surprised to learn that, in the intervening two weeks, she had signed up to train for an Iron Man competition! I asked her whether or not the Iron Man was something that she really wanted to do given the time commitment it would take. Amy agreed that it was not really a top priority (she had achieved this goal of doing an Iron Man the previous year and had never felt inspired about doing more than one). However a month earlier one of her running friends had urged her to sign up again because she needed a training partner and, as Amy put it, "She's a good friend and a great training partner and I didn't have the guts to say no." But when we talked through the things she valued most, she realized that by committing to this friend she had actually undermined the integrity of her commitment to her husband, children and to her business. It became clear to her that she needed to "uncommit" herself. Although her friend was disappointed and she still felt bad about reneging on her commitment, she also felt a whole lot better for restoring alignment between what she was committed to and what she was committing to and with it, her integrity.

Whilst it may be very humbling for you to break your promise to someone, if it means compromising your values, then it is important that you do so. Just practice a little humility by contacting the person you made the commitment to, apologizing (and perhaps admitting your struggle with saying no) and asking if you would be able to "uncommit" yourself. If you are someone who is committed to being a person of your word, reneging on a commitment you have made will call for as much humility as courage. However, it may well be something that will serve you and those you love most well.

Will it be easy for you to say no from here on? *Easier* perhaps, but it may never be truly easy since living a courageous life is never about living an easy life. I mean if no rolled off the tongue as easily as yes then it wouldn't take courage in the first place and people would be managing their commitments with ease, passing up mediocre relationships, okay jobs and good opportunities so they could say yes to even better ones. The fact is, no matter what choices you make in life, there is always something you get and something you have to give up. Let's not pretend otherwise—there is a price tag to saying no. But whatever the price, however great the short-term discomfort, trust that if your no is making a stand for your greatest life then it will be well worth it in the long-term.

So as much as I'd like to tell you otherwise, there is no magic pill you can swallow or mystical formula you can apply that will suddenly enable you to be the most courageous and gracious "no giver" on the planet. It just doesn't work that way. It is more a case of gradually moving toward becoming more courageous and competent in responding with a gracious no, whilst gradually moving away from being a head- nodding, people-pleasing "yes person." As in every new skill or habit, sometimes it is two steps forward and one step back.

My hope is that your commitment to living a life that is meaningful and fulfilling will compel you to draw on your courage and say no as the need arises. It is my firm belief that you have it within you to do just that. And as you begin to say no to that which is not aligned with your deepest values and greatest aspirations, you will discover that you are capable of living a more rewarding and balanced life than you have up until now. But don't take my word for it. Before you sign up for something else or take another step in a direction that does not stir your spirit, take a long deep breath and connect with the power within you to start making new choices which take your life in the direction you *truly* want to travel.

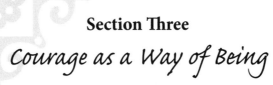

Section Three

Courage as a Way of Being

The Courage to Live with an Open Heart
The Courage to Let Go
The Courage to Be a Leader

"My life is my message."
–Mahatma Gandhi

Chapter 10
The Courage to Live with an Open Heart

"And what is as important as knowledge?" asked the mind.
"Caring and seeing with the heart," answered the soul.
—Author Unknown

Love. What a mighty word. Yet love is the essence of what it means to live with an open heart; indeed, love is the essence of what it means to be human. For love calls upon us to do more than "love thy neighbor as thyself." It calls upon us to open our heart fully to the experience of life itself—with all its uncertainty, its sorrow and its *heart ache*—and to feel its pain as deeply as its joy. For as much as we might want to experience only joy in life, like yin and yang, we cannot have one without the other.

Of the many virtues living with an open heart calls forth—compassion, patience, tolerance, forgiveness, generosity, kindness and many more—the first is courage. Why? Because in the words of Samuel Johnson, "Courage is the greatest of all virtues; because, unless a man has that virtue, he has no security for preserving any other." If it were easy

> *Whilst living a truly loving life is a challenge that human beings have long struggled with, it is a state of being we are called toward.*

to find the courage to live with an open heart, the world would be a fundamentally different place. Yet whilst living a truly loving life is a challenge that human beings have long struggled with, it is a state of being we are called toward. It takes courage to lower your defenses, to open your heart fully to life, to the people you share it with and to allow yourself to become vulnerable to the full spectrum of emotions a full life extracts.

But as scary as it may seem to you, you have all the courage you need to let down the draw bridge and rise to the challenge that opening your heart fully presents. However much pain you have experienced in the past and however high the walls you have erected around your heart to protect it from more, trust that all things are possible in matters of the heart. Indeed, there is no greater force than love to have on your side.

Choosing not to fully open your heart confines you to an experience of life that is desolate—in terms of richness, meaning and love—compared to what it could be. It means forgoing ever tasting the real sweetness of life that can only be savored by embracing all of life openheartedly. Yes, opening your heart to life may bring with it heartache, but not doing so starves the spirit and is the gravest fate of all. As the poet Kahlil Gibran wrote so beautifully, "Life without love is like a tree without blossoms or fruit."

The intention of this chapter is to grow your capacity for love in your life by helping you find the courage to become a warmer, more loving and open-hearted person. In that endeavor, this chapter will explore the three prime emotions which have the potential to undermine both your readiness and ability to open your heart fully—anger, fear and sadness. It will also provide you with ways to help you embrace those emotions more fully in your life and teach you how to express them constructively in ways that unleash you from any negative impact they may be having on you.

> *"The best and most beautiful things in the world cannot be seen, or even touched, they must be felt with the heart."*
> –Helen Keller

Unleashing Your Heart from Anger

If you read the paper or watch TV regularly, you will know that anger gets a lot of bad press these days. So before I go any further, I want to define what anger is and what it is not. Anger *is* an emotional response to a perceived injustice, either to us, or to someone else. Anger *is not* a bad or sinful emotion that comes from the devil which we should seek to avoid and which only bad, violent or unsavory people have. The fact is that throughout our lives we all experience anger whenever we perceive that either our freedom or dignity or someone else's freedom or dignity has been, or might be, violated in some way.

In itself, anger is neither good nor bad. It is a healthy human emotion that can serve a positive purpose since there are many things in the world which we are just and right to feel angry about. Knowing as I write this today (because an email I just received from World Vision tells me so) that fourteen million people in Africa will go to bed (*if* they have one) hungry tonight makes me feel angry. The fact that many people who have so much care so little about things like this makes me angry. However, this does not make me an "angry person" in the traditional sense of the word. Not at all. Rather responding to these situations with anger is a completely reasonable response because they are so unjust. The point here is that anger per se is not the issue. The real issue is how we channel our anger and whether or not that results in a constructive outcome that serves us and others *or* a destructive outcome that serves no one.

You only have to take a look around at some of the greatest changes made during the last century to see the constructive power anger can wield. I was very fortunate to be in Berlin in November 1990 to join in the first anniversary celebrations of the fall of the Berlin Wall. During the previous 40 years the people in West Germany and indeed in the free world had enjoyed the right to choose where they lived, what they did and what they said. As a result their society and economy had flourished. In the east, people had been deprived of such choices and, consequently, they had to pay a steep price.

Anger about the injustice and violation of human dignity has led to the end of many unjust regimes, systems, ideologies, cultural practices, and laws throughout history and will continue to do so. When harnessed in a positive way, anger can lead to great things that benefit many.

Problems do not arise because we have anger, they arises because our anger has us. Of course how each of us express our anger—whether through outward expressions of aggression or internal repression—differs. Whilst neither produces a positive outcome, I will be focusing on repressed anger because it can be so harmful, destructive and restrictive. Not just to the heart, but to life. The reason people repress their anger is because it makes them feel bad thinking about the circumstances that gave rise to their anger, so repression seems like the best and least painful path to take. And so, people end up carrying their anger around with them, often unconsciously, for many years and sometimes their entire life. Often, because they aren't talking about it, they live under the illusion that it doesn't exist. But instead of going away, it festers for lack of oxygen poisoning their relationships, contaminating their life and expressing itself in anti-social behavior, abusive and dysfunctional relationships, depression and addictive behaviors that diminish their physical, mental, emotional and spiritual wellbeing.

> *"If you don't have love in your heart, you have the worst kind of heart trouble."*
>
> –Bob Hope

The word disease broken down is *dis ease* which translates to a lack or *absence* of *ease*. Unresolved anger leads to a lack of ease within the heart which most of us know better as *heart disease*. Indeed many clinical studies have found the people who harbor anger are much more likely to develop heart disease. The Harvard University Gazette reported a study that the risk of heart attacks more than doubles (2.3 times) in the two hours following moderate to intense anger. Another study found that people are three times more likely to experience a heart attack within 5 years of the incident that gave rise to the emotion than those who responded to their anger in a healthy way. Basically, people who hold a lot of anger are far more prone to react negatively to life events. In response, their bodies release stress hormones that eventually lead to an elevation of something called C-reactive protein (or CRP) which is a marker for inflammation that is often elevated in disease processes, such as rheumatoid arthritis, infection or heart disease. In addition to the physiological impact anger causes through heart disease, it can also negatively impact your ability to enjoy healthy, happy and fruitful relationships with people at work and home. Needless to say, the cost of anger on your ability to enjoy life can be profound.

Interestingly enough, a clinical study at Stanford University found that when people merely visualized what it would be like to resolve an issue they were angry about, their stress levels dropped by 50%. If this is the result they got from just picturing in their mind's eye their life without the anger, then imagine the impact it would have on their life if they actually did get resolution and were able to forgive fully.

Releasing Anger through Forgiveness

In order to resolve your anger you must first own it. However, even just acknowledging a long held resentment or bitterness and its accompanying pain takes courage because it requires confronting an aspect of who you are that is not congruent with who you really want to be. This can be very painful because it often means opening the lid on the anger and allowing all the repressed anger to rise up to the surface. However, it is essential that you take full ownership of any resentment you've been carrying around and not suppress or discount it any longer. Otherwise, you will remain stuck in the same cycle of resentment that has been hindering your ability to build the open, respectful and loving kind of relationships with others—and with yourself—that you've been longing for.

After acknowledging the anger that has kept you shackled to the past, you need to connect with the sacred part within you to find the forgiveness to unleash your heart, and your life, from its confining grip. Forgiveness isn't an intellectual exercise but rather an emotional and spiritual one. Intellectually you may be able to see the logic around forgiveness, but real forgiveness takes more than just saying the words. Of course that's not as easy as it sounds. As much as you may like to feel forgiving, forgiving is the last thing you actually feel like doing.

Talking this over with my father recently, he shared with me how he has often needed to pray for the ability to forgive. While he has always intellectually understood the importance of forgiveness, on an emotional level there have been times he has struggled to find it in his heart to do so. Now if you ever met my dad, you would immediately know what a warm loving man he is and so I think it is fair to say that no matter how big-hearted a person you may be, forgiveness may not always come easily for you. So whether or not you are someone who prays, or even believes that there is anyone to pray to, you may still find it helpful to say a silent little prayer asking for help to forgive.

I do not mean to sound so overly grave and dire here, but I believe it is crucial that you be aware of how destructive anger can be and how profound the cost of not releasing it through the act of forgiveness. What I am sharing here is what speaks from my heart and so if this resonates within you, then that is because your heart also recognizes it as the truth and craves to be made complete again. Yes, your *heart*, and *not* your *head*, where your ego often reigns supreme and is far more concerned with proving your rightness (or superiority) and another's wrongness (or inferiority).

Your ego feeds on your anger, justifying your feeling of self-righteousness, moral superiority and that you are a victim. Your ego is not at all interested in letting go your anger because it gets such a tasty pay off from clinging to it, even if it is at the expense of your spirit's deepest longing to be loved and to give love in return. Where will your ego leave you? Where it may well have left you up until now…disconnected, isolated, bitter, resentful and, regardless of how many people you surround yourself with, feeling alone. Without forgiveness, your heart will remain isolated behind the bars you've put around it and your spirit will be weighed down so gravely that all those things which have the potential to lift your spirit will not be able overcome it. Most of all you will be unable to enjoy the fullness of love in your life that the sacred part of your being hungers for at the deepest level.

> *"The weak can never forgive. Forgiveness is the attribute of the strong."*
> —Mahatma Gandhi

When You Don't Believe Others Deserve Forgiveness

Anger predisposes us to want to punish someone or a group of "some ones." So if you are harboring anger or resentment, it's likely there is a voice in your head screaming at you right now "I'm not going to swallow this baloney about forgiveness. I was wronged. They should never have done what they did and they don't deserve my forgiveness. Not now, not ever!"

But it is not a question of deservingness. Perhaps *they* (whether one person or many) aren't deserving. Perhaps what *they* did was incredibly despicable and, even worse, perhaps *they* aren't even sorry! But that's the point exactly. Forgiveness is *not* about *them* or what *they* chose to do to you. It *is* about *you* and how *you* choose to deal with your anger right now and whether or not you continue to allow *them* to have power over *you*! For that is exactly what they have if you are allowing something they did, perhaps a long time ago, to impact the state of your heart and your happiness. You are suffering needlessly. You had to endure pain once, but you do not have to relive it in your relationships and your life today. That is 100% your choice. I once heard someone describe anger as swallowing a bottle of poison and waiting for the other person to die. The problem is the other person doesn't die (well not on your timeline anyway) but you do. By holding onto anger you punish yourself far more than you punish anyone else.

This was the predicament Leanne faced. Although she wanted to be a loving person and enjoy harmonious and loving relationships, her anger was poisoning them and causing her to react to the world and those she cared for most, in hostile and aggressive ways. As a young teenager, Leanne's parents divorced and within a year her mother had remarried. Leanne felt that her mother was now more interested in her new husband than she was in her teenage daughter. Leanne soon found herself in with the "wrong crowd." Her dad had moved to another town about a half hour away, and although she knew he cared about her, he wasn't around much and she felt largely disconnected from him. At 15 she found herself pregnant. When she finally told her mother, she insisted that Leanne have an abortion. Leanne didn't feel she had much choice at the time and didn't question that this was the best thing to do. Eventually she finished high school and went on to college. By the time she had graduated college, she had built up a lot of anger and resentment toward her mother who she felt had largely abandoned her through her teenage years and hadn't been there when she really needed her most. But Leanne didn't own her anger. Rather she said outwardly that, "I've dealt with it. My mom is an emotional basket case who I know I can never depend on. But I love her anyway." Leanne's actions certainly didn't reflect love.

When I met Leanne she was in her 40's, in her second marriage, raising two teenage children from her first, and living a comfortable suburban life. Although Leanne was a friendly outgoing woman, she was also very highly strung and would fly off the handle at the slightest provocation. It was from pressure from her husband that she came to speak to me because he said that he had had enough of her being so controlling and aggressive. Indeed by her language and the way she spoke about her marriage, her children and her life in general, I felt that her friendliness was a thin veil for her unresolved and very deep-seated hostility. Even the way she moved radiated her hostility. Her body and posture reflected her, "Don't mess with me," attitude. As we began to work together, it became apparent to me that Leanne was very attached to her anger and to the feelings of self-righteousness and victim hood she had in regards to her relationship with her mother. The question was whether she was more committed to her anger or to her marriage, which it was undermining. It was my belief that only through owning her anger and forgiving her mother would Leanne be able to move away from her very defensive, controlling and hostile way of being and move toward one that was more open, loving and tolerant.

But anger doesn't impact everyone in the same way. For instance, when I met Carlos I found him to be a soft-spoken, apprehensive and quite timid man. In his mid-thirties, Carlos was single after many ill-fated relationships and just getting by in his work as an automotive technician. He was going through a period of deep soul searching. His father had abandoned him and his four older siblings, when he was only six months old. His mother later told him that his father had hit him with a six-pack of beer. That had been the last straw for her. She packed her husband's belongings and told him to get out and not come back until he was sober. She thought losing his kids, whom she knew he cared for deeply despite his abusive behavior, would be incentive enough to get him off the grog (an Australian term for alcohol). She thought wrong. Carlos and his four siblings grew up without any father from that day on. Now a grown man, Carlos knew that the anger he carried in his heart for so long about what his father had done not only to him, but to his mother and siblings, was preventing him from finding happiness in his own life.

Carlos made the decision to seek his father out (though he wasn't sure if he was even still alive) and tell him that he had forgiven him. Without too much trouble, he was able to track him down to a small but neat house located only a few miles from where he lived himself. He was surprised he'd never run into him. He recounted that when he met him he discovered that his father had given up drinking 16 years earlier and in that time had managed to pick his life up a little and earn enough money in his trade as a carpenter to buy his house and get by. Carlos told him that

> *However deep your bitterness, you have the ability to forgive, to open your heart and to turn the wounds on your heart into badges of honor.*

he forgave him and asked his father to forgive him for the anger he had carried around in his heart toward him for so long. His father's eyes watered. He was unable to speak. Several minutes passed in silence before he thanked his son for finding him, but he really didn't think there was anything he had to forgive him for because he didn't blame his son for feeling angry. He told him that that he had never tried to contact his wife or children, even after he had given up drinking, because he had felt ashamed about all the hurt he had inflicted on them and felt undeserving of their forgiveness or of happiness for himself.

Carlos's act of forgiveness began a beautiful healing for both of them. His father was slowly able find the peace that he had long ago lost and Carlos felt as though a huge weight had been lifted from his heart. In fact, as strange as this may sound, afterward he even walked as though he had a weight literally taken off his chest and suddenly looked inches taller than the Carlos I'd first met whose physical stance has been stooped as though carrying a heavy burden.

What Carlos did took tremendous courage and great love—not necessarily for his father (although that did develop over time), but for himself. Up until the day that Carlos sought out his father, he felt as though he was incapable of forgiveness; that he just didn't have it in him. But the truth was he did. I would like to say that Leanne found the same forgiveness in her heart also but sadly, I cannot. Leanne decided to discontinue coaching after a few sessions (perhaps enough to appease her husband) assuring me that her marriage was doing "just fine" and that she really was "over that issue with my mom." But my intuition tells me otherwise, and it is my fear that the issues which have harmed and limited her relationships up until now will continue to do so. Ultimately, it has and will continue to be her choice whether or not to address the anger in her heart. Sometimes people have so much invested in their anger and the stories which support it that they are unwilling to let it go.

What about you? Is there something weighing on your heart? If so, then know that you, like Carlos, have the ability to forgive whomever you feel resentful toward, to live with an open heart and to turn the wounds on your heart into badges of honor. As you bravely open your heart and let the oxygen into the wounds that have been festering for so long, it will extend what is possible for you in every arena of your life, and enlarge your capacity to give and receive love beyond what you could ever have previously imagined.

Exercise 10.1: Releasing Anger through Forgiveness

In your journal write down the name or names of any people you feel angry and resentful toward. Even if you like to think you are "over it" or "over them," if their face flashes into your head then just write their name down anyway. (Those faces don't flash into your mind for no reason. I promise!)

If you are willing to offload your anger and forgive these people and in so doing, lighten the load on your heart, then make a decision about whether you wish to do this in person or through a letter.

Speaking to someone in person (if that is possible) can be extremely powerful and very healing, particularly if you are still in a relationship with that person (i.e., your mother, father, former spouse or child). What you say is up to you but remember, it's not about justifying your anger but letting it go.

Obviously you don't always have the choice of speaking to someone in person because they are either no longer alive, you do not know where they live or because you really just don't want to be in contact with them. That's okay. Even just the process of putting pen to paper and writing a letter can be a powerful way of releasing years of hurt, resentment and pain. It's completely up to you what you do with this letter (you may like to send it out to sea in a bottle or burn it!) and it's up to you what you say in it. However, I've drafted a sample for you that may help you in figuring out what you want to say.

> *I wish to forgive you. From today onward, I am leaving the past in the past and making a new choice for myself. A choice to give up the resentment and anger that has weighed me down for so long. For too long. Beginning right now, I am starting a new chapter in my life that is unencumbered by the bitterness I have felt toward you. A chapter in which I am fully available to give and receive love and deeply grateful for the opportunity to create for myself a life that is filled with possibility for what I can do and who I can become.*

As I said, what you say is up to you, the main thing is that you release your anger to make way for the love you wish to have in your life.

Forgiveness Is Not Always a One-off Event

The deeper the wound the longer it can take to heal. So as you begin to walk down the path of forgiveness, be patient with yourself when you notice feelings of resentment and anger resurface. It may be that the act of forgiveness will be your greatest life's work which you will continue working toward until your last breath. If that is what is required, so be it. Don't judge it as right or wrong, just be with it. So long as keep your heart open and pointed toward the light you will gradually move toward forgiveness on deeper and deeper levels. The most important thing is to be big enough and brave enough to begin, since in beginning to forgive you are expressing your commitment to releasing the past and enlarging the possibilities for love and for life that exist for you in the future.

I can vividly recall the day I found myself with a gun pointed at my head. It was the 19th day of December in 1996, a Thursday, if I recall correctly. At the time, I was working for a marketing services company in Port Moresby, Papua New Guinea. I was also 19 weeks pregnant with my first child. It was about 11 a.m. and I was sitting in my boss's office—who was out for the morning—with a client called Bruce, a big warm 6'4" man who worked in marketing for one of my biggest clients. We were having a coffee when suddenly several men dressed in dirty clothes stormed into our offices.

> *So long as you keep your heart open and pointed toward the light, you will gradually move toward forgiveness on deeper and deeper levels.*

They were looking for the cash they knew would be on the premises to pay the dozen or so national employees before the office closed for the two-week Christmas break. Since I was sitting in the office in which the safe was located, they assumed that I must have had the keys to open it. Unfortunately, I didn't. One of the men, smelling in desperate need of a bath and with a big mouth stained red from the beetle-nut people chew incessantly in that part of the world, shoved his sawed-off shut gun at my head and demanded I open the safe. I said that I couldn't, that I didn't have the keys. Assuming I was lying, he kept insisting that I open it. With each insistence he got increasingly impatient and pressed the shot gun further and further into my forehead. After a minute or two, I think he must heave realized I really didn't have the keys and told me to lie on the ground beside Bruce while his accomplices went to see if they could find the money elsewhere.

Down on the ground lying on my belly, I felt him run his rough sweaty hand up between my legs under my skirt to the tops of my thighs. In Papua New Guinea, gang rape was a very common occurrence. In fact only a month or so earlier, a New Zealand mother of three children had been kidnapped and gang raped by over 12 men after her car had broken down by the side of the road. So as I lay there on the floor clutching onto Bruce's large strong hand with ferocity unlike I had ever held any person's hand before or since, I remember the most sickening feeling in the bottom of my stomach at the prospect that these men would take me away with them (a white woman being an extra special prize). I recall saying a desperate terrified prayer to God pleading that they wouldn't take me with them. I knew if they did I would almost certainly be raped by all of them and likely many other men back in their settlement area. What they might have done with me after that never really entered my head for at that moment the possibility of being raped was far, *far* more terrifying to me than being murdered.

Time seemed to stand still but I know that it was only a few minutes later when one of his accomplices yelled out from the General Manager's office that he'd found the cash. They all quickly ran out the door and took off in their beaten-up car back to their settlement to divvy up their spoils. I remember in the following hours being in shock, evident by the fact that I could not stop my body from shaking for several hours. Amidst the shock, I also recall feeling incredible relief that they hadn't taken me with them and that no one in my office had been hurt.

The following day, I flew to Australia with Andrew, as we had previously planned to spend Christmas with my family. Eleven days later, on the morning of New Year's Eve, my husband and I went to the local hospital near where my parents lived and where we intended to have our first child (not wanting to risk the hospitals in Port Moresby should there be a complication) for a 19-week ultrasound. My mum and sister Anne also came and decided to stay in the waiting room while we went in to get the ultrasound set up and the baby (the first grandchild in my family) up on the screen. I remember the technician moving the wand over my belly trying to get an image of its development. What happened after that it still is a blur to me and, oddly enough ten years on, I still find my heart pumping loudly, my chest tightening and a lump forming in my throat as I recount this story. In between blurred images I recall the young female technician calling in a second technician to look at the screen and then, in complete disbelief, being told that our baby was not a 19-week-old, healthy baby doing cartwheels in my womb and on target to be born the following May. Instead, we learned that the fetus had died and I had, without knowing it or exhibiting any symptoms, suffered a miscarriage. Although neither my husband or I nor the doctors believed this miscarriage was linked with the robbery 12 days earlier, I include this with the robbery story because, at the time, with both incidents occurring so close together, I couldn't help but wonder if they were connected; if the shock of the robbery had led to the loss of our first child.

I don't know why, but from the outset I just knew that I had to forgive the "rascals" (the inappropriately playful name used to describe the far from comical men who rape and pillage like this throughout Papua New Guinea). Oddly enough, I did not find this particularly difficult because I had lived there long enough to appreciate the wretched existence these men had and the dysfunction of their traditional village system and why they had no qualms behaving as they did. There was nothing personal about it, rather it was a case of being in the wrong place at the wrong time. Of course, I'm sure it would have been more difficult to forgive them had I actually been raped. But then, I also know that it would have made my willingness to forgive them all the more important, because the heavier the burden of bitterness and anger, the more compelling reason there is to forgive.

> *The heavier the burden of anger on your heart, the more compelling the reason to forgive.*

That is not to say that forgiveness means forgetting. Not at all. When we forgive, we are not excusing unacceptable behavior. It is not just our responsibility but our obligation to do what is in our power to ensure that such behavior does not occur again and inflict similar injustice and harm upon others. As Desmond Tutu once said, "In forgiving people we are not being asked to forget. On the contrary it is important to remember so that we do not let such atrocities happen again."

Forgiving Yourself: Two wrongs don't make a right!

After the robbery and the miscarriage, I gradually came to realize that I also had to forgive myself. This proved to be far more challenging. What plagued me was that I had swum in a relay team with my husband's company when I was 12 weeks pregnant. At the time, I had been regularly swimming a kilometer each day and felt fit enough to do it. However, after losing the baby, I began to second-guess my decision and was plagued with regret. Maybe I had over exerted myself and deprived the baby of oxygen. Obviously, there are many women who do far more vigorous physical activity far further along in their pregnancies than this, but I was looking for whatever evidence I could find to heap on myself that it was my fault my baby had died. I'd known my offices didn't have the sort of security they needed, yet I'd kept working there anyway and the list went on. In the end, I simply had to stop raking myself over the coals with all the "what ifs" and all the things that I should or should not have done that might have contributed to losing that baby. It wasn't an easy process. Some days I was more forgiving with myself than others. But I believe that giving myself the gift of forgiveness allowed me to let go of the past and, ultimately, experience the richest joy of my life when my son Lachlan arrived 14 months later on February 13, in perfect time to celebrate Valentine's Day—the day of love!

So is there something that you need to forgive yourself for? Is there something that you did or that you did not do, that you deeply regret and feel deep remorse? Is there something that you feel deeply guilty about which causes you to think to yourself, "I don't deserve to forgive myself?" If that's the case, just take a closer look at your language for a minute. When you say, "I don't deserve to forgive myself," your words carry the implication that you are *two* separate entities: the "I" entity and the "myself'" entity.

When you say that *you* don't deserve to forgive your *self*, the you is speaking from the head and the self is coming from your heart. Your head has it figured out that your heart doesn't deserve to be given the gift of wholeness through the act of forgiveness. No siree! Your clever little head has done a thorough analysis of your transgressions and come to the firm conclusion that you deserve to spend the rest of your life on earth punishing yourself in a state of quiet, tormented, guilt-ridden misery.

Now I'm not ordained to absolve you of your sins, but I am here to ask you whether or not you living in a quiet state of misery is serving anyone, least of all yourself. And if you do believe in God or a power that created you, then do you really think that this is what they would want for you? Yes, you did wrong. Perhaps your actions caused harm, injury or hurt to someone else, perhaps many people. However, as I recall my mother saying to me, as I stormed through the kitchen bent on getting my revenge on one of my siblings for some minor transgression, "Margaret Mary, two wrongs don't make a right!" Choosing to live with a closed heart doesn't make right what you did, but nor does it serve any positive outcome in the world. Only by forgiving yourself, and actively seeking to turn this wrong into a right, will those you may have "wronged" or you be any better off.

Asking for Forgiveness

Just as it takes courage to forgive someone else or yourself, so too does it take courage to ask someone to forgive you. But if there is someone who you know is angry and resentful toward you for something that you did (or something you failed to do) then consider how it would feel for them if you acknowledged their hurt and asked for forgiveness. Consider also the peace you would feel to know that you had been forgiven. And even if they chose not to forgive you, consider how much better you would feel that you had found the courage to ask for forgiveness from them in the first place.

Asking for forgiveness is more than saying you are sorry. Obviously that is important too, but saying "I'm sorry," is only a one-way communication. Asking for forgiveness really calls on the other party to become involved also and with that, to relieve both of you of the weight that goes with guilt and anger alike. At its core, forgiveness is forever waiving the right to hold against another that which you forgave them for. So when you ask someone to forgive you, you are inviting someone else to join with you in putting the past in the past. What a gift all around!

Unleashing Your Heart from Fear

Whereas anger arises from a concern over a real or perceived injustice, fear arises from a concern about the possibility of a future loss. Regardless of whether or not you are clear about what you are afraid of losing, what matters is that you can embrace fear in your life—for all the good and for all the "not so good" ways it affects you. Fear, like anger, can also block your ability to give and receive love in abundance and to live with an open heart. I've said this

> *"Pain nourishes courage. You can't be brave if you've only had wonderful things happen to you."*
> –Mary Tyler Moore

before, but I want to repeat again that there is absolutely nothing wrong with fear, since fear seeks to protect us from pain and ensure we survive life. The hitch with fear is that, if we allow it to run the show in our life, it can also keep us from doing the very things that will ultimately give us the greatest fulfillment.

For Wayne it had been the loss of respect and love from his children. Wayne is a gay man with AIDS in his early 50's. Wayne married when he was 19, had two children by the time he was 23 and left his wife at age 30. Although Wayne had finally come to terms with his own sexuality, he did not want his children to know about it, so he began to live a double life, at times even pretending that he had girlfriends. Over the course of the following ten years, Wayne had a string of relationships with other men, and eventually contracted the AIDS virus. Wayne's shame was deep and his fear even deeper. He thought that if his children ever found out about his homosexuality and that he had AIDS, he would forever lose their respect and their love. But about a year before I met him, Wayne had attended a seminar during which he did an audit of his life to pinpoint the areas where he was failing to live with integrity. This made him aware of the price he was paying for living in fear and failing to be authentic in his relationship with his children and many other people in his life. He got to see how his fear of losing his children was actually keeping him from having the relationship with them he really wanted. So Wayne made the courageous decision to openly share with his children, who were now in their late 20's and early 30's, the lie he had been living and the deep fear and shame he had been feeling. He then asked them if they would forgive him for withholding this from them and love him still. When Wayne did this his whole universe changed. His children each responded not only with love and acceptance (they had long suspected their father was gay), but with deep compassion for the suffering their father had endured. Wayne's courage to rise above his fear and share himself with his children, and later with his ex-wife and siblings, gave him the confidence to open his heart to the world. He was freed to both express his love for others in more meaningful ways and to accept love from others more fully.

Like all parents I know, one of my greatest fears is something terrible happening to one of my children. Such is the price a person pays when they choose to have children for it requires, in the words of Elizabeth Stone, to "forever have your heart go walking around outside your body." Thankfully for humanity, the sacred calling so many people feel toward having children makes the safe option— the one involving the least anguish and fewest sleepless nights—an option too costly to take for it would require foregoing the deep joy that children raising brings.

Fear of opening your heart up fully can be expressed in many ways. Sometimes fear drives us to say and do things for reasons we aren't really clear about. Perhaps you have found yourself in situations where things haven't worked out and you don't fully understand why. But if you will reflect back for a moment, ask yourself did you ever:

- keep your distance from others and avoid situations where you might feel like you should "open up?"

- resist letting down your guard and "keep your cards close to your chest?"
- sabotage your relationships with behavior (through your words or actions or lack thereof) that you knew (on some level of consciousness) would be hurtful, damage trust and convey the message that you weren't fully committed to the relationship?
- keep information to yourself because sharing it would have made you feel vulnerable and given the other person "power" to hurt you?
- avoid commitment and conversations that may have been taking you toward it?

No one gets from childhood to adulthood without experiencing heartache on some level. However, those who fear opening their hearts the most are usually the same people who have suffered an acutely painful experience earlier in their life in which they felt unloved. They equated this experience with being unlovable or, alternately, with not being quite lovable enough. Regardless of how invalid this assessment was, the pain they experienced was so acute and intense that they became determined to never find themselves in circumstances where they might have to experience similar feelings again.

Ann, aged 63, had rang my office and left a message about helping her sort out what she referred to as "what's left of my life." From just the tone of her voice and the language she used, I got the impression that Ann was a woman who did not enjoy much love in her life. Then when I first met Ann I was further struck by her frailty and her deeply lined face. Living in Dallas at the time, I wasn't used to seeing women who wore little makeup, but it was not only the absence of makeup that made Ann look different to other women her age, it was the deep wrinkles which covered her whole face that had her looking far older than she was. Ann was an airline stewardess nearing retirement; she had little money, no family, no friends and she felt like her life had been one long series of misfortune. Her mother was still a teenager when she was born and so Ann had been sent to live with her grandparents. Though, she felt much loved by her grandmother, her grandparents fought all the time, often quite violently. When she was three years old, her mother decided she wanted to have her back. Ann never understood why because her mother was always far more interested in dating than in her. Eventually her mother landed herself a new husband. With a new man permanently on the scene, Ann said she felt she was only an inconvenience. And when her mother went on to have twins with her new husband, she felt so even more acutely, particularly given that her step siblings always got preferential treatment.

What emerged during our conversation was both a deep-seated feeling of inadequacy about herself ("If I'd been more special, then my mother would have loved me.") and an even more painful recollection of abandonment by her grandmother. On an intellectual level she explained her grandmother's choice never to visit her was because her mother would not have wanted her to visit. However, on an emotional level she never was able to reconcile herself with the fact that her grandmother had made no attempt to take her back, to see her or to let her know she missed and loved her. In fact, nine years passed before she saw her grandmother again, nine years during which she felt miserably alone, emotionally abandoned and unloved. She shared with me that she sometimes would walk along the street alone (her mother never seemed to care where she was) and look at people's homes wondering if she went and knocked on their door if they would take her into their family. She figured any family would be better than her own. She longed to be wanted.

Now sixty years later, Ann had never married, had never had children and had never had a lasting or intimate relationship. She didn't even have any friends. For her, opening her heart to another human being was truly more terrifying than death, because as a child the emotion she experienced felt akin to death. At age 63, Ann was still carrying with her the pain of that little girl who just wanted to be loved by her mother, who just wanted to feel special, who just wanted to know that she was lovable and to feel loved. What had torn at her heart then was a deep feeling of rejection and it had scarred her so deeply she had feared ever putting her heart on the line again. As a result, she had lived a very isolated and lonely life.

Sadly, there are many people who, like Ann and Wayne, have held back or shut themselves off from those whom they may otherwise have enjoyed close and meaningful relationships. Often they have grown numb to the absence of love in their lives, as their feeling of aloneness in the world has become the norm. But however deeply buried their fears and numb their hearts to the impact on their life of withholding themselves from others, it does not change the fact that intimacy is something we all need in order to feel whole, complete and connected. Sure, we may still be capable of developing and maintaining relationships with people on a social and superficial level,

Unless you sit with your fear and acknowledge its depth, it will perpetuate and cast long shadows around you.

but unless we are ready to open up our hearts fully, to be completely intimate with another, we can never savor the richness that truly loving relationships make available to us.

In order to overcome the fear that may be hindering you from opening up, you have to first feel the fear fully. You must get down into the core of what it is you fear so much. Unless you sit with your fear and acknowledge its depth, it will perpetuate and cast long shadows around you. If something once happened to you that gave you enormous pain, you must be able to feel that pain fully before you can dissolve the power it still has over you. Don't avoid it— confront it, feel it, embrace it. Only by feeling it deeply can you be unleashed from it. This isn't always easy. You need to go within to find the courage to feel to the core of the pain that left you feeling unloved or unlovable in some way. Feel that pain. Let it just be and know that you are stronger than you think you are. You may also like to try the exercise that follows.

Exercise 10.2: Opening Your Heart from Fear
Get out your journal and write down the following:
1. Describe the kind of relationships you would ideally love to have in your life. They may be with people you already have relationships with or they may be with people you have yet to meet. Describe the way you would like be in those

relationships if you were completely comfortable with being open, intimate and vulnerable.

2. Describe the fears you have that you feel may be hindering your ability to develop the type of relationships you just described. Put down in detail what it is you would really hate to have happen if you did allow yourself to be really open, intimate and vulnerable with another human being (whether a specific person or people in general). What is it you would be most afraid might happen to you if you began to really live with an open heart and become more open, more intimate, more connected and more vulnerable to others?

3. Reflect on the price you will pay in terms of the quality of your relationships if you allow your fears to keep you from opening up to others. Then write down yours answers to these questions:

   a. How will it impact your existing relationships?
   b. How might it limit the relationships you could develop in the future?
   c. How will it impact the amount of joy you feel in your life 5, 10 and 25 years from now?

4. Finally, if you are committed to living with a more open heart, write down a statement of intention that says as much. It could be something like this, "It is my intention to be a more loving, open and warm person." Or, "It is my intention to allow myself to become more vulnerable to others and more available to making more meaningful and intimate relationships." Just write whatever resonates for you. Then stick your intention somewhere where you will see it regularly. Whenever you do, just say it to yourself. In particular, when you find yourself about to go into situations where you will be interacting with other people, repeat this intention to yourself.

5. Share this intention with someone. It doesn't matter who it is—your mum, a child, spouse or friend. By verbalizing your intention it will make it more real and help you to hold yourself accountable on an ongoing basis to fulfilling it.

It obviously takes a lot of courage to begin to share aspects of yourself with people that you have not revealed before and to connect with people more intimately. Obviously if it were easy for you to do so then it wouldn't be a courageous act in the first place. So don't be hard on yourself if you find yourself with a knot in your stomach, feeling very awkward, hesitant or completely terrified. Your fear is natural. Truly! Just get present to that physical sensation (after all, it can't hurt you), take a deep breath, resist the urge to close up and revert to the old, guarded you and reveal yourself anyway. Even if you just share with one person initially, it is still a significant step forward in creating more meaningful, rewarding relationships and experiencing more love in your life.

Unleashing Your Heart from Sadness

Whereas fear arises when we perceive the possibility of a loss, sadness arises from an actual loss—whether of someone or something (including a loss of circumstances). Sadness is the emotion that indicates what really matters to us most deeply. It is therefore through experiencing the emotion of sadness that we are able to find the deepest meaning in our lives and often the greatest sense of purpose. Indeed those people who have been driven by a deep sense of purpose have, at one time, also felt deeply sad.

Just the other day, I was at my children's school waiting for them to come out of their classrooms at the end of the day. Whilst chatting to a mom friend who has a child in one of my children's classes, another mom friend of hers joined us. After being introduced, the conversation somehow got around to the fact that I am a Life Coach. "Oh, one of those happy, positive people," she said exaggerating the "happy" and the "positive" with a big cheesy smile giving me the distinct impression that she was pretty cynical of happy, positive people (and even more cynical of people who call themselves Life Coaches!) I think I fumbled some inane response, the bell rang, the children came pouring out of their classrooms and we

> *We cannot connect with what it is that is most important to us in our lives unless we give ourselves permission to feel sadness in our lives.*

headed home. Mulling the short exchange over in my head afterward, I realized that because of the work that I do there is the expectation that I am, or that I *should* be, always feeling and acting really "up," and "Oh what a glorious day" cheerful, even when I'm having a crappy day. I'm not and Lord knows if I tried to be that way all the time, I would not only fail to do a good job of it, but I would be very *very* inauthentic. The fact is that life, like a rose, has its share of thorns and so during the course of living our lives, there are times we will feel flat and there are times we will feel outright sad. And so whilst I believe it is important to look for the positive in the midst of adversity, I also believe that it's important that we give ourselves permission to also feel unhappy at times and to let go pretending that all is wonderful—to ourselves and to others also.

Facing our sadness is not something that our western culture promotes. Rather, we are bombarded with smiley "Be Happy" faces at every turn and books with similar themes on every counter. There is a gazillion dollar industry invested in convincing us that sad is bad and happy is good and heck, who are we to question the smiley faces bopping up and down at the bottom of our emails?! But who says it's not a good thing to feel sad sometimes? We human beings have an emotional spectrum as colorful and diverse as every shade in the rainbow. Feeling sadness is as important as fear, anger and joy in allowing us to be the whole, emotionally expressed and fully functioning human beings we were born to be. There are times that it is not only appropriate but healthy and therapeutic to feel our sadness fully. In fact, depression can arise not because we feel our sadness, but because we resist feeling it. But not only that, feeling our sadness allows us to connect to what is most important to us in our lives.

Perhaps there is something in your life that at one time you felt very sad about, but because the experience of sadness was so unpleasant, or because you felt it wasn't good to be sad, you resisted or discounted your sadness. Feeling sadness does not mean you are sentencing the rest of your life to one of misery. This is not about indulging in your sadness to the extent that you become a sad, pitiful, miserable, "woe poor me, my life is over" person. Not at all.

There is a distinct difference between feeling sadness and wallowing in it. Rather, when you look into yourself and bring forth into the light any sadness you have kept hidden, you open the doors of your heart releasing yourself from suffering and allowing into the rest of your life love, joy, gratitude and a much deeper sense of meaning than you have ever known before.

You see there is a difference between pain and suffering. Pain in life is unavoidable. The pain of being dumped by your boyfriend, losing someone you love, having your children leaving home, or in my case, leaving my homeland to move to the other side of the world to live. However suffering is something we bring on ourselves when we choose to dwell on the circumstances that created our pain and either refuse to legitimize the pain, or over legitimize the pain.

Just last week, my husband and I caught up with a work colleague of his whose father died suddenly last year leaving his 78-year-old mother a widow after over 50 years of marriage. Asking him how his mum was coping he responded delightedly that she was doing just great. "She's doing things she always wanted to do but never did when dad was alive. She's even gone back to university to study. I don't know what she's studying, but that's not what really matters is it?" Another friend made a joke about how she'd gone back to university to check out the talent and he laughed, "You joke, but I wouldn't be at all surprised

Do not resist your sadness, nor wallow in it, but simply let it be and then... get on with life!

if mum rang to say she had a boyfriend or announce she was getting married again. Truly, she's really enjoying life much more than we ever thought she would be after dad died. It's wonderful."

In contrast to this I think of a friend of mine whose dad died two years ago leaving her mother, who'd been married to him for over 40 years, a widow. Since her dad's death her mother has stopped going out as much as she used to and, in many ways, has stopped living her life fully. Following his death she hardly left the house for 6 months turning it into a shrine for their life together and, along with the other activities she has stopped doing, no longer makes the hour drive to visit her daughter (my friend) and her grandchildren every week as she had done for many years with their Grandpa. She has also begun to suffer a lot more medical ailments since his death and her daughter now has to visit her when she wants her children to see their Grandma.

So there you have it. Two women left widowed after long marriages to men which, I can only assume, they loved very much and felt deeply sad about losing. But there the similarities end. Whilst I am sure that both women have felt enormous loss, only one has chosen to perpetuate the pain and indulge herself in suffering. Ultimately, we always have a choice to acknowledge our sadness and allow it to just be, to pretend not to feel sad at all or to dwell on what is making us sad to the point that it takes over our life and affects the lives of those around us (as it was for my friend). So do not resist your sadness, nor wallow in it, but simply let it be and then get on with life.

You know it's strange but as I write this, I find myself feeling suddenly overcome with sadness. My eyes have filled with tears and I do not really know why they roll down my cheeks as there is no one thing I can identify as feeling particularly sad about. Rather there have been so many things I have felt sad about, and perhaps these tears are for all the sadness I have not felt as fully as I could have over the years—whether because I have failed to acknowledge it fully or I have resisted it and tried to distract myself from it in some way. For the unborn babies I never knew; for my dearest friend Kate who took her life at the age she could have been living it most fully; for the illness which has robbed my brother of so many dreams and so much life; for the special moments, days and years I have missed spending with my mum, my dad, my brothers, sisters and close friends who live on the other side of the world, and for the countless special times they have missed sharing in the delights of my children. I let my tears come and just sit here in my sadness, with my sadness, knowing that before I can be released by it, I must first become truly present to it.

And what about you? What sadness have you not felt fully? Maybe there is some sadness that you also need to feel that you have not. If so, then perhaps the following exercise may be helpful to you.

Exercise 10.3: Connecting with Your Sadness

Get out your journal and write down all the things that make you feel sad—in the past and in the present. Don't censor what you write—just recount times in your life where you experienced a loss of some sort that made you feel sad.

- *Did someone you love die or move away?*
- *Did you lose a friendship with someone you cared about?*
- *Did you miss out on an opportunity to share or participate or enjoy something that is now gone forever?*
- *Did you miss out on a chance to tell someone you cared or to show love?*
- *Did you lose years of your life not enjoying a relationship with someone you would have liked to?*

It may be a loss you are feeling right now. I want you to really let your pen flow and let any tears come with them, and as they do just sit there with your sadness and let it be.

Too often, we resist sharing our sadness with others. We think to ourselves, "I don't want to be a misery guts." Knowing that nobody enjoys people feeling sad, we slap on a smile and greet the world with a big happy face. However, when we keep things to ourselves and suffer in silent solitude we are denying others the opportunity to love us, to care for us, to support us and to share in our pain if they wish to and to become more deeply connected to us.

Sometimes we can even think that no one really cares much about us anyway so we live out that story as though it were "the truth." However, the real truth is that we simply have not made ourselves available for others to care for us. We haven't revealed our humanity, shared our sadness and

"Sharing your sadness provides others an opportunity to love you more deeply."

opened our hearts to receiving the love that others would give us if we allowed them to. Our aloneness is because we have built walls rather than bridges.

Sharing ourselves during times of pain and sadness in life enriches our relationships with those people in ways that just sharing "happy fun times" cannot. Just yesterday, I was sharing these thoughts with my friend Michelle who shared with me how in the playgroup she joined after the birth of her first child initially they were just a group of strangers who had nothing much in common except for the fact that they were all new moms. But now, three years later after sharing the heartache of miscarriages and angst of fertility problems, they have become a very close group of friends. Of course, they probably would have become better friends even if all they had shared were nice chats over coffee and baby showers, but it was through sharing the sad and painful times that this group of women really bonded with each other in a very special intimate way. I know that has certainly been the case myself over the years as my deepest friendships have not developed through just sharing lots of fun times, but more so, through sharing the "not so fun" times.

So if there is something you feel really sad about right now, I encourage you to share you sadness with someone and provide that person with the chance to love you more deeply. Whenever someone shares their sadness, their pain, their suffering with me, it provides me the opportunity to be loving toward them in ways I wouldn't be able to otherwise and this, in its own way, is a gift to me. So too your sadness can be a gift to others if you find within you the courage to reveal it to them. The deeper we dig into ourselves and open our hearts up to the world, the more universal we become, the more deeply we can connect with others and the more meaningful our relationships can be.

Love in Action

It is my belief that service is love in action. After all, love is a verb, not an adjective—*love is as love does.* So whilst how we express love can change over time and across cultures, what it means to be a truly loving person has never changed and never will. The essence of what it means to love is universal and timeless.

Albert Schweitzer, a physician and humanitarian who dedicated much of his life to helping people in Africa, once said, "One thing I know, the only ones among you who are really happy are those who will have sought and found how to serve." Indeed, it is through the service we give to others that we can come to experience the greatest fulfillment in ourselves. It is by serving others that we can discover ourselves fully. We are incomplete beings who long to be made whole by connecting with the hearts of others. Looking only inside ourselves for fulfillment will take us directly into solitude and out of service for who we are, and how we find fulfillment is intrinsically linked to the relationship we have with others.

We cannot fulfill ourselves by ourselves. Our fulfillment occurs through our relationship with others. So for me to find the fulfillment I seek in life, I must serve others—whether my husband, my children or you as you read this book right now—with an open and loving heart in what I say, what I do and who I am. But for you as a reader of this book, I can only do that if I have the courage to risk that you may reject me by rejecting what I am sharing with you in this book. In the case of my husband, it means risking the possibility of losing him and having to deal with the despair, sadness, grief and anger that would arise if that happened. While the former risk is less direct, both are still risks and both have the potential to make me hold back, shelter my heart from the pain of rejection or loss or betrayal and keep me from rendering the service and opening my heart to the extent that I am capable of doing.

> *We cannot fulfill ourselves by ourselves. Our fulfillment occurs through giving of ourselves in our relationships with others.*

It takes a brave heart to serve others fully in a spirit of love. It always has. It always will. For the deepest love requires the greatest risk. It is for this reason that so many people do not live truly loving lives. Of course, one can still give service without being loving. However, unless our service is given in the spirit of love, we are not fulfilling the deepest longing in those we are giving it to. Ultimately, the spirit in which service is rendered matters more than the service itself. For instance, I can cook my family sausages and mashed potatoes tonight in a cheerful spirit of service or I can prepare a five-course gourmet dinner in a spirit of resentment and frustration. Which do you think will have the most positive impact on the joy levels in our family this evening? Besides, my family loves bangers and mash!

Only when we find the courage to open our hearts fully can our service to others touch them fully. Before that, the main person we are really trying to be of service to is ourselves because of the external validation and accolades we get for it. This leads us to being selective and judgmental in whom we give our "loving service" to and from whom we deem fit to receive it. Service is not about doing something because it feeds your ego but because it fulfills your desire to enrich the lives of others through giving what you have and who you are to them…fully and without pre-conditions.

When I first moved to Dallas in the wake of 9/11 with my three very young children, I felt very alone and isolated. With no friends or family in a radius of about 9,000 miles (to round it off to the nearest thousand), I felt very much in need of a little neighborly love. So within a week of arriving, I took my nine-week-old son, 2-year-old daughter and 3-year-old son to a meeting of other pre-school moms affiliated with a local church. I figured this would be a good place to meet some other women who would see my need and extend their friendship. I remember being asked to introduce myself at the beginning of the meeting. When I shared I'd just arrived from Australia seven days earlier with my young family, a volley of "Oh, Bless Your Hearts" came my way. Afterwards, the meeting discussion focused on all the charitable activities the members would be involved in during the following few months. Of course, all the women would have felt that they were being very "Christian" busying themselves in feeding and clothing the poor of their community. But there I was, right in front of their noses, and no one thought to extend a little charity in my direction. The problem was that I wasn't poor, I wasn't homeless, I had clothes on my back and money in my wallet. I didn't need canned beans and wasn't in need of having my heart blessed, I just wanted someone to invite me over for a cup of coffee (or better still, a glass of wine!).

> *"There is more hunger for love and appreciation in this world than for bread."*
> —Mother Theresa

Even though being loving means taking responsibility to help those who are less fortunate than you, it isn't just about doing good deeds for the poor—well not just the materially poor anyway. Real love also requires you to think about how you can make a difference for others through giving who you are and what you have (right down to a simple smile) to help others feel loved, lovable, cared for and appreciated (regardless of how wealthy or in need we judge them to be). Often those who need your love the most are those right under your nose. Without love, being of service is a duty, an obligation, a requirement...not a gift. Therefore service does not require that we have money; it does not require that we have knowledge and initials after our name; it only requires that we have love in our hearts which we are willing to share.

Hallmarks of the Openhearted

Whilst there is as much diversity amongst people who have found the courage to live with an open heart as those who have not, there are common qualities that open-hearted loving people share amongst themselves and with all those whom they encounter in life.

Open: Openhearted people can share their challenges, their struggles, their success and their failures, their joy and their heartache, their temptations and their weakness openly. Whilst they are not people you'd describe as a "closed book," neither are they people you would describe as wearing their heart on their sleeve. Such a description applies only to those who lack self respect and have not yet learnt to love themselves fully. Rather, their openness reflects their lack of need to hide anything about themselves from others and to share who they are freely.

Honest: Openhearted people are honest. They have integrity in who they are and in how they go about living their lives. They are people you know to be sincere in what they say and whom you can trust implicitly. Their words are not products of their ego, so when they speak their truth their words do not raise defenses, but open and touch a place in the heart that deepens their relationships with others.

Generous: Openhearted people are wonderful givers. They are happy to share what they have and have no need to be stingy in how they live their lives. They are generous with their words, with their money, with their time, with their love. They know that the more they give, the richer their life becomes and that the more they love the bigger their heart expands.

Affectionate: Openhearted people are able to express their love freely. Whilst not every loving person may have a "touchy feely" way of being, they are still able to express their affection cleanly, comfortably, consistently.

Deep: Openhearted people think and feel deeply. They do not repress their emotions and their openness to feeling profoundly—be it sorrow, grief, sadness, joy, excitement, disappointment or love—allows them to connect with other people in meaningful and deeply rewarding relationships.

Joyful: Openhearted people have a huge capacity for joy. They can, therefore, sometimes be very childlike (as distinct from childish) because they can show so much delight in so many things. As Mother Teresa said, "A joyful heart is the normal result of a heart burning with love."Openhearted people love to play, joke, laugh at themselves and revel in the wonder of life.

Grateful: Openhearted people embrace a deep sense of gratitude in life. They do not walk through life feeling entitled to all that the world has to offer, but grateful for all that it has given them. It is their gratitude for all that they have that allows them to rise above their challenges in life.

Courageous: Obviously, this goes without saying. Given courage comes from the same place as love, openhearted people are by default courageous people. Though they fear rejection, sorrow, loss and grief, they are loving anyway and allow themselves to be fully vulnerable to all that living with an open heart exposes them to.

Being the remarkable creatures that we are, we human beings have an emotional spectrum as colorful and diverse as every shade in the rainbow. Like a rainbow, we are beautiful when we can express all our emotions in all their depth and glory, however raw they may sometimes be. At times this means experiencing many different emotions all at once. For me there have been times when I have felt very *sad* about being so far from my family in Australia whilst at the same time feeling deeply blessed in my life (*gratitude*), *passionate* about what I am doing in my work and at the same moment mildly *anxious* about how it will all turn out.

Opening your heart up to life and experiencing it fully—with all its complexity and rainbow-like wonder—allows you to know love, to receive love and to leave a legacy long after you are gone. There is nothing richer, nothing greater and absolutely nothing more nourishing to the human spirit.

> *"When you make loving others the story of your life, there's never a final chapter, beause the legacy continues."*
> —Oprah

Chapter 11
The Courage to Let Go

"Learn to Let Go. That is the key to happiness."
—Buddha

It may seem strange to you that a book on courage would include a chapter about letting go. After all, isn't courage about grabbing the bull by the horns, marching boldly onto center stage and taking firm control of your life? Sometimes…but not always. The essence of letting go is finding the courage to give up controlling all the circumstances in your life and trust more deeply that your efforts will ultimately bring you what you *need* most (as distinct from what you *want* most) to enjoy a rewarding and meaningful life.

When I say giving up control, I do not mean giving up effort. Rather, I mean giving up having to control every detail around the outcome of your effort. You see, letting go is not giving up the fight in life; it *is* about giving up having to fight against life. It is also *not* about abdicating responsibility for the state of your life or the results of your efforts, it is not about passivity or resignation, nor is it about relinquishing all your goals and spending your days doing nothing but smelling the roses whilst chanting peace mantras. Not at all. Having inspiring goals and dreams to work toward enriches your experience of life immeasurably. Rather, letting go it is about being purposeful in what you do whilst simultaneously surrendering the need to have it turn out exactly the way you want.

However attached you are to the belief that you must be in control of every aspect of your life, letting go will not impede your ability to achieve *what* you want. It will enhance it. For when

> *When you hold onto control you bound possibilities, when you let go control you create them.*

you hold onto control you bound possibilities; when you let go of control you create possibilities. Possibilities to take advantage of new opportunities; possibilities to learn and develop strengths you didn't know you had; possibilities to savor rich experiences you would never otherwise have; possibilities to experience yourself differently, but most of all, possibilities to be fully present to all that life offers you in any and every given moment.

What It Takes to Let Go

Letting Go Calls for Faith

In his best-selling leadership book, *Good to Great*, Jim Collins wrote about The Stockdale Paradox, which he believed was the hallmark of people who create greatness in their own lives and in leading others. The Stockdale Paradox is that you must retain faith that you will prevail in the end whilst still taking responsibility for confronting the challenges you face, however difficult.

The Stockdale Paradox isn't just relevant to business leaders—it's about getting on with doing what needs to be done in your everyday life whilst also trusting in yourself more fully that it will all work out okay in the end. Recently, I was speaking with one of my children's teachers about her 24 year old son. She shared how on graduating from college less than a year ago, he joined the State Department and found himself with the opportunity of working in Peshawar, Pakistan doing administrative and field work he had never done before. Whilst there, the worst earthquake in recent Pakistani history occurred killing over 70,000 people and leaving many more homeless. On top of that tragedy, there has been ongoing fighting in nearby Afghanistan. Needless to say, her son initially felt a little like he'd been "thrown in the deep end." But now, nearly a year on, she said that not only had his perspective broadened greatly, but his self-confidence has grown immensely. When faced with the opportunity to move to Pakistan he may have been tempted to say no. I'm sure he could have come up with lots of very reasonable excuses for doing so. Instead, he exercised faith in himself even though, in the beginning, he felt very unprepared for the challenges he had to deal with. But because he had the faith to just give it a go and to let go the worry about whether he could rise

> *"Go forward bravely. Fear nothing. Trust in God; all will be well."*
> —Joan of Arc

to the challenge he has not only risen to the challenge but he has also discovered in himself talents, strengths, resourcefulness and courage he never would otherwise have known he had. He now sees many different possibilities for his future that previously he'd never considered.

When speaking of tragedies that have befallen others or challenges that others have had to face, I have often heard people make comments like, "I could never do what they did," "I would die if I had to go through that," and "It would kill me if I had to face that." Perhaps you've said similar things yourself. However, if you were confronted with the same circumstances, you *would* handle it and you would *not* die and it would *not* kill you. You would rise to the challenge and find within you all the courage and strength you needed to deal with whatever confronted you.

Where would this courage and strength come from? It would come from the sacred part of your being that many of us grow disconnected from in the ordinary course of living our lives. Instead, we underestimate how much we are capable of and so we often move through life selling ourselves way short of what we have in us to *do* and to *be*. Trusting in yourself takes courage because it requires you to rise above your self-doubts and the fears you have about your inadequacy to cope with the challenges you may have to face. But regardless of how much or little faith you have in yourself right now, the fact is that you possess within you everything you need to deal with whatever may come your way in life.

Although life may present you with more problems than you *want*, rest assured you will never, never have more problems than you *can* handle. When you fail to trust in your own adequacy, in your own worth, in your own sacredness, you are prevented from experiencing it. Indeed, not trusting in yourself prevents you from ever really knowing that you have everything—absolutely everything—you need within you to deal with each moment as it arrives. However, when you do choose to trust in yourself, you not only get to realize just how amazing you really are but you also spare yourself all the suffering that comes from fretting about what the future may bring because *you know that whatever it brings, you will be able to handle it!*

Finding the courage to let go requires having faith in the source of sacred power from which you came that everything will unfold as it is intended. Indeed, the only thing greater than fear is faith. This does not imply the absence of doubt on your part. Instead, it is simply to say, "I do not know why things happen as they do, nor what the fruits of my labor will bring, but I am willing to trust that so long as what I do is aligned with what I feel is true and right in my heart, everything will work out perfectly. I trust that I will be able to deal with whatever comes my way—*regardless* of the outcome."

Letting Go Calls for a Big Picture View

If you are or have ever been married, think back to your wedding. You likely spent thousands (and thousands) of dollars and countless hours over many months trying to ensure that the big day would be just perfect. The stationery, the menu, the wines, the dress, the bridesmaids dresses, the flowers, the ushers, the bridal registry, the cars, the music, the service booklets, the honeymoon and the list goes on. All this so that your wedding day was exactly how you dreamt it would be. Yet, despite all your effort to control all the variables, there were still things you could not control, from the behavior of your guests to the weather. If you were like many people, the whole period leading up to your wedding was not one of great joy and happiness. It was probably filled with sleepless nights, elevated stress levels, tension headaches, lovers' spats and family quarrels, because your focus was more on having things be "just right" than on what you were actually celebrating. Indeed, for most people the period around their wedding is not a time of great joy, but rather great stress. In fact I clearly remember saying to my then fiancé (now husband) Andrew in the lead up to our wedding in 1993, "I'm really looking forward to when our wedding is behind us so we can actually enjoy being married!" I'm sure I'm not the only person to have felt this way.

Looking back at your own wedding (or if you haven't had one then some other significant event), you might think to yourself, "I wish I could have just loosened up and let go a little." Maybe you wouldn't have been obsessed about getting the right lace for your dress, or so distraught when old Uncle Arthur had one too many beers and fell over on the dance floor, or when the invitations went out on the wrong color paper. I certainly wish I hadn't spent the night before my wedding worrying about the weather forecast for the following day, which called for gale force winds right about the same time as I was due to arrive at the church. As it turned out, the weatherman was spot on with his forecast, but did my worrying serve any positive purpose? Absolutely not. Though it wasn't the weather I'd hoped for, we still had a wonderful day and those gale force winds made for some spectacular photos as my long veil whipped up around in the air (alas my bridesmaids hair styles didn't fare so well).

But what if your life were really just an enlarged version of your wedding or any single "one off" event of significance to you? That being the case, how likely do you think it would be that one day you will find yourself looking back on the event that was your life and thinking to yourself, "I wished I had worried less and enjoyed more." Of course, it's impossible to always live our lives with the wisdom of hindsight, but by using the lessons you have learned up to now you can view how you are living your life today through a much wider lens. In doing so, you can learn to be purposeful in accomplishing the goals that inspire you—whether it be expanding your business, raising your children or organizing an African safari—without having to get so caught up in the minutia required to make everything fit together precisely accordingly to your grand, master plan. Having traveled through Africa and many other less developed parts of the world, I can assure you of one thing, nothing will go perfectly to plan and you really wouldn't want it to, for the richness of travel—as of life—comes from the unexpected.

We cannot always see the perfection of any given situation at the time it's occurring. However, if we were to paint our lives on a large canvas, we would see that it is the unplanned and sometimes unwanted circumstances which add the texture and vibrancy to the canvas of our lives, transforming it from a painting into a masterpiece. Often it takes time to see it…sometimes more time than others (and always more time than we'd like!). But the words in *Ecclesiastes 3:1*, made popular by Simon & Garfunkel back in the 60's, remain as true today as they were when they were written, "To every thing there is a season and a time to every purpose under the heaven".

> *It's the unplanned, sometimes unwanted, circumstances that add the texture and vibrancy to the canvas of our life, transforming it from a painting into a masterpiece*

Just as you can never hope to stem the tides, shorten the winter or add two inches to your height (without heels or what I can only imagine is an extremely painful medical procedure), you will never be able to control all the circumstances you find yourself in. Sometimes things go wrong. Sometimes people let you down, get sick or die. You have your plans all laid out when a curve ball comes at you from left field (one you never even remotely imagined would come your way) and you find yourself indignant and protesting, "This isn't supposed to happen to *me*. This stuff happens to other people. Not to me! It's not right…it's not fair!" But as the saying goes…"shit happens"…and it doesn't only happen to others, it happens to you too, whether it's fair or not.

At the end of the day, life is life, regardless of whether or not you choose to embrace it. The difference is that when you have faith that ultimately everything will work out, it takes an enormous load off your shoulders and frees up your energy to make the most of whatever situation you find yourself. By just letting go of *having* to have *all* the answers to *all* the questions to *all* the dilemmas you face in the course of your life, it lessens your stress and allows you to experience greater ease in your life. The idea of letting go the need to have all the answers and just trusting that I would one day live into the answers was a thought that gave me a tremendous amount of consolation during the period in which I had three miscarriages, back- to-back, prior to the birth of our first child.

That period of my life was only one decade ago and now, with four, absolutely beautiful, noisy, healthy children, I can say with the deepest gratitude that I have already been blessed to live into the answers. What I learnt from that period was that as much as I want to control life, I cannot and nor will I ever be able to. I simply have to trust that in the big picture of life, everything that I experience will all fit together.

Despite this intellectual understanding that we can never try to control everything, we human beings still find it difficult to let go our desire to control. That, of course, is why it serves us to make a regular practice of taking a big step back from the situation we are in and, quit sweating the small stuff. The fact is that you do yourself a huge injustice when you get your knickers in a knot fretting about the "small stuff." As a person with such great ability to do so many worthwhile things with your talent, energy, brains and brawn, you are worthy of so much more. The world needs less people upset by football scores, and more people upset about 29,000 children who die each day from poverty (according to World Vision), the 13 million children who have been orphaned by AIDS and the millions more who will never learn how to read the words in this, or any book.

> *You do yourself a huge disservice fretting about small things that matter little in the big picture of life. You are worthy of so much more.*

Letting Go Calls for Dropping Perfectionism

"Small stuff" is precisely what you need to let go if you want to escape the claws of perfectionism that strangle your ability to enjoy your life fully. When you are hung up with needing to have everything be just perfect, you are by default, saying that things are not okay the way they are. Of course, if you are a heart surgeon, a builder or work in a profession that requires great precision, then that is something else altogether. Too many people live immaculately mediocre lives because they are so obsessed about things that are truly insignificant and unimportant in the larger scheme of life. When you are preoccupied with having everything in your life score a perfect ten—from the size of your chest to the color scheme of your dining room—you cannot be present to, and grateful for all that is great about your life.

You don't have to look too far to notice that our affluent western society is getting increasingly compulsive about achieving an arbitrary standard of perfection, set primarily by merchants wanting to make a profit on their wares. Ultimately, there is nothing wrong with wearing designer jeans, having a designer boob job, living in a designer home and driving a designer car, *but* if you

> *Too many people live immaculately mediocre lives because they get caught up obsessing about things that are unimportant in the larger scheme of life.*

think that all this stuff that makes you look good on the outside is going to make you feel truly happy and fulfilled on the inside, then you're in for one long and fruitless search. The reality is that despite the dramatic increase in the quality of living in the USA, Australia, Western Europe and many other parts of the industrialized world, people are no happier than they were 50 years ago. The facts are that more people are committing suicide or taking anti-depressants than ever before in history. Why? Because the more we seek perfection outside ourselves, the further it recedes and the more deeply we fall into disillusionment.

So continually ask yourself, what really and truly matters? Is your quest for perfectionism robbing you of the rich moments that come from being fully present for those you love, those you work with and from your life itself? Is your need for perfection preventing you from taking action to achieve what is truly meaningful to you? Is it impeding your ability to see the perfection that exists in the messy imperfection of your life?

Winston Churchill said, "The maxim 'nothing avails but perfection' may be spelled PARALYSIS." If the standards you aspire to achieve in everything you *do* require the utmost in perfection, then you will be hard pressed to achieve the kind of truly worthwhile accomplishments you are capable of. Heck, if I had to wait until I was sure I could write the perfect book, you would not be reading this one right now. In order to get on with writing this book, I've had to let go of the idea that I must first possess perfect writing skills, and trust that by doing the best I can at this point in my life and just writing what I believe is important to say right now, then everything will work out.

Likewise, perfectionism can also have a stifling effect on your ability to live fully if you feel that you must *be* a perfect person. Having been born with a very self critical gene (well at least that's the theory I'm working with), I can easily find myself in a state of self-chastisement. During my life, there have been countless times I've verbally whipped myself with self-recriminations for not being as patient, thoughtful, loving, accepting, generous, present, tolerant, self-assured, organized, calm, energetic, articulate, peaceful (and the list goes on) as I'd like to be. Fortunately, in recent years I have become more conscious of when those critical little voices in my head get on their soap box and make me cower for being the far from perfect human that I am. This has enabled me to gradually be kinder to myself and a little better at letting go of perfect. Do I still aspire to be a loving, peaceful, non-judgmental, self-assured person? You betcha I do...more so now than ever. However, I realize that to be a more loving, non-judgmental, tolerant person, I must first be that to myself which, of course, requires that I let go of the idea that I am anything but a fallible imperfect human being with all the foibles, insecurities, egocentricities, and weakness that go with it. You too must learn to let go of having to be perfect and stop making yourself wrong for being a human. But don't just stop at accepting your humanness, embrace it.

By giving up the endless quest for perfection—in yourself, in others and in life—you open your heart to experiencing a sense of gratitude in your life far deeper that anything you have felt before. When you are focused on what's not just right, you can't be present to all that is. So instead of being upset about things not being how you'd like them to be, you can be thankful for the good in them, which includes the opportunity they present for you to learn and grow as a human being.

Letting Go Calls for Accepting What Is

If you've ever been shackled with a pair of Chinese handcuffs you know that the harder you pull your hands apart the tighter they grip around your wrists, and the further away you get from actually releasing yourself from them. The only way to get out of them is to stop resisting them, as doing so loosens their grip and allows you to free yourself from them.

The same is true in life. It is only when we can accept what is and give up resisting it that we can rise above our so-called "problems" and enjoy the ease we seek from life. So often though we expect that things should just go smoothly and when they don't we are up in arms about it and resist the way it is. When this occurs we inflict on ourselves a lot of unnecessary suffering since our suffering is directly proportionate to the gap between how we want things to be and how they are. This is a central part of Buddhist philosophy, which teaches that it is choosing not to accept what *is* that lies at the source of all our suffering. You see, the problem is not that you have problems; the problem is that you expect not to have them.

As human beings, we can be very attached to our vision for how things *should* go (there's that word again!), and we often struggle with accepting what is. Instead, we generally expend a vast amount of time cursing our so called problems and even more energy trying to control circumstances to ensure things go as they are supposed to. This has us living—often unconsciously—in a perpetual state of resistance. Our experience of life becomes one long arduous experience of striving without ever fully arriving. There will always be something else directly ahead on our path that we feel duty bound to work ourselves into a dither worrying about and attempting to control lest it doesn't work out as we think it *should!* But as Marianne Williamson says in her book, *A Return to Love*, "When we stop trying to control events they fall into a natural order, an order that works." Likewise, when we resist the way things are, we cannot be fully present for others, we cannot be fully present to life and we cannot become all we are capable of being.

Of course, acceptance is different from approval. All acceptance means is to say, "It is so." It does not mean that you like or dislike, approve or disapprove of something. It just means that you accept it as it is—for all that it *is* and for all that it *isn't*. The act of acceptance can save you an enormous amount of energy because it means working with what *is* rather than working against and resisting what *is*.

When I was growing up, the closest river to our home was Tambo River. My mum and dad would take us kids "up the Tambo" for a swim on hot summer evenings. I recall how much fun it was to walk up along the muddy banks of the river and then get in the river to float back down to where we'd set up our base. I also remember how much *fun it wasn't* when I tried to swim or even wade upriver against the current. It was hard work, exhausting and sometimes, I'd still end up moving backwards despite all my exertion. It's the same in life. It's not that you may like the way things are flowing in your life, but if you accept what is, then you will be in a far better position to get to where you want to go with ease rather than with anguish.

It is not always easy to go with the flow of life. For me, it's something I need to work at on a daily basis (on some days, a minute-by-minute basis!). With four young children, I often find myself having to give up what I planned to be doing to attend to something else, such as resolving a serious life or death dispute about whose turn it is to play with the big yellow bulldozer or kissing better a scraped knee. Sometimes the path of courage leads to my doing less rather than more. As any parent knows, raising kids is one long lesson in "letting go." If we cursed every time things didn't go according to plan with our children or fretted about everything that might go wrong in the future, we'd have a pretty miserable time raising our kids and would miss out on the countless moments for joy that parenthood provides. Finding the courage to let go allows you to find joy and experience gratitude every day regardless of what happened yesterday, what happened today or what may happen tomorrow.

The problem is not that you have problems; the problem is that you expect not to have them.

The difficulty of accepting what is also applies to accepting others just the way they are. We have expectations about how we want them to be; about how they *should* be (there's that word again!). Indeed, much of our suffering in relationships is caused when people fail to act according to those expectations. We get annoyed or hurt when people are either not thoughtful, trusting, open, adventurous, spontaneous, inviting enough, *or* when they are too closed, conservative, judgmental, shallow, controlling, insecure, self-centered. I remember being very upset with a friend who chose to go away on a vacation instead of coming to my 21st birthday party. Being in the epi-center of my own little universe, I believed that if she really liked me then she would have changed her plans regardless of the hassle or extra expense. I expected her to put *my* party ahead of everything else and, when she didn't, I felt hurt. I'd like to say that I've since outgrown this feeling and no longer get hurt when people don't act the way I want them to. Yes, I'd *like* to say that, but the truth is that to this day, I still sometimes find myself feeling hurt or upset (though not as often). It is a gradual learning to let go of my expectations of others and accept them fully for who they are and where they are right now.

No doubt there have been times when you have experienced similar disappointments. Right now, there may be people in your life who upset you. You may not like what they choose to do or say, but if you want to avoid further suffering, you must accept their behavior and stop expecting them to be different—including attempts to "make them" be the way you think they *should* be.

Sometimes the path of courage leads to doing less rather than doing more.

I must clarify here that acceptance does not mean condoning or tolerating. Acceptance is simply saying *this is so* regardless of whether you agree or disagree, approve or disapprove, like or dislike. For instance, just because you accept that someone is emotionally abusive does not mean you condone their behavior or allow them to be abusive to you. Not at all. But it is simply to say that abusing people emotionally is a pattern of behavior they have developed in their life. When we accept things as they are we are able to respond more effectively and more powerfully to our circumstances and to the people in our lives.

The idea of accepting people as they are is particularly important in raising children. As parents, we have lots of ideas about how we want our children to be and it can come as a bit of a shock the first time we come to realize the fact that our children have their own likes and dislikes, minds and personalities. In letting go of our expectations of how they should be and accepting them as they are, we are then freed up to encourage them to express their own uniqueness and make wise choices for themselves. Once again, this is not saying that we lower the bar for what is and is not acceptable behavior. For instance, I still expect my children to treat others and me with respect and courtesy and to be loving toward one another. Rather, it is letting go of molding them to fit into our often rigid ideas of how they should express themselves in the world.

The fact is we can never experience the peace of mind we yearn for unless we find the courage to let go trying to control the universe and trying to fix all the people in it. Peace cannot exist where frustration, conflict and resistance exist and so when we resist the way things are we cannot enjoy real peace of mind. Instead, our experience of life is one of being continually anxious, disappointed and exhausted. Our resistance also manifests physically as we suffer migraines, tension headaches, skin breakouts, hernias, tightness of muscles in your back, neck, shoulders and the list goes on.

When we stop resisting what we cannot change, a space opens up in our lives for serendipity to occur. The energy of letting go attracts to us all that we need to get to where we are going. People we need to know to help us move forward toward our goals or to meet a challenge appear in our lives, improbable opportunities arise and inexplicable coincidences occur. By giving up resistance and moving to acceptance, we regain the energy previously expended on trying to change what we cannot. We can then channel that energy into what we can change. As we do so, we are able to be fully present to our circumstances, to others and to life.

Letting Go Calls for a Spirit of Adventure

That you will have to experience change in your life is a certainty. Whether your experience of it is one of terror or wonder is a choice. If you are terrified of change, not only will you be unable to adapt to changing circumstances but you will also miss out on the opportunities those circumstances present. In *Who Moved My Cheese?*, Dr. Spencer Johnson taught that to get what we want in life we must be ready to adapt to change. Furthermore, he stated, "that the fastest way to change is to laugh at your own folly—then let go and quickly move on."

Finding the guts to "let go" and "move on" calls on you to open your arms wide to embrace a renewed spirit of adventure. Welcoming the new, the unfamiliar and the unpredictable, regardless of whether it is something you ever previously considered for yourself or included in the master plan for your life, is what will allow you to enjoy your own journey through life.

Before getting married, I traveled a lot on my own around the world. After getting my confidence up back-packing across America and Europe I headed to more exotic destinations. I traveled in India, crossed the Sahara Desert from Algeria into West Africa, spent time in refugee camps in the West Bank, stayed in small Egyptian villages along the Nile and generally had a pretty adventurous time. After meeting Andrew, we both felt it was important to support each other in expanding our horizons further. We made a commitment to embracing a spirit of adventure in the life we would create together as a couple as well as for ourselves individually. We honeymooned on a remote island in the Philippines. A year later, we backpacked through South America, and within eighteen months of being married, found ourselves living in Papua New Guinea where we resisted the urge to put a bone through our noses, but continued to head off on annual adventures (which came to an abrupt halt with our first child). Needless to say, our life since then has continued to be one long adventure, as we

When we accept things as they are we are able to respond more effectively and more powerfully to our circumstances and to the people in our lives.

have moved around the world, furthered our professional studies, pursued careers that excited us, and had our four children along the way (an adventure all its own as every parent knows!). Actually, when I look back I realize that in the six years between getting pregnant with our first child and having our fourth, we lived in six homes in four cities in three countries! As I write, we're now in our 9th home since getting married.

You might be tempted to assume by my description that it has all be one big exciting joyride. It hasn't. At times, having to relocate to new places where we didn't know anyone was incredibly challenging. Perhaps the most challenging period of all was when we moved with our three young children (aged three and under) from Australia to the U.S. in October 2001. Not only was it a difficult time to move to America (just weeks after the September 11 attacks), but Texas proved to be far more alien to me, and far bigger an adventure than I had anticipated. I recall initially being critical about many things. Whereas

> *That you will have to experience change in your life is a certainty. Whether your experience of it is one of terror or wonder is a choice.*

previously I'd relished the differences in cultures and customs, during those first few months in Dallas, I have to admit I just wished for things to be the same as they were back home. Whether or not there were some post-baby hormones still playing havoc with my system, I don't know (it would make for a nice excuse). What I do know is that I was not willing to let go of how I wanted things to be nor to embrace the spirit of adventure I'd committed to with Andrew a decade earlier. As a result, I ended up covered head to toe with psoriasis. Not fun! But as unsightly as those spots were, they did give me the insight to see that it was me, and not Dallas, that was causing all my stress. After that, my experience of life in Texas became much, *much* more enjoyable (as did Andrew's, who no longer had to listen to my whining).

Having a sense of adventure in life is not just about taking on grand adventures around the globe. Indeed you can have a sense of adventure in your life with the life you have right now. It's really not about what you are doing so much as the spirit in which you go about your doing. There are times when the path of courage calls on you not to change what you are doing, but the way you are doing it so that you can achieve what you want out of life without forfeiting the experience of joy or ease in your life. A Chinese proverb says this beautifully: "If you climb to the top of the mountain, but you haven't enjoyed the climb, then it wasn't a successful climb." Likewise, if you are courageously charging ahead in pursuit of your goals—your own Mt Everest—but are so caught up criticizing the current view, planning your next step, berating yourself over your last one, fretting about what may lie around the corner or preoccupied trying to control any number of factors you believe could stifle your plans, then you will miss out on the sights of wonder and moments for joy that are there for the taking each step of your journey. By embracing a sense of adventure in the way you live your life each day, you will be able to lighten up when the going gets tough and relish the journey so much more!

Having traveled, lived or worked in over 50 countries around the world, I have met many people who have also found themselves a long way from home. Whether they are there to travel or work, the factor that makes all the difference to how much they enjoy the "foreignness" of the other cultures is their willingness to embrace a spirit of adventure (and with that adopt a good sense of humor!) and to let go having to have everything be the way it is "back home." By embracing a spirit of adventure in your life, you can more easily laugh when things don't quite go to plan (or go completely off plan), make the most of the opportunities that come your way and find the positive in any situation.

There are times when the path of courage calls on you not to change what you are doing, but the way you are doing it.

I remember one time in Peru finding myself in a predicament that really called for me to laugh rather than cry. Andrew and I had just spent 4 days hiking the Inca trail. On the final day we'd gotten up at 5:00 a.m. to get down to Machu Picchu to watch the sun rise over the ancient Inca ruins. We were scheduled to catch a train out of a little town called Aguas Calientes back to Cusco at around 5:00 that afternoon. To our dismay, we learned as we arrived at the train platform that there had been no train for several days due to a strike and there were over one hundred locals and backpackers also eager to get on the next train. When the train finally did roll slowly into the station, there were already people hanging out the windows, so we knew it was going to be a tussle to get our two bodies (and one hefty backpack) onto the train along with everyone else who was there waiting. But we were determined to get on that train as missing it meant losing at least a day if not more of our time, missing connections out of Cusco and missing out on getting to other places we wanted to visit in South America. It was not a time for frailty or timidity.

Mustering up all our resolve, we literally squeezed ourselves onto the train that was packed like a can of sardines with hot sweaty people (and the odd chicken) pressed up so hard against each other that it made breathing a challenge. As we moved back into the train away from the door and as more people pushed up behind me to climb on, I saw some space through a narrow door so I slowly maneuvered my way toward it while Andrew planted himself nearby with our backpack. When I got there, I realized I had maneuvered myself into a toilet ("restroom" just isn't a word I could use for this space), but having no choice but to move forward, on I went until I found myself crammed in this small and extremely foul smelling room with three Sherpas (the men who carry tourists backpacks along the Inca trail). To spare myself being pressed up hard against them I had to stand up on the toilet seat. With a low ceiling that meant crouching my head over. The Sherpas looked at me strangely (I guess not many women would demean themselves so easily) and then turned back to continue spitting out of the small filthy window (why, I have no idea). What bothered me was not so much that I had to stand on this toilet seat (hey, it was less crowded than in the passage outside), but that 1) it had feces all over it and on the floor, which stunk beyond description, and 2) some of the local people actually came in and sat down between my legs, which straddled each side of the toilet seat and relieved themselves (I kid not!) I mean it was one of the weirdest experiences of my life. Throughout the whole four hour trip (yes, four bloody hours!), I just kept thinking to myself, "This is going to be one of those stories that I laugh about once I'm actually out of here…assuming I don't die of the fumes first!" Indeed it has been exactly that.

So when you find yourself in circumstances that you would never have chosen for yourself (or never even conceived of happening to you), just let go having to have it all work out the way you want and instead think about how you will one day be able to look back on your situation and laugh about it. I promise you, embracing a spirit of adventure, where you are and whatever your circumstances, can make life a whole lot more fun and whole lot less stressful!

Practices for Letting Go

Peace activist and author, Thich Nhat Hanh, once said, "By taking good care of the present moment, we are taking care of the future." However finding the courage to let go and enjoy the moment more fully isn't something you can just permanently "switch on." Nor is there one particular practice that will leave you forever in a Zen-like state of calm and tranquility. I can assure you, if there was, I'd be doing it! Rather, letting go and developing a way of being that allows you to be more present in the moment is something you will gradually move toward with ongoing commitment and practice. Sometimes two steps forward, one step back. Sometimes, one step forward, two steps back. Such is life.

As you develop a greater level of awareness you will begin to discern just how much (or how little) you are "letting go" and how available you are to enjoying where you find yourself at any given moment. You will gradually learn how to do this without judging yourself as being either right or wrong, but simply by noticing what *is*. As you do, you can simply say to yourself, "Ah ha…there I go trying to control things again." It is in that moment of self-awareness that you have the power to choose to let go, to reaffirm your faith in something greater than yourself and to accept whatever is. In doing so, you will become centered again and reconnect back into the present moment—into the "now."

There are many different ways that you can begin to cultivate a more peaceful and less controlling way of being. All of them can help you to connect with the sacred part of yourself in which your courage resides and in which peace and ease can flow. Different ways resonate and work better for different people. You will need to experiment with what works best for you. How you go about doing this doesn't matter so much as that you make a commitment to deepening your current level of self awareness. This will help you to find the courage you need to let go more fully in *every* area of your life, throughout the *everyday* course of your life.

Exercise 11.1: Mantras for Letting Go

In chapter five I wrote about the power of affirmations in relation to helping you find the courage to just be yourself and let go having to prove yourself to others. But mantras can also be very helpful when it comes to embracing a particular outlook on life. Although the traditional meaning of a mantra is a religious syllable or poem, typically from the Sanskrit language, you can create your own personal mantra for letting go. Like an affirmation, they need to be positively phrased so that they focus on what you want rather than on what you don't want (e.g., "My life is not stressful and exhausting," is *not* what I'd call positively phrased).

Sue, one of my dear friends, has a mantra that goes "All there is to do today, is all there is to do today." She finds saying this lifts from her the pressure she feels to get more done in the day than she realistically has time to do. One that I use a lot is, "I move calmly and peacefully through my day." Just the words "calm and peaceful" are helpful reminders that what is more important to me than how much I get done in a day is how I go about doing it.

So get out your journal and just brainstorm a few affirmations that resonate for you and would help you to let go and enjoy more ease and less angst as you move through your day. Here are a few ideas:
- *The future will take care of itself.*
- *I surrender this present moment trusting all is as it should be.*
- *I live life fully in the moment.*
- *Grace, ease and abundance run through my life.*

- *I let go and move calmly through my day.*
- *All is perfect.*
- *Let Go and Let God.*
- *Whatever happens, I can handle it.*

Exercise 11.2: Visualizations for Letting Go

In Chapter 4, I wrote about the importance of having the courage to dream inspiring dreams. The practice of visualization is a form of dreaming where you decide exactly what you want to create in reality, and then try to paint it in as much detail in your mind's eye. By picturing it internally in your minds eye, you are setting the stage for it to become your external reality. This is something that sports psychologists and top athletes have known for a long time. Now technological advances in MRIs are able to clinically verify, as they detect the same sequence of neuron patterns in the same areas of the brain, when someone is visualizing something as when they are actually doing it.

If you've never tried visualization before, you might like to begin by visualizing how you would like to experience the following 24-hour period. Take yourself somewhere quiet where no one will interrupt you. Close your eyes and visualize how you would like to experience your day ahead or even your week ahead. Visualize yourself dealing with whatever happens (planned or unplanned) in a calm way where you take everything in your stride. Picture how you would deal with others if you were feeling calm, centered, confident and peaceful.

> *"Learn to get in touch with the silence within yourself and know that everything in this life has a purpose."*
> —Elisabeth Kubler Ross

By visualizing yourself the way you ideally want to be, you will find it much easier to be this way in reality. You can also use visualization to prepare yourself for a specific event, e.g., a job interview, a presentation, a sensitive conversation you plan to have with someone. Even if things take an unexpected turn, you will find it easier to let go of having to control everything and respond more effectively and calmly to whatever the circumstances are. Should someone make a disparaging comment about something that relates to you, you will be far better placed to respond graciously, confidently and calmly rather than on the defensive. Should someone put you on the spot, instead of clamming up, getting annoyed and reacting awkwardly, you will instead be able to respond more articulately and with greater self-assurance and ease.

Exercise 11.3: Meditations for Letting Go

Can one be courageous and learn how to "let go" without meditating? Sure. However, the reason I suggest you consider meditating is that meditation has proven itself over many years and in diverse cultures as a powerful way to help people become "centered." It does this by quieting your busy mind enough to connect you with the sacred part of your being that holds unlimited strength, courage and wisdom. This enables you to rise above all the small stuff, to view your circumstances and challenges from a larger perspective and to see with greater clarity the best direction for you to move forward. In doing so, meditation can undermine the power that fear may be wielding in your life and free you to trust in yourself more fully. Suddenly, obstacles that previously seemed insurmountable are less intimidating. Meditation can be particularly valuable during periods of high stress, anxiety and overwhelm, when you are more likely to become spiritually disconnected and react negatively to the stress triggers around you.

There are countless wonderful resources available to learn more about meditation (some are listed in the resources section on my website). Yoga Centers often also have meditation centers, for the two are closely linked. I am by no means an expert on this subject. All that I know I have learnt from my efforts to practice meditation rather than from what I have read on the subject. So whilst I do recommend that you explore meditation—the *why* and *how*—I don't recommend waiting until you are a meditation expert to find a quiet time and place. Close your eyes and just focus on your breath going into your body and exhaling out again. If you are like me, you'll probably last about 10 seconds before your mind begins to wander. When it does (for it most definitely will!), don't judge yourself but just catch your thought and bring your focus back to your breath again. In the beginning, just aim for about five minutes. As you practice meditation, you will gradually find it easier to stay focused on your breath for longer periods. As you do, you will move into what is called a state of flow, or what Wayne Dyer (a master on meditation) refers to as being "in the gap" between your thoughts.

Whether through affirmations, visualization, meditation or other means such as prayer, the intention behind all of these practice is to help you shift your way of being in the world—your experience of yourself, of life and how others experience you—by finding within yourself the courage to let go more often and more deeply. As you do, you will become more fruitful and effective in your "doing." You will gradually begin to move with a greater sense of ease; you will be more present to those around you, to life and to the sacred nature of your own being. You will be able to experience joy more intensely and you will know more fully that whatever happens, you have everything you need within you to handle the situation. By finding the courage to let go and trust more deeply in yourself, you will grow into the greatness of the person you have the potential to become.

> *"When I let go of what I am, I become what I might be.*
> *When I let go of what I have, I receive what I need."*
> –Lao Tzu

Chapter 12
The Courage to Be a Leader

> *"If your actions inspire others to dream more, learn more, do more and become more, you are a leader."*
> —John Quincy Adams

From the time I was 12 until I turned 18, I attended Nagle College, a Catholic school in a rural part of Victoria, Australia. The motto for our school was Luceat Lux Vestra which is Latin for "Let Your Light Shine." I always thought it was a pretty neat little saying and as I left home at eighteen and set off to "make my way in the world", I took it with me.

In the 20 or so years since I left Nagle, what it means for me to "let my light shine" has evolved into something much deeper, more compelling and...more challenging. Nowadays, Luceat Lux Vestra for me means to express your unique greatness fully and unreservedly in the world in all that you say, in all that you do and in all that you are. Of course, this is no easy task for it requires having the guts to step out from the safety of the world you've created around you—with all the stories you have of what is not possible for you and who you need to "get by" and "make it" in life—and expose your full splendor to the world. In doing so you will honor the light that exists within us all and touch the lives of those around you in the most profound way by inspiring them to do the same. This is the essence of what it is to be a leader.

Leadership Is a Choice, Not a Position or Personality Type

Leading others through what you do and say is not *one of the ways* to influence people and bring out their best; it is the *only way*. Up until now you may have had a narrow view on what it means to be a leader. Perhaps you hold the traditional view that leadership requires holding a position of formal authority and title like Chair, Captain, Director, CEO, Boss or President. Or, perhaps you have felt that to be a leader one must be a "natural leader" possessing superior communication skills, stellar strategic ability, brilliant business acumen, a high IQ, a charismatic personality, political savvy and academic brilliance.

In reality, leadership doesn't necessitate any of these qualities or abilities. Nor do these qualities or abilities guarantee you will be a leader. There have been many people throughout history, who could be described as "intellectual giants" or charismatic, who haven't demonstrated strong leadership. Why? Because true leadership is not a position or personality type—it's a choice. Indeed, real leadership goes way beyond any one attribute because real leadership is inspiring people to move in a direction they otherwise may not have gone, to accomplish more than they may otherwise have sought to accomplish and to grow into someone they may otherwise never have become.

The word *inspire* comes from the same root as respire, which literally translates to breathing life into someone. So when you inspire others, you touch their spirit in a way that they can live their life more fully. Peter Drucker, the founding father in the study of modern management, defined leadership as the art of "lifting a person's vision to higher sights, the raising of a person's performance to a higher standard, the building of a personality beyond its normal limitations." So when you influence another person's thoughts, words, actions or the spirit in which they use them—intentionally or not—you are being a leader since the essence of leadership is really about, to rephrase Drucker, "inspiring a person beyond who they would otherwise be."

Mahatma Gandhi was a man who displayed extraordinary leadership through his ability to touch and inspire those around him. Like all great leaders, Gandhi was not born with some extra leadership gene. No, he was an ordinary human being who had the courage to dream a dream that was so big, so *extra-ordinary* that he inspired millions of people to make a bold stand they may never have made otherwise. He did not lead millions of people by being forceful, domineering or threatening. Nor did he lead because he was the most charismatic orator the world had known. And he most certainly did not gain India independence from Britain because he held formal power. Rather, he achieved what he did and became the extraordinary leader we all know today because he had

At every moment of every day, you have a bank of courage waiting on you to draw on it to live a little bigger, a little bolder and to reveal the full brilliance of your own light, such that it radiates outward onto others revealing to them the splendor of their own.

the courage and integrity to do what inspired him deeply whilst respecting the dignity of his fellow human beings. At the core, he was a very loving man and, because his actions came from his heart, he was able to touch the hearts of millions of others.

Of course, there will only ever be one Gandhi. But so too there will only ever be one you. It doesn't matter that resources at your disposal may be more modest than those of the CEO of a Fortune 500 company and you don't have the profile of Oprah. The only resources that truly matter are those that reside within you. At every moment of every day, you have a bank of courage waiting on you to draw on it to live a little bigger, act a little bolder and to reveal the full brilliance of your own light, such that it radiates outward onto others revealing to them the splendor of their own. Indeed, your doing so is a priceless gift for the greatest deed you can ever do for someone is not to share your riches, but to reveal to them their own.

Just as your light spills onto others, so too does your courage infect them. Why? Because courage is contagious. I can think of countless times that I've done something gutsy, from jumping into a pool of frigid spring water to jumping out of a plane at 5,000 feet, because someone else has had the courage to go before me—a case of "If you do it, I'll do it!" Likewise, when you act with courage, you cause others to reflect on their choices. You create new possibilities for them and inspire them to plunge into things they may not have found the guts to do otherwise.

You may recall seeing on television a remarkable young man called Mattie Stepanek, who died three weeks shy of his 14th birthday in 2004. Mattie was born with a rare form of Muscular Dystrophy which claimed the lives of his three siblings. His disability interrupted the functioning of the automatic nervous system and ultimately left him confined to a wheel chair and dependent on intensive medical care and apparatus to stay alive. Yet Mattie didn't just withdraw from the world and give up. Rather right throughout the course of his life, Mattie found within him enormous courage and a beautiful gift for writing poetry, which he called "Heartsongs." Mattie used his Heartsongs poetry books to fulfill his personal mission of spreading the message of peace in the world. In an interview with Oprah, Mattie said, "We each have an equal purpose, whether that purpose is big or small, and mine is huge. But I have to choose to use that bigness. Nobody ever got anywhere by sitting around, right?"

Right! In Mattie's short life, he became a great leader, for he touched and inspired countless people to live bigger lives themselves. You, too, have a choice about whether or not you will live a purposeful life. How grand your purpose may seem to others is unimportant because just as leadership isn't limited by the position you have at work or status you hold in society, neither are the ways you can exhibit leadership confined to large-scale changes in the way you affect those around you. That is, you don't have to inspire people to lay down their life for you in order to be a leader. In fact, leadership is often just about the small, sometimes seemingly insignificant, ways that we can inspire those around us. Even small changes in the way people live their daily lives can, over time, make a profound difference on a large scale. Indeed, only by exercising our own individual courage can humanity, as a collective of individual human beings, find its courage and evolve into a society that nurtures uniqueness and respects the dignity of all its members.

This is exactly the impact that my friend Mona had on me a couple years ago. At the time, Mona and I had between us eight children under the age of seven. Needless to say, getting together with our broods was not just a noisy experience but also a scheduling challenge. I remember calling Mona to organize a time to catch up with her and suggesting a few different dates that would work for me over the following couple of weeks. Mona looked through her schedule and said to me, "You know, Margie, I'd really love to catch up but none of those times work for me. We're already partially booked on those days and if I commit to anything else, the weeks just get too busy. Let's touch base again in a couple weeks and see if we can find a good time then." I remember after the call I felt somewhat deflated. I thought, "If Mona really valued our friendship she would make the time to catch up." This wasn't the truth of the situation for I knew that Mona did really value our friendship. After brewing on it awhile I realized I was making it mean something it did not. What I came to see that what Mona had done was display the kind of courage that I'd not found myself. She'd had the courage to have integrity by keeping her commitments aligned with what she valued most deeply (that is having quality time with her own family and not being a stressed out mom). This required her to say no when there was a part of her that would have liked to please me and say yes. After reflecting on this, I became much more aware that I too had the power to say no to similar types of requests (which, at the time, I often didn't). The lesson I learned from Mona was to be more courageous in how I managed my time, my commitments and my responsibility to being the best mother I can be to my own children. Yes, I know this is a very simple example, but Mona's way of quietly living her life courageously continues to influence how I live mine. What a gift she is to me. What a gift you too can be to those around you.

The Paradox of Being Human

You don't have to wait for *someday* when you are more wise, more professionally established, more financially secure with a few extra initials beside your name, to really get "out there", to take on the world and be the outstanding person that somewhere, however deeply inside you, you aspire to be. No, no, no, no, NO! Greatness is not about your future potential; it's about who you are being *right now!* Only by participating fully in life in the present can you become bigger, wiser and feel truly powerful in the future. As Anne Frank wrote in her famous diary, "How wonderful it is that nobody need wait a moment before starting to improve the world."

What often prevents us from daring to express our greatness fully is our failure to reconcile ourselves with the paradox of what it is to be a human being: to be scared to death about our inadequacy whilst simultaneously terrified of how powerful we truly are. Claiming your brilliance and owning it fully takes great courage, for it requires feeling the deep well of doubt about your shortcomings and, in the same moment, your fear that you are powerful beyond measure... and then, stepping forward anyway.

"For everyone to whom much is given, from him much will be required." (Luke 12:48, NKJV) is one of my favorite Bible verses because it reminds me of the responsibility I have to give back to the world which has blessed me so greatly. Of course it also often leaves me feeling daunted at the size of the responsibility, but then I am sure that the sense of responsibility that comes from connecting with the power that resides within each of us—to create change and wield influence—has left even the greatest men and women feeling deeply inadequate and humbled.

So, if you are uncomfortable with the idea that you have extraordinary power that's okay. Consider yourself normal. Just sit with that thought, however uncomfortable it makes you feel, and let the vastness of your power sink into your bones. You may continue to feel daunted by the mystery of your humanity until your last breath, but if you keep looking within yourself, you will find the courage you need to answer your unique call to greatness, to express your true magnificence and to give back to the world that has given you so much. Yes, it takes courage to unleash the full bounty of who you are on the world, but oh, what a more splendid world it will be when you do.

Perhaps you aren't at all conscious of fear in your life—be it fear of your inadequacy, your power or both. Of course, only you can know what lies deep in your heart but it is my experience that those who are least present to their fears are those who are most terrified. Thomas Edison once said, "Show me a thoroughly satisfied man and I will show you a failure." Whilst I do not believe that anyone is a failure, I do believe there are people who have failed to honor their potential in the world. They have erected barriers so high to protect themselves from their fear and their power that they have grown numb and the spark within them has grown dormant. They pretend (to themselves most of all) that they are "just fine" and claim to live an enlightened life. But the surest indication of someone who lacks enlightenment is their confidence in claiming it.

Everyday Acts of Courage for Leaders

By finding the courage to honor your values, heed your calling and respect the dignity of others, you will become a leader with the power to affect change in others, and in the world, in your own unique way. Every single day—in your family, in your community, in your workplace—you have the opportunity to be a leader. Of course, life being life, every day your commitment to living with courage (and, by default, to being a leader) will be challenged as there will be a continual stream of things that will threaten to pour a bucket of water over that light that burns within you. However, its when you feel like throwing in the towel that you have the greatest opportunity to be truly courageous (remember, courage is action in the presence of doubt and fear and misgivings, not in their absence). By tapping the power of choice and making a conscious decision about how you will respond to your circumstances moment-by-moment, day-by-day, throughout the course of your life you can live the life of courage to which you aspire. The question is, as you are confronted by each challenge, which path will you choose? *The path of blame or responsibility? Resignation or possibility? Safety or growth? Conformity or authenticity? Expediency or integrity? Hope or resignation? Fear or faith? Mediocrity or leadership? Cowardice or courage?*

The choice is always yours. However, if you wish to choose the path of leadership then, by default, you are committed to…

...taking responsibility

Taking responsibility is to know that no matter what challenges you face, you have the power to make the ultimate choice about whether to let the world influence you or to go out and influence the world. It is to resist the temptation to go blaming others and looking for excuses when things don't work out and instead to look inward taking personal responsibility for the situation you find yourself in and for doing something about it even when circumstances play a definitive role. It is to recognize the timeless truth that you are always in a position to choose how you will respond to your circumstances in any given moment. By being a person who takes full ownership of their experience of life—a person who does not stand for blame, complaint or excuses to explain their woes and misfortunes—you will be an example for others to do the same.

Reflection: *Where am I complaining about something, but have no intention of doing anything about it? Where am I blaming someone else for a problem and failing to see how my actions have contributed to it? Where have I been claiming to be completely powerless in specific situations? Where have I not taken responsibility for my role in the circumstances and instead made excuses for why things aren't working out in my life as well as I'd like? What is one thing I could do today that would make a difference in my situation?*

...living with integrity

Living with integrity means to place integrity at the cornerstone of every decision you make and every action you take. It calls upon you to make choices which are aligned with your deepest values and principals such that there is alignment and harmony between what you know is right, what you are doing and who you are being. At times this may require you to veer off the safe, convenient, or well-traveled path others around you are taking and on to a less traveled one, or, to forge your own. It may at times require you to take a politically incorrect stand on issues and to risk ridicule or scorn. It will mean making a habit of regularly reflecting on and challenging the decisions you are making, the actions you are taking and the person you are being. By being a person who is honest, ethical and principled and who therefore can be relied upon for doing the right thing, you will gain the deep and abiding trust of those who come to know you. It is this trust that will allow you to lead others effectively and powerfully and to encourage them to live with greater integrity.

Reflection: *Which aspects of how I have been living my life do I not feel proud of or would be ashamed for others to know about? Where am I taking shortcuts I know are not right? Where am I compromising what is right for what is convenient or politically expedient? Is there something I feel inspired about doing that I am not doing? What is one thing I could do today to act with greater integrity?*

...challenging your stories

Challenging your stories is to be open to the idea that, throughout the course of your life, you will need to embrace new ways of observing your life and the world around you. It means never assuming that the way you view any situation or person is the way it really is and to be willing to regularly question your assumptions, your beliefs, your logic...your "stories". It means acknowledging that you do not see things the way they are but as you are and that, no matter how long you live or how wise you become, you will never possess a monopoly on

You have the power to make the ultimate choice about whether to let the world influence you or to go out and influence the world!

"the truth." By having the guts to challenge your stories, you will become a person others can count on as being both open-minded and amenable to changing your opinion about what you believe is possible for yourself, for those around you and for the world in which you live. In doing so, you will encourage others to challenge their own limiting beliefs which may be confining their experience of life and limiting their potential in life.

Reflection: *Which aspect of my life do I feel stuck or which would I like to be working better? What assumptions and beliefs do I have in this area of my life that I could be challenging but haven't? Why is it that I am so reluctant to view my situation or life from an alternative* perspective? What evidence is there that refutes my story about a person or situation or even myself? If I were to approach one of my current problems or challenges from the perspective of someone I admire how would that shift my approach?

...dreaming bigger

Dreaming bigger is daring to create a vision for your life and for the world in which you live that is more inspiring and more daring than the one you've been living. It is to move out of a state of resignation and away from the belief that, "This is as good as it's gonna get," and to have the guts to want more from yourself and more out of life. It is to dig deep inside yourself and connect with what would truly inspire you and bring a deep sense of meaning and fulfillment to your relationships, your career and your life in general. By having the courage to create for yourself a vision that leaves you feeling purposeful and passionate, your passion rubs off on others, igniting their own imagination and inspiring them to set their sights higher in life, to ask more from it and to give more to it!

Reflection: *Which aspects of my life do I feel resigned, uninspired, dissatisfied or without any sense of vision? Where might I have set my sights low and so avoided risking the possibility of failing, feeling disappointed or embarrassed? Where have I been "putting up with" or tolerating less than what I'd really like for myself in either my relationships, career or any aspect of life? Where could I dare to dream bigger and create a vision that would truly inspire me—in both what I am doing with my time, energy and talents each day, and in who I am being as a person? If, with the wave of a magic wand, I could do or be anything I wanted in my life, what would it be?*

...being who you are

Being "yourself" is expressing yourself fully and authentically in every relationship and in every encounter—whether with one person or many—without pretending to be any more or less or different than you are requires relinquishing the need to prove yourself and letting go the masks you wear to "fit in," gain approval or avoid disapproval. It is to have the courage to rise above the pressures to conform and to reveal yourself to others as the unique individual that you are, knowing that when you hide who you really are, you keep from others what makes you most attractive. When you reveal yourself authentically to others you can connect with them more fully and embolden them to reveal their own humanness and become more authentic, genuine and real themselves.

Reflection: *How have I been trying to impress others and convey an image about myself to them? If I did not have a need to prove myself in anyway to anyone, how would that alter how I was around people—at work, socially, in life? What aspects of who I am have I been hiding? What aspects could I reveal more? With whom could I be more open and authentic in my life today?*

...speaking up

Speaking up is about daring to engage in conversations that you have been reluctant to have before in ways that build trust and strengthen relationships. It's about being more committed to your own sense of integrity and self-expression than you are to proving you are right, making someone else wrong or just playing it safe! By speaking your truth in ways that respect the dignity of all, you can bring forth greater alignment, closer cooperation and stronger partnerships to make significant and lasting changes in the organizations you are part of and the world around you.

Reflection: *What issues are causing me to feel resentful or dissatisfied in my relationships that I am not speaking up about? Where have I been holding back from sharing what I think or how I feel? Where have I been expressing my opinion in ways that may leave others feeling a lack of respect or care on my part? What requests could I be making of others that I have not been making? What is one conversation I could have today that I have been putting off?*

...stepping boldly into action

Stepping boldly into action is about mustering up the guts to move out of your comfort zone to make the changes and take the chances necessary to transform your life into one that makes you feel fully and exhilaratingly alive. It means trading excuses and procrastination for a renewed commitment to creating for yourself a life you truly love living. It also requires that you risk making mistakes and even the possibility of failure, but taking the risk anyway in the knowledge that the far greater risk is to risk nothing at all. In the end, stepping boldly into action is about acknowledging that nothing changes if nothing changes and that only through taking action can we ever hope to have what we want most in life. By stepping into action and rising above your own fears, you empower others to rise above theirs to make changes in their own life and live more boldly.

Reflection: *Where am I procrastinating about doing some things I truly want to do? In what specific areas of my life is my fear of messing up or "not having what it takes" preventing me from giving it a try in the first place? Where have I interpreted a mistaken action on my part as meaning I was a failure as a person? What actions may I regret not taking 5, 10 or 30 years from now? What actions could I take today that would move me one step closer toward a goal that inspires me?*

...persevering

Perseverance is about staying the course and facing your challenges with deep determination and commitment to honoring that which calls you forward. It means resisting succumbing to resignation in the face of adversity and knowing that any goal worth pursuing will not be achieved without its share of disappointments, setbacks and obstacles. It requires embracing the motto of the Special Olympics which originally came from the gladiators of Ancient Rome as they entered the arena: "Let me win but if I cannot win let me be brave in the attempt." Through your braveness and determination you show those around you that he who is ordinary can become *extra* ordinary simply by refusing to hand over the reigns of power to fear and doubt, not giving up on your dreams and persevering in the face of adversity.

Reflection: *Which aspects of my life or goals have I given up on? Where have I failed to give something a second or third shot because, on my first try, I didn't get the results I wanted? What might I one day regret because I failed to persevere? Is there one specific area of my life where I could be more persistent? If I had no fear of failing, at what would I persevere?*

...saying no!

Saying no means being willing to sacrifice the immediate gratification a yes can bring—in people-pleasing, approval, convenience, security and pleasure—in order to pursue the dreams and fulfill the aspirations which inspire you most deeply in the longer term. It requires taking time to reflect on what it is you want *most* out of your life so that you can effectively manage the many demands on your time, your responsibilities and your commitments in a way that ensures you achieve it! It is, in the midst of being pulled in many directions at once, having the fortitude to set boundaries for yourself and to put your own sense of wellbeing and purpose in life ahead of everything else. In doing so, you empower others to find the courage to say no themselves—to the everyday things and to the big things—and so inspiring them to give up the good to make room for the great!

Reflection: *What commitments have I made that don't touch my heart and ignite my spirit? In what areas of my life have I consistently been putting the needs of others ahead of my own? What aspect of my life is heading in a direction I no longer wish to travel? Starting today, what can I begin saying no to?*

...opening your heart fully

Living with an open heart means letting down the barriers which isolate you from others and making yourself available to share yourself and your love fully with others, recognizing that the more we open our hearts with each other, the more connected we become. It requires opening yourself up to the experience of life and allows you to become vulnerable to the full spectrum of human emotion that living a full life gives rise to—from its rich joy to its deepest sorrow—and not to avoid it, repress it or deny it. For only by being in touch with yourself can you touch the lives of others. In doing so, you give others the experience of feeling valued, respected and loved, inspiring them to also open their hearts to love more fully and live more deeply.

Reflection: *In what areas of my life am I afraid to show my vulnerability to others? In what circumstances have I failed to be truly intimate with people? What is it that I am afraid of? What issues do I feel resentful, guilty or sad about that might be undermining how open and loving I am in my relationships? Where am I not being very loving in my life? Whom could I be more open, loving and encouraging toward today?*

…letting go

Letting go is to surrender to something bigger than yourself and to trust that you have within you all that you need, at any moment, to deal with what life presents to you. It is to be detached from the outcome of your efforts and understand that who you are is not the results you produce. It is to let go regrets of the past, anxiety for the future and to live fully in the present moment. By letting go having to control the universe, you make yourself available to enjoy where you are at each moment. The new-found sense of ease in which you live your life helps others find more ease, lighten up and let go a little more in their own life.

Reflection: *Where could I enjoy experiencing more ease and less angst in my life by giving up resisting what is? In what specific situations am I trying to force an outcome? Where have I not been taking a "big picture perspective" in life and instead, been preoccupied with the "small stuff?" In what areas of my life could I ease the pressure I put on myself by not having to have everything lined up just perfectly? Where am I failing to trust in my ability to handle things fully? Where could I benefit from embracing more of a spirit of adventure? What person or circumstances in my life can I be fully present to for today? Where could I be living with more gratitude and less resistance?*

Stepping Up to the Leadership Plate

"The noblest question in the world," observed Benjamin Franklin in Poor Richard, "is what good may I do in it?" Which begs me to ask you the question—are you ready to step up to the plate of leadership? Are you willing to rise to the challenge of being a leader in the truest sense of the word? And if so, what do you intend to do about it?

By finding the courage to live your life fully you are, by default, being a leader. But the magnificence of finding the courage to live your life more boldly is that you cannot change your own life without also changing the lives of others. In shining your light brightly, you reveal to others the majesty of their own. I can think of no greater act of service.

Of course, it is important you realize that you will not always know whether or how you are affecting the lives of others; whether, in the words of John Quincy Adams, you are inspiring them to, "...dream more, learn more, do more or become more..." *or not.* There will be times you will notice the impact you are having on others by something they say or do. But more often you will just have to trust that as you go about

> *The beauty of finding the guts to live your life more boldly is that you can't change your own life without changing the lives of others.*

living your life courageously and wholeheartedly that you will, in however subtle a way, be affecting the way others see, think and feel in their own lives.

So, to Franklin's question—what good would you like to do in the world? If you are committed to living a more courageous life, then I suggest you begin by doing a "performance review" (to use the language of corporate leadership) on how you've been living your life up until now. Now, I am not talking about a "one off," one time only, review of how well you've been doing, your wins and your losses. Rather I encourage you in making it a habit to regularly reflect on how you have been living your life. Just looking over the "reflection questions" posed in the previous few pages will help you identify any gaps between who you are being right now in the world and who you aspire to be.

Some days you will be moving forward beautifully. You decline an invitation to something you previously would have accepted. You speak up about something you previously would have remained silent about. You get started on accomplishing something that you have procrastinated about forever. You make yourself vulnerable by sharing something you've never shared before or you go out of your way to be friendly toward someone you never would have bothered to otherwise. As you do this you will be living the essence of leadership and it will feel good. Other days you won't…and it will not feel so good.

It is on those "other days" that you need to practice a little self-forgiveness and surrender to what *is*—that your life is a continual process of learning and that you are not perfect. You never have been, you never will be. There will constantly be a gap between the person you aspire to be and the person you are being. Heck, there are going to be countless times you won't even be the kind of person you want to be for yourself, much less the leader you aspire to be for others (I say this from experience. A lot of it!) Such is the lot of we human beings. The most important thing is that you are now armed with a heightened level of self-awareness enabling you to discern whether the choices you are making and the person you are being is aligned with who you feel committed to being in the world…*or not*. Let go of having to be perfect and reconnect with who you feel inspired to be, then choose to be that person again.

> *"True nobility isn't about being better than anybody else, but about being better than you use to be."*
> –Wayne Dyer

As you begin to shift your way of being and allow yourself to express all that you are—your greatness, vulnerability and fallibility alike—you will initially feel strange, awkward and sometimes not particularly comfortable. That's natural. But stand up straight (Have you ever met a truly powerful person who slouches?), get your chin off the ground, put a smile on your dial and get on with it anyway! It is the challenges you face in becoming the person you aspire to be that gives your life its texture, its richness, its meaning and your humility the practice it needs to keep you grounded. Ultimately, this is the essence of what it is to find your courage, to get on with expressing your greatness and to show up as a great big bright light in the faces of those you encounter, such that they cannot help but be lit up by it!

Luceat Lux Vestra: How Bright Will You Shine?

As human beings we each carry responsibility for leadership. The question is are you willing to take it?

Today, and every day, you have countless opportunities to make a difference for those around you. It all begins with your willingness to accept the possibility that you are more powerful than you have ever imagined yourself to be, to accept your personal call to leadership. Doing so will allow you, in your own unique and special way, to change the world, one life at a time, starting with your own.

If you have children, you have the greatest opportunity of all. It is my strongest belief that as parents, we hold the greatest leadership role on earth. For the children we are nurturing into adults will one day be passed the baton of responsibility for charting the course of humanity. As the most important role models our children will ever have, we must live our lives with courage and integrity and as we do, teach and empower them to do the same. Children often don't do what we say but they nearly always do what we do. As parents we all want our children to one day go out into the world and live their dreams. The question we must continually ask ourselves is will they learn how to live their dreams by watching us?

> *There is a light that beckons you forward and it comes from within you. Embrace it. Don't try to hide in the shadow of fear it casts behind you. For if you are committed to having the courage to live with an open heart, there is no greater way to love others or to love yourself than to fulfill your unique potential, to express your unique greatness and to become the unique leader you have it within you to become. Finding the courage to be a leader and to touch the lives of others in ways that only you can do, is the most profound act of love and service and significance.*
>
> *Dare to want more from your life and to dig deeper into yourself to experience its mystery, its richness and its sacredness more fully. For when you do, you will see with greater clarity just how universal*

> *we all are. And sensing that we are all part of a bigger whole, you will come to know, perhaps for the first time, that your life is truly holy and that it is not just your responsibility to honor the sacred within you, it is your obligation.*
>
> *This is the truth that speaks from my heart. I invite you to open yours to receive it.*

On finishing this book, it is my prayer that you will come to experience the miracle that you are and the greatness you have within you. I do not pray that your life be free of pain or sadness or struggle. This would deprive you of the human experience and the great richness that comes from experiencing their opposites—joy and happiness and peace.

I pray that you find it in your heart to accept what is and discover the wonder of what could be.

I pray that you find your courage and use it to fulfill the one true mission you have with your years on earth, to do the best you can do with what you have been given.

Finally, I pray that in doing this you will enrich the lives of others profoundly and so forever touch the world we share together.

> *"Give the world the best you have, and it may never be enough;*
> *Give the world the best you've got anyway."*
> —Mother Teresa

ABOUT THE AUTHOR

MARGIE WARRELL is an executive and life coach, speaker, writer and mother of four rowdy children. From her childhood on a dairy farm in rural Australia, Margie has long sought to embrace a spirit of adventure in life. She has traveled extensively around the world, venturing independently to many places throughout the Middle East, North Africa, South America and Asia (including three years working in Papua New Guinea).

With bachelor's degrees in business and psychology, Margie has worked in marketing for multi-national corporations and as an independent consultant in the adventure travel industry. She is also a certified ontological coach, an accredited coach with the International Coach Federation and a member of the International Association of Certified Coaches.

Passionate about empowering people to find the courage to pursue the goals that inspire them, Margie works with individuals, teams and organizations globally to achieve the success and make the difference they are capable of. She has also spoken to audiences in Fortune 500 companies, universities, not-for-profit organizations and national associations.

Together with best-selling authors including Jack Canfield, Richard Carlson and John Gray, Margie is a contributor to *101 Ways to Improve Your Life (Vol 2)*. She is also an internationally published writer (and photographer) and syndicated columnist.

Having lived in many homes in many cities in many time zones around the world, Margie currently resides in northern Virginia with her husband and children.

For free resources, to subscribe to Margie's free online newsletter "Live Your Greatest Life!", or for more information on her coaching and speaking services please visit www.margiewarrell.com.